NO FEAR SHAKESPEARE

NO FEAR SHAKESPEARE

As You Like It

Hamlet

Henry V

Julius Caesar

King Lear

Macbeth

The Merchant of Venice

A Midsummer Night's Dream

Much Ado About Nothing

Othello

Richard III

Romeo and Juliet

Sonnets

The Taming of the Shrew

The Tempest

Twelfth Night

NO FEAR SHAKESPEARE

RICHARD III

SPARK
NOTES

The original text and translation for this edition were prepared by John Crowther.

Spark Publishing
A Division of Barnes & Noble, Inc.
120 Fifth Avenue, 8th Floor
New York, NY 10011

Please submit all comments and questions or report errors to www.sparknotes.com/errors

Library of Congress Cataloging-in-Publication Data

Shakespeare, William, 1564–1616.
  Richard III / edited by John Crowther.
    p. cm.—(No fear Shakespeare)
  ISBN: 978-1-4114-0102-0
1. Richard III, King of England, 1452-1485—Drama. 2. Great Britain—History—Richard III,
1483-1485—Drama. I. Crowther, John (John C.) II. Title.
PR2821.A2C76 2004
822.3'3—dc22

                              2004009849

Printed and bound in the United States of America

20 19 18 17

There's matter in these sighs, these profound heaves.
You must translate: 'tis fit we understand them.

(Hamlet, 4.1.1–2)

FEAR NOT.

Have you ever found yourself looking at a Shakespeare play, then down at the footnotes, then back at the play, and still not understanding? You know what the individual words mean, but they don't add up. SparkNotes' *No Fear Shakespeare* will help you break through all that. Put the pieces together with our easy-to-read translations. Soon you'll be reading Shakespeare's own words fearlessly—and actually enjoying it.

No Fear Shakespeare puts Shakespeare's language side-by-side with a facing-page translation into modern English—the kind of English people actually speak today. When Shakespeare's words make your head spin, our translation will help you sort out what's happening, who's saying what, and why.

RICHARD III

CHARACTERS

Richard—The play's protagonist and villain, deformed in body and twisted in mind. At the beginning of the play Richard is the Duke of Gloucester and brother to King Edward IV. Later, he becomes King Richard III. He is evil, corrupt, sadistic, and manipulative, and willing to stop at nothing to become king. His intelligence, political brilliance, and dazzling use of language keep the audience fascinated—and his subjects and rivals under his thumb.

Buckingham—Richard's right-hand man in his schemes to gain power. A willing accomplice in Richard's murders and machinations, Buckingham is almost as amoral and ambitious as Richard himself. Unlike Richard, however, Buckingham eventually reaches the limit of his willingness to kill.

King Edward IV—The older brother of Richard and Clarence, and the king of England at the start of the play. Edward was deeply involved in the Yorkists' brutal overthrow of the Lancaster regime, but as king he is devoted to achieving a reconciliation among the various political factions of his reign. He is unaware that Richard attempts to thwart him at every turn.

Clarence—The gentle, trusting brother born between Edward and Richard in the York family. Richard has Clarence murdered in order to get him out of the way. Clarence leaves two children, a son and a daughter.

Queen Elizabeth—The wife of King Edward IV and the mother of the two young princes (the heirs to the throne) and their older sister, young Elizabeth. After Edward's death, Queen Elizabeth (also called Lady Gray) is at Richard's mercy. Richard rightly views her as an enemy because she opposes his rise to power, and because she is intelligent and fairly strong-willed. Elizabeth is part of the Woodeville family. Her kinsmen—Dorset, Rivers, and Gray—are her allies in the court.

Dorset, **Rivers**, and **Gray**—The kinsmen and allies of Elizabeth and members of the Woodeville and Gray families. Rivers is Elizabeth's brother, while Gray and Dorset are her sons from her first marriage. Richard eventually executes Rivers and Gray, but Dorset flees and survives.

Anne—The young widow of Prince Edward, who was the son of the former king, Henry VI. Lady Anne hates Richard for the death of her husband, but for reasons of politics—and for sadistic pleasure—Richard persuades Anne to marry him.

Duchess of York—Widowed mother of Richard, Clarence, and King Edward IV. The Duchess of York is Elizabeth's mother-in-law, and she is very protective of Elizabeth and her children, who are the Duchess's grandchildren. She is angry with, and eventually curses, Richard for his heinous actions.

Margaret—Widow of the dead King Henry VI and mother of the slain Prince Edward. In medieval times, when kings were deposed, their children were often killed to remove any threat from the royal line of descent—but their wives were left alive because they were considered harmless. Margaret was the wife of the king before Edward, the Lancastrian Henry VI, who was subsequently deposed and murdered (along with their children) by the family of King Edward IV and Richard. She is embittered and hates both Richard and the people he is trying to get rid of, all of whom were complicit in the destruction of the Lancasters.

The princes—The two young sons of King Edward IV and his wife, Elizabeth, their names are actually Prince Edward and the Duke of York, but they are often referred to collectively. Agents of Richard murder these boys—Richard's nephews—in the Tower of London. Young Prince Edward, the rightful heir to the throne, should not be confused with the elder Edward, prince of Wales (the first husband of Lady Anne, and the son of the former king, Henry VI), who was killed before the play begins.

Young Elizabeth—The former Queen Elizabeth's daughter. Young Elizabeth enjoys the fate of many Renaissance noblewomen. She becomes a pawn in political power-brokering, and is promised in marriage at the end of the play to Richmond, the Lancastrian rebel leader, in order to unite the warring houses of York and Lancaster.

Ratcliffe, Catesby—Two of Richard's flunkies among the nobility.

Tyrrell—A murderer whom Richard hires to kill his young cousins, the princes in the Tower of London.

Richmond—A member of a branch of the Lancaster royal family. Richmond gathers a force of rebels to challenge Richard for the throne. He is meant to represent goodness and justice and fairness—all the things Richard does not. Richmond is portrayed in such a glowing light in part because he founded the Tudor dynasty, which still ruled England in Shakespeare's day.

Hastings—A lord who maintains his integrity, remaining loyal to the family of King Edward IV. Hastings winds up dead for making the mistake of trusting Richard.

Stanley—The stepfather of Richmond. Lord Stanley, Earl of Derby, secretly helps Richmond, although he cannot escape Richard's watchful gaze.

Lord Mayor of London—A gullible and suggestible fellow whom Richard and Buckingham use as a pawn in their ploy to make Richard king.

Vaughan—A friend of Elizabeth, Dorset, Rivers, and Gray who is executed by Richard along with Rivers and Gray.

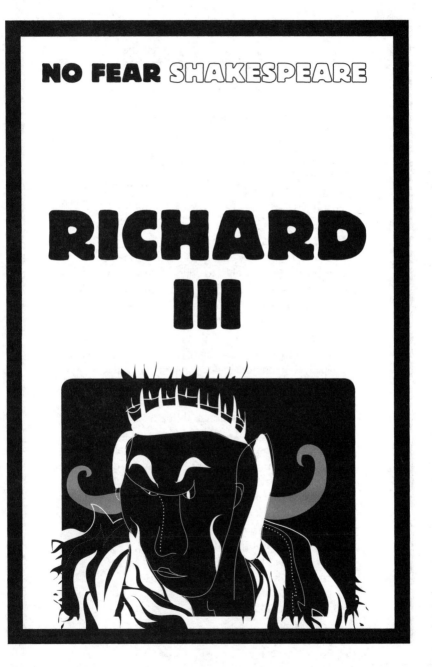

ACT ONE

SCENE 1

Enter RICHARD, *Duke of Gloucester, solus*

RICHARD

Now is the winter of our discontent
Made glorious summer by this son of York,
And all the clouds that loured upon our house
In the deep bosom of the ocean buried.

5   Now are our brows bound with victorious wreaths,
Our bruisèd arms hung up for monuments,
Our stern alarums changed to merry meetings,
Our dreadful marches to delightful measures.
Grim-visaged war hath smoothed his wrinkled front;

10   And now, instead of mounting barbèd steeds
To fright the souls of fearful adversaries,
He capers nimbly in a lady's chamber
To the lascivious pleasing of a lute.
But I, that am not shaped for sportive tricks,

15   Nor made to court an amorous looking glass;
I, that am rudely stamped and want love's majesty
To strut before a wanton ambling nymph;
I, that am curtailed of this fair proportion,
Cheated of feature by dissembling nature,

20   Deformed, unfinished, sent before my time
Into this breathing world, scarce half made up,
And that so lamely and unfashionable
That dogs bark at me as I halt by them—
Why, I, in this weak piping time of peace,

25   Have no delight to pass away the time,
Unless to see my shadow in the sun
And descant on mine own deformity.

ACT ONE
SCENE 1

RICHARD, *Duke of Gloucester, enters alone.*

RICHARD

Now all of my family's troubles have come to a glorious end, thanks to my brother, King Edward IV. All the clouds that threatened the York family have vanished and turned to sunshine. Now we wear the wreaths of victory on our heads. We've taken off our armor and weapons and hung them up as decorations. Instead of hearing trumpets call us to battle, we dance at parties. We get to wear easy smiles on our faces rather than the grim expressions of war. Instead of charging toward our enemies on armored horses, we dance for our ladies in their chambers, accompanied by sexy songs on the lute. But I'm not made to be a seducer, or to make faces at myself in the mirror. I was badly made and don't have the looks to strut my stuff in front of pretty sluts. I've been cheated of a nice body and face, or even normal proportions. I am deformed, spit out from my mother's womb prematurely and so badly formed that dogs bark at me as I limp by them. I'm left with nothing to do in this weak, idle peacetime, unless I want to look at my lumpy shadow in the sun and sing about *that*.

And therefore, since I cannot prove a lover
To entertain these fair well-spoken days,
30   I am determinèd to prove a villain
And hate the idle pleasures of these days.
Plots have I laid, inductions dangerous,
By drunken prophecies, libels and dreams,
To set my brother Clarence and the king
35   In deadly hate, the one against the other;
And if King Edward be as true and just
As I am subtle, false, and treacherous,
This day should Clarence closely be mewed up
About a prophecy which says that "G"
40   Of Edward's heirs the murderer shall be.
Dive, thoughts, down to my soul. Here Clarence comes.

Enter CLARENCE, *guarded, and* BRAKENBURY

Brother, good day. What means this armèd guard
That waits upon your Grace?

CLARENCE
                                    His majesty,
Tend'ring my person's safety, hath appointed
45   This conduct to convey me to the Tower.

RICHARD
    Upon what cause?

CLARENCE
                    Because my name is George.

RICHARD
    Alack, my lord, that fault is none of yours.
He should, for that, commit your godfathers.
O, belike his majesty hath some intent
50   That you shall be new christened in the Tower.
But what's the matter, Clarence? May I know?

Since I can't amuse myself by being a lover, I've decided to become a villain. I've set dangerous plans in motion, using lies, drunken prophecies, and stories about dreams to set my brother Clarence and the king against each other. If King Edward is as honest and fair-minded as I am deceitful and cruel, then Clarence is going to be locked away in prison today because of a prophecy that "G" will murder Edward's children. Oh, time to hide what I'm thinking—here comes Clarence.

Edward interprets "G" to mean George, Duke of Clarence, though ironically it could just as well mean Richard, Duke of Gloucester.

CLARENCE *enters, surrounded by guards, with* BRAKENBURY.

Good afternoon, brother. Why are you surrounded by these armed guards?

CLARENCE

His majesty is so concerned about my personal safety that he has ordered them to conduct me to the Tower.

The Tower of London, where political prisoners were kept.

RICHARD

You're being arrested? Why?

CLARENCE

Because my name is George.

RICHARD

That's not your fault! He should imprison the person who named you, instead. Maybe the king is sending you to the Tower to have you renamed. But, really, what's going on, Clarence? Can you tell me?

CLARENCE

    Yea, Richard, when I know, for I protest
    As yet I do not. But, as I can learn,
    He hearkens after prophecies and dreams,
55   And from the crossrow plucks the letter *G*,
    And says a wizard told him that by "G"
    His issue disinherited should be.
    And for my name of George begins with *G*,
    It follows in his thought that I am he.
60   These, as I learn, and such like toys as these
    Have moved his Highness to commit me now.

RICHARD

    Why, this it is when men are ruled by women.
    'Tis not the king that sends you to the Tower.
    My Lady Grey his wife, Clarence, 'tis she
65   That tempers him to this extremity.
    Was it not she and that good man of worship,
    Anthony Woodeville, her brother there,
    That made him send Lord Hastings to the Tower,
    From whence this present day he is delivered?
70   We are not safe, Clarence. We are not safe.

CLARENCE

    By heaven, I think there is no man is secure
    But the queen's kindred and night-walking heralds
    That trudge betwixt the king and Mistress Shore.
    Heard ye not what an humble suppliant
75   Lord Hastings was to her for his delivery?

RICHARD

    Humbly complaining to her deity
    Got my Lord Chamberlain his liberty.
    I'll tell you what: I think it is our way,
    If we will keep in favor with the king,
80   To be her men and wear her livery.
    The jealous o'erworn widow and herself,
    Since that our brother dubbed them gentlewomen,
    Are mighty gossips in this monarchy.

CLARENCE

I'll tell you as soon as I know, Richard, because at this point I have no idea. All I've been able to find out is that our brother the king has been listening to prophecies and dreams. He picked out the letter "G" from the alphabet and said a wizard told him that "G" will take the throne away from his children. He thinks "G" is me. I've learned that this, along with other frivolous reasons like it, is what prompted the king to send me to prison.

RICHARD

Well, this is what happens when men let themselves be ruled by women. The king isn't the one sending you to the Tower, Clarence. It's his wife, Lady Grey, who got him to do this. Remember how she and her brother, Anthony Woodeville, made him send Lord Hastings to the Tower? Hastings was just released. We're not safe, Clarence, we're not safe.

CLARENCE

By God, I think the only people who *are* safe are the queen's own relatives and the late-night messengers the king uses to fetch his mistress, Mistress Shore. Did you hear how Lord Hastings had to beg the queen to be freed?

RICHARD

Hastings got his freedom by bowing down to that goddess. And I'll tell you what. If we want to stay in the king's good graces, we're going have to act like the mistress's servants, too. Ever since our brother made them gentlewomen, Mistress Shore and the queen have become mighty busybodies in our kingdom.

Richard implies that Mistress Shore and the queen did not belong to the rank of gentry.

BRAKENBURY

I beseech your Graces both to pardon me.
85　　His majesty hath straitly given in charge
That no man shall have private conference,
Of what degree soever, with his brother.

RICHARD

Even so. An please your Worship, Brakenbury,
You may partake of anything we say.
90　　We speak no treason, man. We say the king
Is wise and virtuous, and his noble queen
Well struck in years, fair, and not jealous.
We say that Shore's wife hath a pretty foot,
A cherry lip, a bonny eye, a passing pleasing tongue,
95　　And that the queen's kindred are made gentlefolks.
How say you, sir? Can you deny all this?

BRAKENBURY

With this, my lord, myself have naught to do.

RICHARD

Naught to do with Mistress Shore? I tell thee, fellow,
He that doth naught with her, excepting one,
100　　Were best he do it secretly, alone.

BRAKENBURY

What one, my lord?

RICHARD

Her husband, knave. Wouldst thou betray me?

BRAKENBURY

I do beseech your Grace to pardon me, and withal
Forbear your conference with the noble duke.

BRAKENBURY

I beg your pardon, my lords, but the king gave me orders that no one, however high in rank, should speak privately to Clarence.

RICHARD

All right. If you like, Brakenbury, you can listen to anything we say. We're not saying anything treasonous, man. We say the king is wise and good, and his noble queen is getting old, pretty, and not jealous. And that Mr. Shore's wife has nice feet, cherry lips, pretty eyes, and a very pleasant way of expressing herself. And, finally, that the queen's relatives have all been elevated in rank. What do you think? Is there anything inaccurate in that?

BRAKENBURY

I have nothing to do with what you're talking about, my lord.

RICHARD

To do "nothing," or "naught," meant to have sex. Richard is playing off Brakenbury's innocent, frightened remark.

"Nothing to do" with Mrs. Shore! I tell you, mister, there's only one man who gets to do "nothing" with her and not be punished for it. Everyone else had better keep their "nothings" to themselves.

BRAKENBURY

Who is that, my lord?

RICHARD

Her husband, you rascal. Are you going to get me in trouble?

BRAKENBURY

"Grace" is a title of address for nobility and royalty and might apply to a king, queen, duke, duchess, or archbishop.

I beg your Grace to pardon me, and now please stop talking to Clarence.

CLARENCE
105   We know thy charge, Brakenbury, and will obey.

RICHARD
        We are the queen's abjects and must obey.—
        Brother, farewell. I will unto the king,
        And whatsoe'er you will employ me in,
        Were it to call King Edward's widow "sister,"
110   I will perform it to enfranchise you.
        Meantime, this deep disgrace in brotherhood
        Touches me deeper than you can imagine.

CLARENCE
        I know it pleaseth neither of us well.

RICHARD
        Well, your imprisonment shall not be long.
115   I will deliver you or else lie for you.
        Meantime, have patience.

CLARENCE
        I must perforce. Farewell.

                        Exeunt CLARENCE, BRAKENBURY, *and guard*

RICHARD
        Go tread the path that thou shalt ne'er return.
        Simple, plain Clarence, I do love thee so
120   That I will shortly send thy soul to heaven,
        If heaven will take the present at our hands.
        But who comes here? The new-delivered Hastings?

        Enter HASTINGS

HASTINGS
        Good time of day unto my gracious lord.

RICHARD
        As much unto my good Lord Chamberlain.
125   Well are you welcome to the open air.
        How hath your lordship brooked imprisonment?

CLARENCE

> We know you have a job to do, Brakenbury, and we'll do what you say.

RICHARD

> We are required to serve the queen, and we must obey her. Farewell, brother. I will go to the king and do whatever you want me to, even if it's to call my brother's wife "sister," in order to set you free. But just so you know, I am very angry about how our own brother has treated you, angrier than you can imagine.

CLARENCE

> It doesn't make either of us happy, I know.

RICHARD

> Well, your imprisonment won't last long. I will either get you out, lying if I have to, or stay in prison in your place. In the meantime, be patient.

CLARENCE

> I have no choice. Goodbye.

CLARENCE, BRAKENBURY, *and the guards exit.*

RICHARD

> Go walk the path that you will never return from. Dumb, honest Clarence. I love you so much that I'll send your soul to heaven very soon—if heaven will accept anything from me, that is. But who's coming? The newly released Hastings?

HASTINGS *enters.*

HASTINGS

> Good afternoon, my dear lord!

RICHARD

> The same to you, my lord! Welcome to the open air again. How did you tolerate prison?

HASTINGS

With patience, noble lord, as prisoners must.
But I shall live, my lord, to give them thanks
That were the cause of my imprisonment.

RICHARD

130 No doubt, no doubt; and so shall Clarence too,
For they that were your enemies are his
And have prevailed as much on him as you.

HASTINGS

More pity that the eagle should be mewed
While kites and buzzards prey at liberty.

RICHARD

135 What news abroad?

HASTINGS

No news so bad abroad as this at home:
The king is sickly, weak and melancholy,
And his physicians fear him mightily.

RICHARD

Now, by Saint Paul, that news is bad indeed.
140 O, he hath kept an evil diet long,
And overmuch consumed his royal person.
'Tis very grievous to be thought upon.
Where is he, in his bed?

HASTINGS

He is.

RICHARD

145 Go you before, and I will follow you.

Exit HASTINGS

ACT 1, SCENE 1

NO FEAR SHAKESPEARE

HASTINGS

With patience, noble lord, as prisoners must. But I will live to thank those who sent me there.

RICHARD

No doubt, no doubt. And so will Clarence, for your enemies are his enemies, and they have gotten the upper hand of him as well as of you.

HASTINGS

It's a shame that we eagles are caged up while the vultures are free to do whatever they please.

RICHARD

What's the news abroad?

HASTINGS

No news as bad as the news at home: The king is sickly, weak, and depressed, and his doctors are very afraid he's going to die

RICHARD

Now, by George, that really is terrible news. Oh, the king has abused his body with bad habits for a long time, and it's finally taking its toll on him. Very sad. Where is he, in his bed?

HASTINGS

He is.

RICHARD

You go ahead, and I will follow you.

HASTINGS exits.

He cannot live, I hope, and must not die
Till George be packed with post-horse up to heaven.
I'll in to urge his hatred more to Clarence
With lies well steeled with weighty arguments,
150   And, if I fail not in my deep intent,
Clarence hath not another day to live;
Which done, God take King Edward to His mercy,
And leave the world for me to bustle in.
For then I'll marry Warwick's youngest daughter.
155   What though I killed her husband and her father?
The readiest way to make the wench amends
Is to become her husband and her father;
The which will I, not all so much for love
As for another secret close intent
160   By marrying her which I must reach unto.
But yet I run before my horse to market.
Clarence still breathes; Edward still lives and reigns.
When they are gone, then must I count my gains.

Exit

The king won't live, I hope. But he'd better not die till Clarence is sent packing to heaven. I'll go see the king and, with carefully argued lies, get him to hate Clarence even more than he already does. If my plan succeeds, Clarence doesn't have another day to live. Then God's free to send King Edward to heaven, too, and leave me the world to run around in! I'll marry the earl of Warwick's youngest daughter, Lady Anne. So what if I killed her husband and her father? The best way to make up for the girl's losses is to become what she's lost: a husband and a father. So that's what I'll do, not because I love her but because I'll get something out of it. But I'm running ahead of myself. Clarence is still alive; Edward is not only alive, he's king. Only when they're dead can I start to count my gains.

He exits.

ACT 1, SCENE 2

Enter the corse of Henry the Sixth, on a bier, with halberds to guard it, Lady ANNE *being the mourner, accompanied by gentlemen*

ANNE

Set down, set down your honorable load,
If honor may be shrouded in a hearse,
Whilst I awhile obsequiously lament
Th' untimely fall of virtuous Lancaster.

They set down the bier

5   Poor key-cold figure of a holy king,
Pale ashes of the house of Lancaster,
Thou bloodless remnant of that royal blood,
Be it lawful that I invocate thy ghost
To hear the lamentations of poor Anne,
10   Wife to thy Edward, to thy slaughtered son,
Stabbed by the selfsame hand that made these wounds.
Lo, in these windows that let forth thy life
I pour the helpless balm of my poor eyes.
O, cursèd be the hand that made these holes;
15   Cursèd the heart that had the heart to do it;
Cursèd the blood that let this blood from hence.
More direful hap betide that hated wretch
That makes us wretched by the death of thee
Than I can wish to wolves, to spiders, toads,
20   Or any creeping venomed thing that lives.
If ever he have child, abortive be it,
Prodigious, and untimely brought to light,
Whose ugly and unnatural aspect
May fright the hopeful mother at the view,
25   And that be heir to his unhappiness.

ACT 1, SCENE 2

A "bier" is a framework for carrying or displaying a corpse or coffin.

The corpse of KING HENRY VI *is carried in on a bier, followed by Lady* ANNE, *dressed in mourning clothes, and armed guards.*

ANNE

Set down your honorable load, men, if there is ever any honor in being dead. I want to mourn the cruel death of this good man. Look at the noble king's poor cold body—the measly remains of the Lancaster family.

They put down the bier.

Anne's husband was Prince Edward, King Henry's son and a Lancaster.

His royal blood has drained right out of him. I hope I can talk to your ghost, Henry, without breaking church laws. I want you to hear my sorrow. My husband was murdered by the same man who stabbed you. My tears now fall into the holes where your life leaked out. I curse the man who made these holes. I curse the man's heart who had the heart to stab you. And I curse the man's blood who shed your blood. I want the man who made me suffer by killing you to face a more terrible end than I could wish on spiders, toads, and all the poisonous, venomous things things alive. If he ever has a child, let it be born prematurely, and let it look like a monster—so ugly and unnatural that the sight of it frightens its own mother.

If ever he have wife, let her be made
More miserable by the death of him
Than I am made by my poor lord and thee.—
Come now towards Chertsey with your holy load,
30   Taken from Paul's to be interrèd there.

They take up the bier

And still, as you are weary of this weight,
Rest you, whiles I lament King Henry's corse.

Enter RICHARD, Duke of Gloucester

RICHARD
Stay, you that bear the corse, and set it down.

ANNE
What black magician conjures up this fiend
35   To stop devoted charitable deeds?

RICHARD
Villains, set down the corse or, by Saint Paul,
I'll make a corse of him that disobeys.

GENTLEMAN
My lord, stand back and let the coffin pass.

RICHARD
Unmannered dog, stand thou when I command!—
40   Advance thy halberd higher than my breast,
Or by Saint Paul I'll strike thee to my foot
And spurn upon thee, beggar, for thy boldness.

They set down the bier

And if he ever has a wife, let her be more miserable
when he dies than I am now. Guards, let's continue on
to Chertsey monastery, carrying this holy burden you
picked up at St. Paul's monastery.

They pick up the bier.

When it gets too heavy, rest, and I'll lament over King
Henry's corpse some more.

RICHARD *enters.*

RICHARD

Halt, corpse bearers, and put down your load.

ANNE

What wicked magician has conjured up this devil to
interrupt this sacred burial rite?

RICHARD

Villains, set down the corpse, or I'll make a corpse of
you.

GENTLEMAN

My lord, stand back and let the coffin pass.

RICHARD

Rude dog! Stop when I command you to! And put up
your weapon so it's not pointing at my chest, or I'll
strike you to the ground and trample on you, you beggar, for being so bold.

They put down the bier.

ANNE

(to gentlemen and halberds)
What, do you tremble? Are you all afraid?
Alas, I blame you not, for you are mortal,
45   And mortal eyes cannot endure the devil.—
Avaunt, thou dreadful minister of hell.
Thou hadst but power over his mortal body;
His soul thou canst not have. Therefore begone.

RICHARD

Sweet saint, for charity, be not so curst.

ANNE

50   Foul devil, for God's sake, hence, and trouble us not,
For thou hast made the happy earth thy hell,
Filled it with cursing cries and deep exclaims.
If thou delight to view thy heinous deeds,
Behold this pattern of thy butcheries.

She points to the corse

55   O, gentlemen, see, see dead Henry's wounds
Open their congealed mouths and bleed afresh!—
Blush, blush, thou lump of foul deformity,
For 'tis thy presence that exhales this blood
From cold and empty veins where no blood dwells.
60   Thy deeds, inhuman and unnatural,
Provokes this deluge most unnatural.—
O God, which this blood mad'st, revenge his death!
O earth, which this blood drink'st revenge his death!
Either heaven with lightning strike the murderer dead,
65   Or earth gape open wide and eat him quick,
As thou dost swallow up this good king's blood,
Which his hell-governed arm hath butcherèd!

ANNE

(to the gentlemen and guards) What, are you trembling? You're all afraid of him? Well, I can't blame you. You're only human, after all, and mortals can't stand to look at the devil. *(to* RICHARD*)* Begone, you dreadful servant of hell. You only had power over my father-in-law's body; you can't have his soul. So get out.

RICHARD

Sweet saint, for goodness's sake, don't be so angry.

ANNE

Ugly devil, for God's sake, get out of here and leave us alone. You have made the happy world into your hell, filling it with cursing cries and lamentations. If you enjoy looking at your awful deeds, take a look at this noteworthy example of your butcheries.

She points to the corpse.

Oh, gentlemen, look, look! Dead Henry's wounds have opened up and are bleeding again! —Shame on you, you deformed lump. It's your presence that draws out this blood from his empty veins. Your inhuman and unnatural actions have provoked this unnatural flood of blood. Oh God, who made this blood, revenge his death! Oh earth, which soaks up this blood, revenge his death! Either let heaven send lightning to strike the murderer dead or let the earth open wide and devour him, as it does this good king's blood.

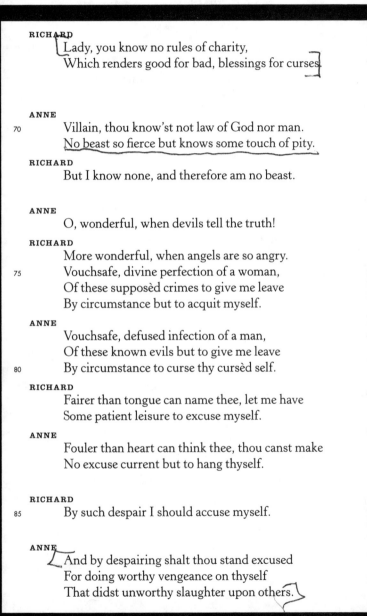

RICHARD
Lady, you know no rules of charity,
Which renders good for bad, blessings for curses.

ANNE
70   Villain, thou know'st not law of God nor man.
No beast so fierce but knows some touch of pity.

RICHARD
But I know none, and therefore am no beast.

ANNE
O, wonderful, when devils tell the truth!

RICHARD
More wonderful, when angels are so angry.
75   Vouchsafe, divine perfection of a woman,
Of these supposèd crimes to give me leave
By circumstance but to acquit myself.

ANNE
Vouchsafe, defused infection of a man,
Of these known evils but to give me leave
80   By circumstance to curse thy cursèd self.

RICHARD
Fairer than tongue can name thee, let me have
Some patient leisure to excuse myself.

ANNE
Fouler than heart can think thee, thou canst make
No excuse current but to hang thyself.

RICHARD
85   By such despair I should accuse myself.

ANNE
And by despairing shalt thou stand excused
For doing worthy vengeance on thyself
That didst unworthy slaughter upon others.

RICHARD

Dear woman, you don't know the rules of charity. When faced with bad, you're supposed to turn it into good, and when subject to curses, you're supposed to convert them into blessings.

ANNE

Villain, you don't know the laws of God or of man. Even the fiercest wild animal has some touch of pity.

RICHARD

If I know nothing about pity, that must mean I'm not an animal.

ANNE

It's amazing to hear a devil speak the truth!

RICHARD

It's even stranger when an angel is so angry. Divine, perfect woman, give me a chance to prove in detail that I'm innocent of the evils you accuse me of.

ANNE

Contagious infection of humanity, give me a chance to condemn you for the evils I know you've committed.

RICHARD

You who are beautiful beyond words, calm down and let me explain myself.

ANNE

You who are wicked beyond belief, the only "explanation" I'll accept from you is for you to hang yourself.

RICHARD

Such an expression of despair would only prove that I was guilty.

ANNE

Maybe, but if you killed yourself, it would also show that you felt some guilt for killing others.

RICHARD
    Say that I slew them not.

ANNE
90   Then say they were not slain.
    But dead they are, and devilish slave, by thee.

RICHARD
    I did not kill your husband.

ANNE
    Why then, he is alive.

RICHARD
    Nay, he is dead, and slain by Edward's hands.

ANNE
95   In thy foul throat thou liest. Queen Margaret saw
    Thy murd'rous falchion smoking in his blood,
    The which thou once didst bend against her breast,
    But that thy brothers beat aside the point.

RICHARD
    I was provokèd by her sland'rous tongue,
100   That laid their guilt upon my guiltless shoulders.

ANNE
    Thou wast provokèd by thy bloody mind,
    That never dream'st on aught but butcheries.
    Didst thou not kill this king?

RICHARD
    I grant you.

ANNE
105   Dost grant me, hedgehog? Then, God grant me too
    Thou mayst be damnèd for that wicked deed.
    O, he was gentle, mild, and virtuous.

RICHARD
    The better for the King of heaven that hath him.

ANNE
    He is in heaven, where thou shalt never come.

RICHARD
110   Let him thank me, that holp to send him thither,
    For he was fitter for that place than earth.

RICHARD

Let's say I didn't kill them.

ANNE

Then you might as well say they're not dead. But they are dead, and you killed them, you slave of the devil.

RICHARD

I did not kill your husband.

ANNE

Well, then he must be alive.

RICHARD

No, he is dead. Edward killed him.

ANNE

You're lying. Queen Margaret saw your sword steaming with his blood. It was the same sword you almost killed her with—and you would have killed her if my brothers hadn't fought you off.

RICHARD

She provoked me with her lying mouth, accusing me of crimes I didn't commit.

ANNE

No, what provoked you was your own bloody mind, which never thinks about anything but butchering. You killed this king, didn't you?

RICHARD

Yes, I'll grant you that.

ANNE

You'll grant me, you hedgehog? Then let God grant me that you'll be damned for that wicked deed. Oh, he was gentle, mild, and virtuous.

RICHARD

That will please God, who has him now.

ANNE

He is in heaven, where you will never go.

RICHARD

Let him thank me, who helped him get there. He's better suited to be there than here.

ANNE
> And thou unfit for any place but hell.

RICHARD
> Yes, one place else, if you will hear me name it.

ANNE
> Some dungeon.

RICHARD
115 > Your bedchamber.

ANNE
> Ill rest betide the chamber where thou liest!

RICHARD
> So will it, madam till I lie with you.

ANNE
> I hope so.

RICHARD
>   I know so. But, gentle Lady Anne,
> To leave this keen encounter of our wits
120 > And fall something into a slower method—
> Is not the causer of the timeless deaths
> Of these Plantagenets, Henry and Edward,
> As blameful as the executioner?

ANNE

And you're not suited for any place except hell.

RICHARD

Yes, and one other place, if you'll only let me name it.

ANNE

Some dungeon.

RICHARD

Your bedroom.

ANNE

There is no rest to be had in any bedroom where you are!

RICHARD

Exactly, madam, until I sleep with you.

ANNE

I hope you're right.

Anne assumes that she's never going to sleep with him.

RICHARD

I know I am. But, gentle Lady Anne, let's stop this rapid-fire argument and move more slowly. Isn't the person who caused the untimely deaths of these two Plantagenets, Henry and Edward, as much to blame as the person who actually executed the murders?

Plantagenet was the name of the royal family that ruled England from the twelfth to the fifteenth centuries. Both the Lancasters, the family to which Lady Anne's husband and father-in-law belonged, and the Yorks, the family to which Richard and his brothers belong, are descended from the Plantagenets.

ANNE
          Thou wast the cause and most accursed effect.

RICHARD
125   Your beauty was the cause of that effect—
          Your beauty, that did haunt me in my sleep
          To undertake the death of all the world,
          So I might live one hour in your sweet bosom.

ANNE
          If I thought that, I tell thee, homicide,
130   These nails should rend that beauty from my cheeks.

RICHARD
          These eyes could never endure that beauty's wrack.
          You should not blemish it, if I stood by.
          As all the world is cheered by the sun,
          So I by that. It is my day, my life.

ANNE
135   Black night o'ershade thy day, and death thy life.

RICHARD
          Curse not thyself, fair creature; thou art both.

ANNE
          I would I were, to be revenged on thee.

RICHARD
          It is a quarrel most unnatural
          To be revenged on him that loveth thee.

ANNE
140   It is a quarrel just and reasonable
          To be revenged on him that killed my husband.

RICHARD
          He that bereft thee, lady, of thy husband
          Did it to help thee to a better husband.

ANNE
          His better doth not breathe upon the earth.

obsession with

Perfection

ANNE

You're both those people—responsible for both cause and effect.

RICHARD

Your beauty caused what I did. It haunted me in my sleep. I would have killed the whole world just to be able spend one hour next to you.

ANNE

If I believed you, murderer, I would take my nails and scratch that beauty right off my cheeks.

RICHARD

I couldn't stand to see you destroy your beauty; you won't touch it as long as I'm standing next to you. Just as everyone becomes cheerful from the sun, I'm cheered up by your looks. They are my daylight, my life.

ANNE

Then I hope night shadows your day, and death takes your life!

RICHARD

Don't damn yourself. You, fair lady, are both my day and my life.

ANNE

I wish I were, so I could deprive you of both day and life.

RICHARD

It's strange that you want to take revenge on the person who loves you.

ANNE

It's just and reasonable that I want to take revenge on the person who killed my husband.

RICHARD

The man who killed your husband, dear lady, only did it to help you get a better husband.

ANNE

There is no better one on earth.

RICHARD

145   He lives that loves thee better than he could.

ANNE

Name him.

RICHARD

Plantagenet.

ANNE

Why, that was he.

RICHARD

The selfsame name, but one of better nature.

ANNE

Where is he?

RICHARD

Here.

She spitteth at him

Why dost thou spit at me?

ANNE

Would it were mortal poison for thy sake.

RICHARD

150   Never came poison from so sweet a place.

ANNE

Never hung poison on a fouler toad.   *Talking to the King.*
Out of my sight! Thou dost infect mine eyes.

RICHARD

Thine eyes, sweet lady, have infected mine.

ANNE

Would they were basilisks to strike thee dead.

RICHARD

Wrong. There is a man who loves you better than your husband could.

ANNE

Name him.

RICHARD

Plantagenet.

ANNE

Yes, that's my husband's name.

RICHARD

Someone else has the same name, but he's a better man.

ANNE

Where is this man?

RICHARD

Here.

ANNE *spits at him.*

Why do you spit at me?

ANNE

If only I could spit poison.

RICHARD

Poison never came from such a sweet place.

ANNE

Poison never landed on such an ugly toad. Get out of my sight! You're poisoning my eyes.

RICHARD

Your beautiful eyes, sweet lady, have infected mine with love.

ANNE

Basilisks were mythical creatures whose glances killed the people they landed on.

I wish my eyes were basilisks, so they could strike you dead!

RICHARD

155 I would they were, that I might die at once,
For now they kill me with a living death.
Those eyes of thine from mine have drawn salt tears,
Shamed their aspect with store of childish drops.
These eyes, which never shed remorseful tear—
160 No, when my father York and Edward wept
To hear the piteous moan that Rutland made
When black-faced Clifford shook his sword at him;
Nor when thy warlike father, like a child,
Told the sad story of my father's death
165 And twenty times made pause to sob and weep,
That all the standers-by had wet their cheeks
Like trees bedashed with rain—in that sad time,
My manly eyes did scorn an humble tear;
And what these sorrows could not thence exhale
170 Thy beauty hath, and made them blind with weeping.
I never sued to friend, nor enemy;
My tongue could never learn sweet smoothing word.
But now thy beauty is proposed my fee,
My proud heart sues, and prompts my tongue to speak.

She looks scornfully at him

175 Teach not thy lip such scorn, for it were made
For kissing, lady, not for such contempt.
If thy revengeful heart cannot forgive,
Lo, here I lend thee this sharp-pointed sword,
Which if thou please to hide in this true breast
180 And let the soul forth that adoreth thee,
I lay it naked to the deadly stroke
And humbly beg the death upon my knee.

He kneels and lays his breast open; she offers at it with his sword

RICHARD

I wish they were, so that I could die right now, because, at this point, I live a living death. Your eyes have made me cry, shamefully, like a child. I never cried before this. I didn't cry when my father, York, and my brother Edward both wept at the death of my brother Rutland, whom Clifford slaughtered. And when your warrior-father recounted the sad story of my father's death, pausing to sob twenty times in the course of the story so that all the bystanders ended up dripping tears like trees in a rainstorm—even then, I refused to cry. But your beauty has made me cry until I couldn't see. I never tried to win over a friend or enemy with sweet words. I'm too proud for that. But if your beauty is the reward for sweet talk, I'll talk.

ANNE *looks at him with disgust.*

Don't curl your lips in scorn. They were made for kissing, not for contempt. If your vengeful heart can't forgive me, here—take my sword and bury it in my heart so that my soul, which adores you, can be free. I open myself to being stabbed. In fact, I beg for death on my knees.

He opens his shirt to expose his chest, and she points the sword toward it.

[handwritten note, left margin: Admits to Murder / Dumb?]

Nay, do not pause; for I did kill King Henry—
But 'twas thy beauty that provokèd me.
185 Nay, now dispatch; 'twas I that stabbed young Edward—
But 'twas thy heavenly face that set me on.

[handwritten note, right: Tells her to kill him]

She falls the sword

Take up the sword again, or take up me.

ANNE

Arise, dissembler. Though I wish thy death,
I will not be the executioner.

RICHARD

190 *(rising)* Then bid me kill myself, and I will do it.

ANNE

I have already.

RICHARD

                    That was in thy rage.
Speak it again and, even with the word,
This hand, which for thy love did kill thy love,
Shall for thy love kill a far truer love.
195 To both their deaths shalt thou be accessory.

ANNE

I would I knew thy heart.

RICHARD

'Tis figured in my tongue.

ANNE

I fear me both are false.

RICHARD

Then never man was man true.

ANNE

200 Well, well, put up your sword.

RICHARD

Say then my peace is made.

ANNE

That shall you know hereafter.

No, don't pause, because I *did* kill King Henry, though it was your beauty that made me do it. Go ahead. And it *was* me who stabbed young Edward, though it was your heavenly face that set me to work.

ANNE *lets the sword drop.*

Take up the sword again, or take me up.

ANNE

Get up, liar. Though I wish you were dead, I'm not going to be the one to kill you.

RICHARD

(rising) Then tell me to kill myself, and I will.

ANNE

I have already.

RICHARD

You said it when you were furious. Say it again—just one word, and my hand, which killed your lover out of love, will kill your far truer lover. You will be an accessory to both crimes.

ANNE

I wish I knew what was in your heart.

RICHARD

I've told you.

ANNE

I fear that your words and your heart are both false.

RICHARD

Then no man has ever been honest.

ANNE

Well, then, put your sword away.

RICHARD

Tell me that you'll accept my love.

ANNE

You'll know about that later.

RICHARD
But shall I live in hope?

ANNE
All men I hope live so.

RICHARD
205   Vouchsafe to wear this ring.

ANNE
To take is not to give.

He places the ring on her finger

RICHARD
Look, how this ring encompasseth finger;
Even so thy breast encloseth my poor heart.
Wear both of them, for both of them are thine.
210   And if thy poor devoted servant may
But beg one favor at thy gracious hand,
Thou dost confirm his happiness forever.

ANNE
What is it?

RICHARD
That it would please you leave these sad designs
215   To him that hath more cause to be a mourner,
And presently repair to Crosby House,
Where, after I have solemnly interred
At Chertsey monast'ry this noble king
And wet his grave with my repentant tears,
220   I will with all expedient duty see you.
For divers unknown reasons, I beseech you,
Grant me this boon.

ANNE
With all my heart, and much it joys me too
To see you are become so penitent.—
225   Tressel and Berkeley, go along with me.

RICHARD
Bid me farewell.

RICHARD

But can I have some hope?

ANNE

I'd like to think all men have some hope.

RICHARD

Please wear this ring.

ANNE

I'll take the ring, but don't assume I'm giving you anything in return.

He places the ring on her finger.

RICHARD

See how my ring encircles your finger? That's how your heart embraces my poor heart. Wear both the ring and my heart, because both are yours. And if I, your poor devoted servant, may ask you for one small favor, you will guarantee my happiness forever.

ANNE

What's that?

RICHARD

Please leave it to me to take care of the burial, as I have more reason to mourn than you do. Meanwhile go to my estate at Crosby Place. After I have performed the solemn burial rites for this noble king at Chertsey monastery and cried with regret at his grave, I'll hurry to meet you. For various reasons that must remain secret, please do this for me.

ANNE

I'll do it with all my heart. I'm happy to see you've come to repent for what you've done. Tressel and Berkeley, come with me.

RICHARD

Say goodbye to me.

ANNE
                              'Tis more than you deserve;
              But since you teach me how to flatter you,
              Imagine I have said "farewell" already.

                                    Exeunt Lady ANNE *and two others*

RICHARD
              Sirs, take up the corse.

GENTLEMAN
230   Towards Chertsey, noble lord?

RICHARD
              No, to Whitefriars. There attend my coming.

                                    Exeunt all but RICHARD

              Was ever woman in this humor wooed?
              Was ever woman in this humor won?
              I'll have her, but I will not keep her long.
235   What, I that killed her husband and his father,
              To take her in her heart's extremest hate,
              With curses in her mouth, tears in her eyes,
              The bleeding witness of my hatred by,
              Having God, her conscience, and these bars against me,
240   And I no friends to back my suit at all
              But the plain devil and dissembling looks?
              And yet to win her, all the world to nothing!
              Ha!
              Hath she forgot already that brave prince,
245   Edward, her lord, whom I some three months since
              Stabbed in my angry mood at Tewkesbury?
              A sweeter and a Lovellier gentleman,
              Framed in the prodigality of nature,
              Young, valiant, wise, and, no doubt, right royal,
250   The spacious world cannot again afford.

ANNE

It's more than you deserve. But since you're already teaching me how to flatter you, pretend I've said goodbye already.

ANNE and two others exit.

RICHARD

Sirs, take up the corpse.

GENTLEMEN

Toward Chertsey, noble lord?

RICHARD

No, to the Whitefriars monastery. Wait for me there.

Everyone exits except RICHARD.

Has anyone ever courted a woman in this state of mind? And has anyone ever won her, as I've done? I'll get her, but I won't keep her long. What! I, who killed her husband and his father, managed to win her over when her hatred for me was strongest, while she's swearing her head off, sobbing her eyes out, and the bloody corpse, proof of why she should hate me, right in front of her? She has God, her conscience, and my own acts against me, and I have nothing on my side but the ugly devil and my false looks. And yet, against all odds, I win her over! Ha! Has she already forgotten her brave husband, Prince Edward, whom I stabbed on the battlefield three months ago in my anger? The world will never again produce such a sweet, lovely gentleman. He was graced with lots of natural gifts, he was young, valiant, wise, and no doubt meant to be king.

And will she yet abase her eyes on me,
That cropped the golden prime of this sweet prince
And made her widow to a woeful bed?
On me, whose all not equals Edward's moiety?
255   On me, that halts and am misshapen thus?
My dukedom to a beggarly denier,
I do mistake my person all this while!
Upon my life, she finds, although I cannot,
Myself to be a marv'lous proper man.
260   I'll be at charges for a looking glass
And entertain a score or two of tailors
To study fashions to adorn my body.
Since I am crept in favor with myself,
I will maintain it with some little cost.
265   But first I'll turn yon fellow in his grave
And then return lamenting to my love.
Shine out, fair sun, till I have bought a glass,
That I may see my shadow as I pass.

Exit

And yet she cheapens herself by turning her gaze on me, who cut her sweet prince's life short and made her a widow? On me, though I am barely half the man that Edward was? On me, though I am limping and deformed? I bet I've been wrong about myself all this time. Even though I don't see it, this lady thinks I'm a marvelously good-looking man. Time to buy myself a mirror and employ a few dozen tailors to dress me up in the current fashions. Since I'm suddenly all the rage, it will be worth the cost. But first, I'll dump this fellow in his grave, then return to my love weeping with grief. Come out, beautiful sun—until I've bought a mirror to admire my reflection in, I'll watch my shadow as I stroll along.

He exits.

ACT 1, SCENE 3

Enter QUEEN ELIZABETH, *Lord Marquess of* DORSET, *Lord*
RIVERS, *and Lord* GREY

RIVERS

    Have patience, madam. There's no doubt his majesty
    Will soon recover his accustomed health.

GREY

    In that you brook it ill, it makes him worse.
    Therefore, for God's sake, entertain good comfort
5   And cheer his grace with quick and merry eyes.

QUEEN ELIZABETH

    If he were dead, what would betide on me?

RIVERS

    No other harm but loss of such a lord.

QUEEN ELIZABETH

    The loss of such a lord includes all harms.

GREY

    The heavens have blessed you with a goodly son
10   To be your comforter when he is gone.

QUEEN ELIZABETH

    Ah, he is young, and his minority
    Is put unto the trust of Richard Gloucester,
    A man that loves not me nor none of you.

RIVERS

    Is it concluded that he shall be Protector?

QUEEN ELIZABETH

15   It is determined, not concluded yet;
    But so it must be if the king miscarry.

ACT 1, SCENE 3

QUEEN ELIZABETH, *the lord marquess of* DORSET, RIVERS, *and Lord* GREY *enter.*

RIVERS

Be patient, madam. I'm sure his majesty will recover his health soon.

GREY

You'll only make him worse with all your worry. For God's sake, let people comfort you. Then you'll be able to cheer *him* up.

QUEEN ELIZABETH

If he were dead, what would happen to me?

GREY

Nothing more than that you'd lose your husband.

QUEEN ELIZABETH

Losing *this* husband will cause me all sorts of harm.

GREY

You have been blessed with an excellent son, who will comfort you when the king is dead.

QUEEN ELIZABETH

But he's young, and as long as he's too young to become king, Richard, the duke of Gloucester, has power over him. Richard loves neither me nor any of you.

RIVERS

Has it been decided that Richard will be Protector?

A "Protector" acted for a king until he was old enough to rule on his own.

QUEEN ELIZABETH

It's been decided, though not yet officially announced. But that's what will happen if the king dies.

Enter BUCKINGHAM *and Lord* STANLEY, *Earl of Derby*

GREY
>Here comes the lord of Buckingham, and Derby.

BUCKINGHAM
>*(to* QUEEN ELIZABETH*)* Good time of day unto your
>royal Grace.

STANLEY
20 >God make your Majesty joyful, as you have been.

QUEEN ELIZABETH
>The countess Richmond, good my lord of Derby,
>To your good prayer will scarcely say amen.
>Yet, Derby, notwithstanding she's your wife
>And loves not me, be you, good lord, assured
25 >I hate not you for her proud arrogance.

STANLEY
>I do beseech you either not believe
>The envious slanders of her false accusers,
>Or if she be accused in true report,
>Bear with her weakness, which I think proceeds
30 >From wayward sickness and no grounded malice.

QUEEN ELIZABETH
>Saw you the king today, my lord of Derby?

STANLEY
>But now the duke of Buckingham and I
>Are come from visiting his majesty.

QUEEN ELIZABETH
>What likelihood of his amendment, lords?

BUCKINGHAM
35 >Madam, good hope. His grace speaks cheerfully.

The duke of BUCKINGHAM *and Lord* STANLEY, *Earl of Derby, enter.*

GREY

Here come Lord Buckingham and Lord Derby.

BUCKINGHAM

(to QUEEN ELIZABETH*)* Good afternoon, your royal Highness!

STANLEY

I hope God makes you happy again, like you once were.

QUEEN ELIZABETH

My good Lord Derby, the countess Richmond would hardly say "amen" to your kind words. But don't worry. I don't hold it against *you*, even though she's your wife, that she's so unfriendly and arrogant.

Before the Countess of Richmond was Stanley's wife, she was married to Edmund Tudor. She is the mother of the earl of Richmond, the future Henry VII, who will prove to be an important character later in this play.

STANLEY

Please don't believe the false rumors you've heard about her feelings toward you, or if they're true, then forgive her, since she's only acting that way because she's sick, not because she hates you.

QUEEN ELIZABETH

Did you see the king today, Lord Derby?

STANLEY

Yes, the duke of Buckingham and I have just returned from visiting him.

QUEEN ELIZABETH

What are the chances of his getting better, lords?

BUCKINGHAM

Madam, keep up hope. He seems cheerful.

QUEEN ELIZABETH
God grant him health. Did you confer with him?

BUCKINGHAM
Ay, madam. He desires to make atonement
Betwixt the duke of Gloucester and your brothers,
And betwixt them and my Lord Chamberlain,
40   And sent to warn them to his royal presence.

QUEEN ELIZABETH
Would all were well—but that will never be.
I fear our happiness is at the height.

Enter RICHARD, *Duke of Gloucester, and* HASTINGS

RICHARD
They do me wrong, and I will not endure it!
Who is it that complains unto the king
45   That I, forsooth, am stern and love them not?
By holy Paul, they love his grace but lightly
That fill his ears with such dissentious rumors.
Because I cannot flatter and look fair,
Smile in men's faces, smooth, deceive and cog,
50   Duck with French nods and apish courtesy,
I must be held a rancorous enemy.
Cannot a plain man live and think no harm,
But thus his simple truth must be abused
With silken, sly, insinuating jacks?

RIVERS
55   To whom in all this presence speaks your Grace?

RICHARD
To thee, that hast nor honesty nor grace.
When have I injured thee? When done thee wrong?—
Or thee?—Or thee? Or any of your faction?
A plague upon you all! His royal grace,
60   Whom God preserve better than you would wish,
Cannot be quiet scarce a breathing while
But you must trouble him with lewd complaints.

QUEEN ELIZABETH

> God give him health. Did you talk with him?

BUCKINGHAM

> Yes, madam. He wants to patch things up between Richard and your brothers, and between your brothers and Hastings. He has summoned them all.

QUEEN ELIZABETH

> I wish I could believe you that all was well! But I'm worried that things can only go downhill from here.

RICHARD, HASTINGS, *and* DORSET *enter.*

RICHARD

> They're out to get me, and I won't stand for it! Which of you has been complaining to the king that I don't like them? By God, whoever is worrying the king with these lies doesn't love him very much. Just because I don't know how to flatter and act nice, to smile in men's faces and, as soon as their backs are turned, spread rumors about them, to bow and scrape like a nobleman trained in the French court, people have to think I'm their enemy. Can't a plain man live and do no harm to anyone without being taken advantage of by a bunch of slick, sneaky lowlifes?

RIVERS

> Which of us are you referring to?

RICHARD

> You, who are neither honest nor good. When did I ever do you any harm? Or you? Or you? Or any of you? Damn you all! The king—whom I hope God will protect better than you would like—can't get a minute's rest without you bothering him with your outrageous complaints.

QUEEN ELIZABETH
Brother of Gloucester, you mistake the matter.
The king, on his own royal disposition,
65   And not provoked by any suitor else,
Aiming belike at your interior hatred
That in your outward actions shows itself
Against my children, brothers, and myself,
Makes him to send, that he may learn the ground.

RICHARD
70   I cannot tell. The world is grown so bad
That wrens make prey where eagles dare not perch.
Since every jack became a gentleman,
There's many a gentle person made a jack.

QUEEN ELIZABETH
Come, come, we know your meaning, brother Gloucester.
75   You envy my advancement, and my friends'.
God grant we never may have need of you.

RICHARD
Meantime God grants that we have need of you.
Our brother is imprisoned by your means,
Myself disgraced, and the nobility
80   Held in contempt, while great promotions
Are daily given to ennoble those
That scarce some two days since were worth a noble.

QUEEN ELIZABETH
By Him that raised me to this careful height
From that contented hap which I enjoyed,
85   I never did incense his majesty
Against the duke of Clarence, but have been
An earnest advocate to plead for him.
My lord, you do me shameful injury
Falsely to draw me in these vile suspects.

QUEEN ELIZABETH

Brother, you've made a mistake. The king himself noticed your hatred toward my children, my brothers, and myself. No one had to point it out to him—it's obvious. He *asked* people to visit him. He wanted to find out the reason for your ill will, so he could do something about it.

RICHARD

I can't tell what's going on. The world has become so bad that now little wrens have settled where eagles used to roost. Since every peasant has been made into a nobleman, many noblemen have been dragged down to the level of peasants.

QUEEN ELIZABETH

Come, come, I know what you're referring to, Richard. You resent my friends' rise in society, and my own. Let's hope we never need your help for anything.

RICHARD

Meanwhile, we're the ones who need you. My brother is imprisoned because of you, I am disgraced, and the nobility are held in contempt while those who two days ago weren't worth a dime have suddenly been promoted.

QUEEN ELIZABETH

By the Lord who raised me to this weighty post from the happy and carefree life I used to enjoy, I promise you I never did anything to get the king to turn against the duke of Clarence. In fact, I've always been on his side and have pleaded for him. My lord, you're doing me a huge injustice to suggest otherwise.

RICHARD

90   You may deny that you were not the mean
        Of my Lord Hastings' late imprisonment.

RIVERS

        She may, my lord, for—

RICHARD

        She may, Lord Rivers. Why, who knows not so?
        She may do more, sir, than denying that.
95   She may help you to many fair preferments
        And then deny her aiding hand therein,
        And lay those honors on your high desert.
        What may she not? She may, ay, marry, may she—

RIVERS

        What, marry, may she?

RICHARD

100   What, marry, may she? Marry with a king,
        A bachelor, a handsome stripling too.
        I wis, your grandam had a worser match.

QUEEN ELIZABETH

        My Lord of Gloucester, I have too long borne
        Your blunt upbraidings and your bitter scoffs.
105   By heaven, I will acquaint his majesty
        With those gross taunts that oft I have endured.
        I had rather be a country servant-maid
        Than a great queen with this condition,
        To be so baited, scorned, and stormèd at.

        Enter old QUEEN MARGARET, *apart from others*

110   Small joy have I in being England's queen.

QUEEN MARGARET

        (aside) And lessened be that small, God I beseech Him!
        Thy honor, state, and seat is due to me.

RICHARD

Oh, and I'll bet you'll also deny you were responsible for Lord Hastings's recent stay in prison.

RIVERS

She may deny that, my lord, because—

RICHARD

She may, Lord Rivers? Everybody knows she *may*. She may do a lot more than that, sir. She may help you to get many nice promotions, and then deny she helped you, claiming you won them on your own merits. What can't she do? She could even—

RIVERS

She could even what?

RICHARD

She could even what? She could marry a king, a bachelor, a handsome young lad. Certainly, your grandmother had a worse match.

QUEEN ELIZABETH

My lord of Gloucester, I have suffered your blunt upbraidings and your bitterness toward me for too long. By God, I will tell the king about these taunts. I would rather be a country serving maid than a great queen if it meant I could escape your scorn and constant harassment.

Old QUEEN MARGARET *enters without being seen.*

I've had very little joy as England's queen.

QUEEN MARGARET

Queen Margaret is the widow of King Henry VI, who was deposed and murdered by the Yorkists.

(speaking so no one else can hear) God, give her even less joy, I beg you! Elizabeth, your honor, your high rank, and your position as queen are all owed to me.

RICHARD
    (to QUEEN ELIZABETH*)* What, threat you me with telling of
        the king?
    Tell him, and spare not. Look, what I have said,
115   I will avouch 't in presence of the king;
    I dare adventure to be sent to th' Tower.
    'Tis time to speak. My pains are quite forgot.

QUEEN MARGARET
    (aside) Out, devil! I do remember them too well:
    Thou killed'st my husband Henry in the Tower,
120   And Edward, my poor son, at Tewkesbury.

RICHARD
    (to QUEEN ELIZABETH*)* Ere you were queen, ay, or your
        husband king,
    I was a packhorse in his great affairs,
    A weeder-out of his proud adversaries,
    A liberal rewarder of his friends.
125   To royalize his blood, I spent mine own.

QUEEN MARGARET
    (aside) Ay, and much better blood than his or thine.

RICHARD
    (to QUEEN ELIZABETH*)* In all which time, you and your
        husband Grey
    Were factious for the house of Lancaster.—
    And, Rivers, so were you. —Was not your husband
130   In Margaret's battle at Saint Albans slain?
    Let me put in your minds, if you forget,
    What you have been ere this, and what you are;
    Withal, what I have been, and what I am.

QUEEN MARGARET
    (aside) A murd'rous villain, and so still thou art.

RICHARD

> *(to* QUEEN ELIZABETH*)* What! You're threatening to tell the king? Go ahead, and don't spare a single detail. Look, what I have said to you I will repeat in the presence of the king. If it means I'll be sent to the Tower, so be it. It's time for me to speak the truth. All the pains I took on King Edward's behalf have been forgotten.

QUEEN MARGARET

> *(speaking so no one else can hear)* You devil! I remember these pains all too well. You killed my husband, Henry, in the Tower and my poor son, Edward, at Tewksbury.

RICHARD

> *(to* QUEEN ELIZABETH*)* Before you were queen—in fact, before your husband was king—I was a packhorse for his great affairs, a weeder-out of his proud enemies, a generous rewarder of his friends. In order to make his blood royal, I spent my own blood.

QUEEN MARGARET

Margaret is referring to the deaths of her own husband and son.

> *(speaking so no one else can hear)* Yes, and you spent better blood than his or your own.

RICHARD

> *(to* QUEEN ELIZABETH*)* In all that time, you and your first husband, Sir John Grey, were fighting for the Lancasters.—And so were you, Rivers.—Elizabeth, wasn't your first husband killed while fighting in Queen Margaret's army at Saint Alban's? In case you've forgotten, I want to remind you where you come from and what side you were on before you arrived here. And I want you to remember whom I fought for, who I have been, and who I am.

QUEEN MARGARET

> *(speaking so no one else can hear)* You were a murderous villain, and you still are.

RICHARD
135   *(to* QUEEN ELIZABETH*)* Poor Clarence did forsake his
          father Warwick,
    Ay, and forswore himself—which Jesu pardon!—

QUEEN MARGARET
    (aside) Which God revenge!

RICHARD
    To fight on Edward's party for the crown;
    And for his meed, poor lord, he is mewed up.
140   I would to God my heart were flint, like Edward's,
    Or Edward's soft and pitiful, like mine.
    I am too childish-foolish for this world.

QUEEN MARGARET
    (aside) Hie thee to hell for shame, and leave the world,
    Thou cacodemon! There thy kingdom is.

RIVERS
145   My Lord of Gloucester, in those busy days
    Which here you urge to prove us enemies,
    We followed then our lord, our sovereign king.
    So should we you, if you should be our king.

RICHARD
    If I should be? I had rather be a peddler.
150   Far be it from my heart, the thought thereof.

QUEEN ELIZABETH
    As little joy, my lord, as you suppose
    You should enjoy were you this country's king,
    As little joy may you suppose in me
    That I enjoy, being the queen thereof.

RICHARD

In Henry VI, Part 3, Clarence constantly shifted his loyalties from the Yorks (his own family) to th Lancasters, to which his father-in-law belonged.

(to ELIZABETH*)* Poor Clarence abandoned his father-in-law, a Lancaster, and broke his own oath—may Jesus forgive him!—

QUEEN MARGARET

(speaking so no one else can hear) May God take revenge on him!

RICHARD

(to QUEEN ELIZABETH*)* —in order to fight on Edward's side to help him win the crown. And now he is rewarded by being thrown in prison! I wish to God my heart were made of stone, like Edward's is. Or I wish Edward's were soft and full of feeling, as mine is, so that he would let Clarence go. I am too childish, too innocent, for this world.

QUEEN MARGARET

(speaking so no one else can hear) Hurry to hell, then, and leave the world alone, you demon! Hell is where your kingdom is.

RIVERS

My Lord of Gloucester, in those busy days, which you're bringing up now to prove we're your enemies, we followed the lawful king. If you were king, we would do the same.

RICHARD

If I were king? I'd rather be a peddler. The thought of being king doesn't appeal to me in the least.

QUEEN ELIZABETH

You're right to imagine that being this country's leader brings no pleasure. As queen, I have felt none.

QUEEN MARGARET

155   *(aside)* As little joy enjoys the queen thereof,
    For I am she, and altogether joyless.
    I can no longer hold me patient.

    She steps forward

    Hear me, you wrangling pirates, that fall out
    In sharing that which you have pilled from me!
160   Which of you trembles not that looks on me?
    If not, that I am queen, you bow like subjects,
    Yet that, by you deposed, you quake like rebels.—
    Ah, gentle villain, do not turn away.

RICHARD

    Foul, wrinkled witch, what mak'st thou in my sight?

QUEEN MARGARET

165   But repetition of what thou hast marred.
    That will I make before I let thee go.

RICHARD

    Wert thou not banishèd on pain of death?

QUEEN MARGARET

    I was, but I do find more pain in banishment
    Than death can yield me here by my abode.
170   A husband and a son thou ow'st to me;
    (to QUEEN ELIZABETH*)*
    And thou a kingdom; —all of you, allegiance.
    The sorrow that I have by right is yours,
    And all the pleasures you usurp are mine.

RICHARD

    The curse my noble father laid on thee
175   When thou didst crown his warlike brows with paper,
    And with thy scorns drew'st rivers from his eyes,
    And then, to dry them, gav'st the duke a clout
    Steeped in the faultless blood of pretty Rutland—
    His curses then, from bitterness of soul

QUEEN MARGARET

>*(speaking so no one else can hear)* No pleasure for the queen, indeed: I am the real queen, and the experience is completely joyless. I can no longer hold my tongue.

>*She moves forward so that everyone can see her.*

>Hear me, you wrangling pirates. You're quarreling over what doesn't even belong to you—you stole it from me! Which of you does not tremble when you see me? If you aren't trembling because you know I am queen and you are my subjects, then you're shaking because you threw me from the throne! *(to* RICHARD*)* Oh highborn villain, do not turn away!

RICHARD

>Ugly, wrinkled witch, what are you doing here?

QUEEN MARGARET

>Only describing what you have ruined. Or at least that's what I plan to do before I let you go.

RICHARD

>Weren't you banished on pain of death?

QUEEN MARGARET

>I was. But I felt more pain from exile than I would have from being dead here at home. You, Richard, owe me a husband and a son. The rest of you owe me a kingdom. And all of you owe me allegiance. The sorrow that I feel actually belongs to you, and the high life you enjoy actually belongs to me. You stole it from me.

RICHARD

Richard refers to events Shakespeare dramatizes in King Henry VI, Part 3 (Act 1, Scene 4). Queen Margaret has Richard's father, the third duke of York, killed.

>The curse my noble warrior-father laid on you when you set a paper crown on his head just before slaying him has finally borne fruit. Your scorn for him was so shocking that he cried rivers.

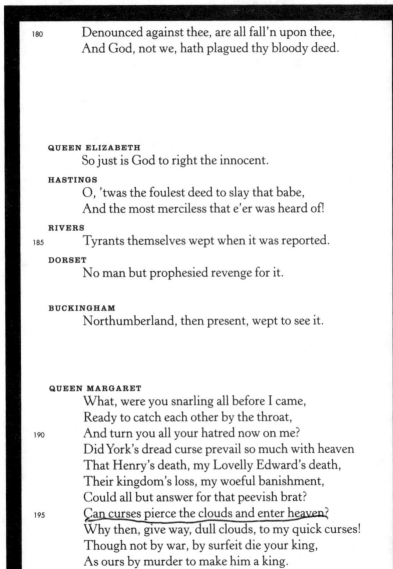

180   Denounced against thee, are all fall'n upon thee,
           And God, not we, hath plagued thy bloody deed.

QUEEN ELIZABETH
           So just is God to right the innocent.

HASTINGS
           O, 'twas the foulest deed to slay that babe,
           And the most merciless that e'er was heard of!

RIVERS
185   Tyrants themselves wept when it was reported.

DORSET
           No man but prophesied revenge for it.

BUCKINGHAM
           Northumberland, then present, wept to see it.

QUEEN MARGARET
           What, were you snarling all before I came,
           Ready to catch each other by the throat,
190   And turn you all your hatred now on me?
           Did York's dread curse prevail so much with heaven
           That Henry's death, my Lovelly Edward's death,
           Their kingdom's loss, my woeful banishment,
           Could all but answer for that peevish brat?
195   Can curses pierce the clouds and enter heaven?
           Why then, give way, dull clouds, to my quick curses!
           Though not by war, by surfeit die your king,
           As ours by murder to make him a king.

But before she kills him, she sets a paper crown on his head to mock him and hands him a rag soaked in his son Rutland's blood. He begs God to destroy her.

To stop up his tears, you handed him a rag soaked with the blood of his own child. God, not us, is responsible for punishing you for your bloody deed.

QUEEN ELIZABETH

God is just. He rewards the innocent.

HASTINGS

Oh, killing that child was the dirtiest, most merciless deed there ever was!

RIVERS

Tyrants themselves wept when they heard about it.

DORSET

Everyone understood there would be a heavy payback.

BUCKINGHAM

Even Northumberland wept to see it.

The earl of Northumberland was an enemy of Richard's family, the House of York.

QUEEN MARGARET

What, were you all snarling before I arrived, ready to catch each other by the throat like dogs, but now that I'm here, you turn your hatred toward me? Did the duke of York's terrible curse have so much weight with God that God repaid him not only with Henry's death and my lovely Edward's death but with the loss of their kingdom and with my banishment, too? All because of what happened to that brat Rutland? If curses can pierce the clouds and enter heaven that easily, then open up, thick clouds, and listen to *my* curses!

(to QUEEN ELIZABETH*)*
Edward thy son, that now is Prince of Wales,
200 For Edward our son, that was Prince of Wales,
Die in his youth by like untimely violence.
Thyself a queen, for me that was a queen,
Outlive thy glory, like my wretched self.
Long mayst thou live to wail thy children's death
205 And see another, as I see thee now,
Decked in thy rights, as thou art stalled in mine.
Long die thy happy days before thy death,
And, after many lengthened hours of grief,
Die neither mother, wife, nor England's queen.—
210 Rivers and Dorset, you were standers-by,
And so wast thou, Lord Hastings, when my son
Was stabbed with bloody daggers. God I pray Him
That none of you may live his natural age,
But by some unlooked accident cut off.

RICHARD
215 Have done thy charm, thou hateful, withered hag.

QUEEN MARGARET
And leave out thee? Stay, dog, for thou shalt hear me.
If heaven have any grievous plague in store
Exceeding those that I can wish upon thee,
O, let them keep it till thy sins be ripe
220 And then hurl down their indignation
On thee, the troubler of the poor world's peace.
The worm of conscience still begnaw thy soul.
Thy friends suspect for traitors while thou liv'st,
And take deep traitors for thy dearest friends.
225 No sleep close up that deadly eye of thine,
Unless it be while some tormenting dream
Affrights thee with a hell of ugly devils.

(to QUEEN ELIZABETH*)* Though your king did not die in battle, let him die from overindulging his appetites, as my husband was murdered to make your husband king. May your son Edward, who is currently the prince of Wales, die young and violently, as payback for the death of my son Edward, the former prince of Wales. And may you outlive your glory just as miserably as I have, to make up for taking *my* position as queen. May you live long enough to mourn your children's deaths and watch another woman enjoy the throne, as I now watch you. Let your happy days die long before you do. After many extended hours of grief, may you die neither a mother, a wife, nor England's queen. Rivers, Dorset, and Lord Hastings, you all stood by as my son was stabbed. For his sake, I pray to God that none of you die a natural death but have your lives cut short by some unforeseen accident.

RICHARD

Enough of your magic spells, you hateful, withered hag.

QUEEN MARGARET

And leave you out? Don't move, dog. It's your turn now. If heaven has any plagues beyond what I can drum up, let it wait until your sins are piled high and then hurl them down on you, you destroyer of a whole world of peace! May conscience eat away at your soul constantly. May you suspect your true friends of being traitors and take the worst traitors as your closest friends. May you never sleep a wink except to dream of a hell full of ugly devils.

Margaret wants Richard to die only after committing the maximum number of sins, so he can be guaranteed a greater punishment in Hell.

Thou elvish-marked, abortive, rooting hog,
Thou that wast sealed in thy nativity
230   The slave of nature and the son of hell,
Thou slander of thy heavy mother's womb,
Thou loathèd issue of thy father's loins,
Thou rag of honor, thou detested—

RICHARD

                                                                Margaret.

QUEEN MARGARET
    Richard!

RICHARD
                Ha?

QUEEN MARGARET
235   I call thee not.

RICHARD
    I cry thee mercy, then, for I did think
    That thou hadst called me all these bitter names.

QUEEN MARGARET
    Why, so I did, but looked for no reply.
    O, let me make the period to my curse!

RICHARD
240   'Tis done by me, and ends in "Margaret."

QUEEN ELIZABETH
    (to QUEEN MARGARET)
    Thus have you breathed your curse against yourself.

QUEEN MARGARET
    Poor painted queen, vain flourish of my fortune,
    Why strew'st thou sugar on that bottled spider,
    Whose deadly web ensnareth thee about?
245   Fool, fool, thou whet'st a knife to kill thyself.
    The day will come that thou shalt wish for me
    To help thee curse that poisonous bunch-backed toad.

HASTINGS
    False-boding woman, end thy frantic curse,
    Lest to thy harm thou move our patience.

You deformed, prematurely born, rooting hog, you evil birth defect, you insult to your mother's womb, you hated disgrace to your father's sperm, you disgusting—

RICHARD

Margaret.

QUEEN MARGARET

Richard.

RICHARD

Yes?

QUEEN MARGARET

I didn't call you.

RICHARD

I beg your pardon—I thought it was me whom you were calling all those terrible names.

QUEEN MARGARET

Yes, I was, but I don't want an answer from you. Let me finish my curse.

RICHARD

I've finished it for you, and it ends in "Margaret."

QUEEN ELIZABETH

He's turned your curse against you, Margaret.

QUEEN MARGARET

Poor imitation queen, why do you align yourself with this humpbacked spider when he's got you trapped in his deadly web? Fool! You're sharpening a knife to cut yourself. The day will come when you'll wish I could help you cast spells against this poisonous, hunchbacked toad.

HASTINGS

Woman, stop your frantic curses and false prophesies before we run out of patience and do something bad to you.

is Richard Just really Emotional?

QUEEN MARGARET
250   Foul shame upon you, you have all moved mine.

RIVERS
        Were you well served, you would be taught your duty.

QUEEN MARGARET
        To serve me well, you all should do me duty:
        Teach me to be your queen, and you my subjects.
        O, serve me well, and teach yourselves that duty!

DORSET
255   *(to* RIVERS*)* Dispute not with her; she is lunatic.

QUEEN MARGARET
        Peace, Master Marquess, you are malapert.
        Your fire-new stamp of honor is scarce current.
        O, that your young nobility could judge
        What 'twere to lose it and be miserable!
260   They that stand high have many blasts to shake them,
        And if they fall, they dash themselves to pieces.

RICHARD
        Good counsel, marry. —Learn it, learn it, marquess.

DORSET
        It touches you, my lord, as much as me.

RICHARD
        Ay, and much more; but I was born so high.
265   Our aerie buildeth in the cedar's top,
        And dallies with the wind and scorns the sun.

QUEEN MARGARET
        And turns the sun to shade. Alas, alas,
        Witness my son, now in the shade of death,
        Whose bright out-shining beams thy cloudy wrath
270   Hath in eternal darkness folded up.
        Your aerie buildeth in our aerie's nest.
        O God, that seest it, do not suffer it!
        As it was won with blood, lost be it so.

QUEEN MARGARET

Shame on you; I've already run out of patience with you all.

RIVERS

If you got what you deserved, you would learn some respect.

QUEEN MARGARET

What I deserve is that you treat me like a queen, and what you deserve is to act like my subjects. Give me what I deserve, and do your duty!

DORSET

(to RIVERS*)* Don't argue with her. She's crazy.

QUEEN MARGARET

Enough from you, mister, you're being impertinent. Unlike those born into nobility, your claim to royalty is so recent that you hardly even know what it means to lose it. People in high positions are shaken by many blasts of wind, and when they fall, they shatter into pieces.

RICHARD

Good advice, indeed. Take it to heart, Dorset.

DORSET

It applies to you as much as to me, my lord.

RICHARD

Yes, and much more so. But I was born that high. Like an eagle, which builds its nest at the top of a high tree, I play in the wind and am not afraid to look at the sun.

QUEEN MARGARET

But you turn that sun into a shadow. Take my son, for example. He is dead now. You put out his bright life forever. You are building your nest in *our* nest. Oh God who's watching, don't let him get away with this! He won his position violently. Let him lose it that way, too.

BUCKINGHAM
Peace, peace, for shame, if not for charity.

QUEEN MARGARET
275   Urge neither charity nor shame to me.
        (addressing the others)
        Uncharitably with me have you dealt,
        And shamefully my hopes by you are butchered.
        My charity is outrage, life my shame,
        And in that shame still live my sorrows' rage.

BUCKINGHAM
280   Have done, have done.

QUEEN MARGARET
        O princely Buckingham, I'll kiss thy hand
        In sign of league and amity with thee.
        Now fair befall thee and thy noble house!
        Thy garments are not spotted with our blood,
285   Nor thou within the compass of my curse.

BUCKINGHAM
        Nor no one here, for curses never pass
        The lips of those that breathe them in the air.

QUEEN MARGARET
        I will not think but they ascend the sky,
        And there awake God's gentle-sleeping peace.
        (aside to BUCKINGHAM*)*
290   O Buckingham, take heed of yonder dog!
        Look when he fawns, he bites; and when he bites,
        His venom tooth will rankle to the death.
        Have not to do with him. Beware of him.
        Sin, death, and hell have set their marks on him,
295   And all their ministers attend on him.

RICHARD
        What doth she say, my lord of Buckingham?

BUCKINGHAM
        Nothing that I respect, my gracious lord.

BUCKINGHAM

Stop—if you can't be kind, at least have some shame.

QUEEN MARGARET

How dare you talk about kindness or shame. *(to the others)* You have only been unkind to me, and you have shamefully butchered my hopes. My kindness to you is to be outraged at what has happened, and my sad, sad shame is in what you have done to my life.

BUCKINGHAM

Enough, enough.

QUEEN MARGARET

Oh noble Buckingham, I'll kiss your hand to show my friendship and support for you. I wish only good things upon you and your noble family! Your clothes aren't spattered with my family's blood, and you aren't affected by my curse.

BUCKINGHAM

No one here is affected by your curse, because curses are just words with no power.

QUEEN MARGARET

I think they rise up to heaven and arouse God from his gentle sleep. *(so that only* **BUCKINGHAM** *hears)* Oh Buckingham, watch out for that dog, Richard! When he seems to be fawning on you, he's actually about to bite. And his poisonous bite kills. Have nothing to do with him. Beware of him. All the powers of sin, death, and hell are doing his bidding.

RICHARD

What is she saying, my lord?

BUCKINGHAM

Nothing that interests me, my good lord.

QUEEN MARGARET
What, dost thou scorn me for my gentle counsel,
And soothe the devil that I warn thee from?
300   O, but remember this another day,
When he shall split thy very heart with sorrow,
And say poor Margaret was a prophetess.—
Live each of you the subjects to his hate,
And he to yours, and all of you to God's.

Exit

HASTINGS
305   My hair doth stand an end to hear her curses.

RIVERS
And so doth mine. I muse why she's at liberty.

RICHARD
I cannot blame her. By God's holy mother,
She hath had too much wrong, and I repent
My part thereof that I have done to her.

QUEEN ELIZABETH
310   I never did her any, to my knowledge.

RICHARD
Yet you have all the vantage of her wrong.
I was too hot to do somebody good
That is too cold in thinking of it now.
Marry, as for Clarence, he is well repaid;
315   He is franked up to fatting for his pains.
God pardon them that are the cause thereof.

RIVERS
A virtuous and a Christian-like conclusion
To pray for them that have done scathe to us.

RICHARD
So do I ever *(aside)* being well-advised,
320   For had I cursed now, I had cursed myself.

Enter CATESBY

QUEEN MARGARET

What, you ignore my kind advice and try to please the devil I'm warning you about? Oh, just remember this another day, when he splits your heart in two with sorrow. Then you'll say poor Margaret was a prophet. Richard will come to hate everyone here, as you will come to hate him—and as God will come to hate you all.

She exits.

BUCKINGHAM

Her curses have made my hair stand on end.

RIVERS

Mine, too. I don't understand why she's not locked up.

RICHARD

I can't blame her. She has been wronged too often. I regret what I have done to hurt her.

QUEEN ELIZABETH

I never caused her any harm, as far as I know.

RICHARD

But you have all the advantages from the harm done. For my part, I was too eager to do King Edward good. He doesn't even seem to notice now. And look how he's repaid poor Clarence for his loyalty—penned him up like a pig being fattened for slaughter. God pardon those who are responsible for Clarence's troubles.

RIVERS

That's very virtuous and Christian of you, Richard, to pray for those who have done us harm.

RICHARD

I always pray for them (*to himself*) because "they" are none other than myself. If I cursed Clarence's wrong-doers, I'd be cursing myself.

CATESBY *enters.*

CATESBY
> Madam, his majesty doth call for you,—
> And for your Grace, —and yours, my gracious lords.

QUEEN ELIZABETH
> Catesby, I come. —Lords, will you go with me?

RIVERS
> We wait upon your Grace.

Exeunt all but RICHARD, *Duke of Gloucester*

RICHARD
325 > I do the wrong, and first begin to brawl.
> The secret mischiefs that I set abroach
> I lay unto the grievous charge of others.
> Clarence, whom I indeed have cast in darkness,
> I do beweep to many simple gulls,
330 > Namely, to Derby, Hastings, Buckingham,
> And tell them 'tis the queen and her allies
> That stir the king against the duke my brother.
> Now they believe it and withal whet me
> To be revenged on Rivers, Dorset, Grey;
335 > But then I sigh and, with a piece of scripture,
> Tell them that God bids us do good for evil;
> And thus I clothe my naked villainy
> With odd old ends stolen out of Holy Writ,
> And seem a saint when most I play the devil.

Enter two MURDERERS

340 > But, soft! here come my executioners.—
> How now, my hardy, stout, resolvèd mates?
> Are you now going to dispatch this thing?

FIRST MURDERER
> We are, my lord, and come to have the warrant
> That we may be admitted where he is.

CATESBY

Madam, his majesty asks for you, and for you, Duke of Gloucester, and for you, my noble lords.

QUEEN ELIZABETH

Catesby, we'll be there soon.—Lords, will you come with me?

RIVERS

We will wait on you, your majesty.

Everyone but RICHARD *exits.*

RICHARD

Incredible. I do the wrong and am the first to start quarrels. What I did in secret I blame on others. I cry about Clarence, whom I had imprisoned, in front of these simple fools—namely, Hastings, Derby and Buckingham—and tell them that the queen and her allies roused the king against my brother Clarence. They believe me and urge me to take revenge on Rivers, Vaughan, and Grey. But then I sigh and quote a chunk of the Bible—how God says do good in return for evil. Ha! Dressing my out-and-out wickedness in scraps of Scripture, I look like a saint exactly when I'm most like the devil.

Two MURDERERS *enter.*

But quiet. Here come the murderers I've hired. How's it going, hardy, reliable friends! Are you going to take care of this thing now?

FIRST MURDERER

We are, my lord. We've come to get the warrant so we can be let into his cell.

RICHARD
345   Well thought upon. I have it here about me.

He gives a paper

When you have done, repair to Crosby Place.
But, sirs, be sudden in the execution,
Withal obdurate; do not hear him plead,
For Clarence is well-spoken and perhaps
350   May move your hearts to pity if you mark him.

FIRST MURDERER
Tut, tut, my lord, we will not stand to prate.
Talkers are no good doers. Be assured
We go to use our hands and not our tongues

RICHARD
Your eyes drop millstones, when fools' eyes drop tears.
355   I like you lads. About your business straight.
Go, go, dispatch.

MURDERERS
We will, my noble lord.

Exeunt

RICHARD

Good thinking. I have it on me here. *(he hands over the warrant)* When you're done, go to Crosby Place. But, sirs, do the job fast. And stick to your mission. Don't let him plead for his life, because Clarence is a good talker and may make you pity him if you let him get started.

FIRST MURDERER

Tut, tut, my lord, we're not going to stand around chit-chatting. Talkers aren't good doers. Rest assured that we're going there to use our hands, not our tongues.

RICHARD

When fools cry, you remain stony. I like you guys. Go straight to work. Hurry now, get the job done.

MURDERERS

We will, my noble lord.

They all exit.

ACT 1, SCENE 4

Enter CLARENCE *and* KEEPER

KEEPER
> Why looks your grace so heavily today?

CLARENCE
> O, I have passed a miserable night,
> So full of ugly dreams, of ugly sights,
> That, as I am a Christian faithful man,
> I would not spend another such a night
> Though 'twere to buy a world of happy days,
> So full of dismal terror was the time.

KEEPER
> What was your dream, my lord? I pray you tell me.

CLARENCE
> Methoughts that I had broken from the Tower
> And was embarked to cross to Burgundy,
> And in my company my brother Gloucester,
> Who from my cabin tempted me to walk
> Upon the hatches. Thence we looked toward England
> And cited up a thousand fearful times,
> During the wars of York and Lancaster
> That had befall'n us. As we paced along
> Upon the giddy footing of the hatches,
> Methought that Gloucester stumbled, and in falling
> Struck me, that thought to stay him, overboard
> Into the tumbling billows of the main.
> O Lord, methought what pain it was to drown,
> What dreadful noise of waters in my ears,
> What sights of ugly death within my eyes.
> Methoughts I saw a thousand fearful wracks,
> A thousand men that fishes gnawed upon,
> Wedges of gold, great anchors, heaps of pearl,
> Inestimable stones, unvalued jewels,
> All scattered in the bottom of the sea.

ACT 1, SCENE 4

CLARENCE *and the* KEEPER *enter.*

KEEPER

Why do you look so depressed today, your Grace?

CLARENCE

Oh, I had a miserable night. I had such dark and terrifying dreams that I swear I wouldn't spend another night like that if it guaranteed me a whole lifetime of happy days.

KEEPER

What was your dream? Tell me.

CLARENCE

I thought I had escaped from the Tower and was on a ship to France with my brother Richard, who persuaded me to leave my cabin and walk on deck with him. Looking toward England, we reminisced about the countless frightening experiences we'd had in the wars between the Yorks and the Lancasters. As we were pacing the deck, which was tipping heavily, Richard seemed to stumble, and as I tried to grab hold of him and keep him from falling, he knocked me overboard into the crashing waves. Lord, how painful it was to drown. The sound of the rushing water was terrible, and so were the sights. I saw a thousand shipwrecks, a thousand men whom fish had gnawed to the bone, huge anchors, chunks of gold, heaps of pearls, and precious jewels—all scattered on the bottom of the sea.

Some lay in dead men's skulls, and in the holes
30   Where eyes did once inhabit, there were crept—
As 'twere in scorn of eyes—reflecting gems,
That wooed the slimy bottom of the deep
And mocked the dead bones that lay scattered by.

KEEPER
Had you such leisure in the time of death
35   To gaze upon the secrets of the deep?

CLARENCE
Methought I had, and often did I strive
To yield the ghost, but still the envious flood
Stopped in my soul and would not let it forth
To find the empty, vast, and wand'ring air,
40   But smothered it within my panting bulk,
Who almost burst to belch it in the sea.

KEEPER
Awaked you not in this sore agony?

CLARENCE
No, no, my dream was lengthened after life.
O, then began the tempest to my soul.
45   I passed, methought, the melancholy flood,
With that sour ferryman which poets write of,
Unto the kingdom of perpetual night.

The first that there did greet my stranger-soul
Was my great father-in-law, renownèd Warwick,
50   Who spake aloud, "What scourge for perjury
Can this dark monarchy afford false Clarence?"
And so he vanished. Then came wand'ring by

Some of the gems had wedged themselves like imitation eyes into the dead men's skulls. The fake eyes gazed dully at the bones scattered around.

KEEPER

So you had time as you were dying to look around?

CLARENCE

I thought I did, and I often tried to die. But the terrible water always held me back. It wouldn't let my soul find its way to air but smothered it inside my gasping body. My body wanted so badly to vomit up my spirit that it almost burst.

KEEPER

And didn't you wake up during this terrible agony?

CLARENCE

Oh, no, my dream went on even after I died. In fact, the real nightmare had only just begun. With the help of the grim ferryman that poets like to write about, my soul crossed the river into the kingdom of endless night.

According to Greek mythology, an old man, Charon, ferries the dead across the river Styx to Hades, the underworld for the good and bad alike. Shakespeare adds a certain Christian flavor here to alter this tradition: the underworld of Clarence's dream is hellish.

Clarence abandoned Warwick, who fought for the Lancasters, to join forces with his own brother King Edward IV.

The first to greet me there was my great father-in-law, the famous earl of Warwick. He cried aloud, "What terrible punishment can this dark realm devise for the oath-breaker Clarence?" And he vanished. Then a

A shadow like an angel, with bright hair
Dabbled in blood, and he shrieked out aloud
55   "Clarence is come—false, fleeting, perjured Clarence,
That stabbed me in the field by Tewkesbury.
Seize on him, furies. Take him unto torment."
With that, methoughts, a legion of foul fiends
Environed me and howlèd in mine ears
60   Such hideous cries that with the very noise
I trembling waked, and for a season after
Could not believe but that I was in hell,
Such terrible impression made my dream.

KEEPER
No marvel, lord, though it affrighted you.
65   I am afraid, methinks, to hear you tell it.

CLARENCE
Ah keeper, keeper, I have done those things,
That now give evidence against my soul,
For Edward's sake, and see how he requites me.—
O God, if my deep prayers cannot appease thee,
70   But thou wilt be avenged on my misdeeds,
Yet execute thy wrath in me alone!
O, spare my guiltless wife and my poor children!—
Keeper, I prithee sit by me awhile.
My soul is heavy, and I fain would sleep.

KEEPER
75   I will, my lord. God give your Grace good rest.

CLARENCE *sleeps*

Enter BRAKENBURY *the lieutenant*

BRAKENBURY
Sorrow breaks seasons and reposing hours,
Makes the night morning, and the noontide night.
Princes have but their titles for their glories,
An outward honor for an inward toil,

ghost like an angel with its hair spattered in blood wandered by, and shieked,

"Clarence has arrived—lying, cowardly Clarence, who stabbed me at Tewksbury. Grab him, avenging spirits, and torment him." With that, a legion of ugly demons surrounded me and howled so loudly in my ears that I woke up trembling and for a long time thought I was still in hell.

The ghost in Clarence's dream was Prince Edward, Queen Margaret's and King Henry VI's son. Clarence helped kill Prince Edward.

KEEPER

I'm not surprised it scared you, my lord. It scares me just to hear you talk about it.

CLARENCE

Oh, keeper, keeper, the bad things I've done are finally taking their toll. I did them for Edward's sake—and look how he rewards me.—Oh God, if my prayers don't satisfy you, and you have to avenge the wrongs I've done, at least punish me alone! Please spare my innocent wife and children!—Kind warden, please stay with me for a while. I'm feeling very low, and I need to sleep.

KEEPER

I'll stay, my lord. May God bring you sleep!

CLARENCE *sleeps.*

BRAKENBURY *the lieutenant enters.*

BRAKENBURY

Sorrow interrupts all hours and seasons. It turns everything around—the night into morning and noon into night. The only glory princes have are their titles.

80   And, for unfelt imaginations,
        They often feel a world of restless cares,
        So that betwixt their titles and low name
        There's nothing differs but the outward fame.

        Enter the two MURDERERS

FIRST MURDERER
        Ho, who's here?

BRAKENBURY
85   What wouldst thou, fellow? And how cam'st thou hither?

SECOND MURDERER
        I would speak with Clarence, and I came hither on my legs.

BRAKENBURY
        What, so brief?

FIRST MURDERER
        'Tis better, sir, to be brief than tedious.—Let him see our
        commission, and talk no more.

        BRAKENBURY *reads the paper*

BRAKENBURY
90   I am in this commanded to deliver
        The noble duke of Clarence to your hands.
        I will not reason what is meant hereby
        Because I will be guiltless from the meaning.
        There lies the duke asleep, and there the keys.

        He hands them the keys

95   I'll to the king and signify to him
        That thus I have resigned my charge to you.

FIRST MURDERER
        You may, sir. 'Tis a point of wisdom. Fare you well.

Instead of the pleasures we think they're enjoying, they experience a whole world of worries. It turns out the only difference between them and peasants is their fame.

The two MURDERERS *enter.*

FIRST MURDERER

Ho! Who's there?

BRAKENBURY

What do you want, fellow? And how did you get in here?

SECOND MURDERER

I want to speak with Clarence, and I came here on my legs.

BRAKENBURY

That's it? Nothing to add?

FIRST MURDERER

Well, sir, it's better to say little than to be tedious. *(to* SECOND MURDERER*)* Show him our orders and keep your mouth shut.

BRAKENBURY *reads the paper.*

BRAKENBURY

It orders me to hand the noble duke of Clarence over to you. I won't ask why because I'd rather not know than feel guilty if you're doing something you shouldn't be. Here are the keys, and there is the duke, sleeping. *(he hands them the keys)* I'll go to the king to let him know I've handed my prisoner over to you.

FIRST MURDERER

You may, sir. That's a wise idea. Goodbye.

Exit BRAKENBURY *and* KEEPER

SECOND MURDERER
What, shall I stab him as he sleeps?

FIRST MURDERER
No. He'll say 'twas done cowardly, when he wakes.

SECOND MURDERER
100   Why, he shall never wake until the great Judgment Day.

FIRST MURDERER
Why, then he'll say we stabbed him sleeping.

SECOND MURDERER
The urging of that word "judgment" hath bred a kind of
remorse in me.

FIRST MURDERER
What, art thou afraid?

SECOND MURDERER
105   Not to kill him, having a warrant, but to be damned for
killing him, from the which no warrant can defend me.

FIRST MURDERER
I thought thou hadst been resolute.

SECOND MURDERER
So I am—to let him live.

FIRST MURDERER
I'll back to the duke of Gloucester and tell him so.

SECOND MURDERER
110   Nay, I prithee stay a little. I hope this passionate humor of
mine will change. It was wont to hold me but while one tells
twenty.

FIRST MURDERER
How dost thou feel thyself now?

SECOND MURDERER
Faith, some certain dregs of conscience are yet within me.

BRAKENBURY *and the* KEEPER *exit.*

SECOND MURDERER
What, should I stab him while he sleeps?

FIRST MURDERER
No. When he wakes up, he'll say we killed him like cowards.

SECOND MURDERER
When he wakes up! Why, he won't wake up till Judgment Day.

FIRST MURDERER
Okay, so that's when he'll say we stabbed him in his sleep.

SECOND MURDERER
That word "judgment" makes me feel a bit guilty.

FIRST MURDERER
What, are you afraid?

SECOND MURDERER
Not of killing him, because I have a warrant for it, but of being damned for killing him, which no warrant can protect me from.

FIRST MURDERER
I thought you were resolved to do this.

SECOND MURDERER
I am resolved—to let him live.

FIRST MURDERER
I'll go back to the duke of Gloucester and tell him so.

SECOND MURDERER
Please, just wait a minute. I'm hoping my holy mood will pass. It usually only lasts about twenty seconds.

FIRST MURDERER
How are you feeling now?

SECOND MURDERER
Actually, I'm still feeling some pangs of conscience.

FIRST MURDERER

115 Remember our reward when the deed's done.

SECOND MURDERER

Zounds, he dies! I had forgot the reward.

FIRST MURDERER

Where's thy conscience now?

SECOND MURDERER

O, in the duke of Gloucester's purse.

FIRST MURDERER

So when he opens his purse to give us our reward, thy

120 conscience flies out.

SECOND MURDERER

'Tis no matter. Let it go. There's few or none will entertain it.

FIRST MURDERER

What if it come to thee again?

SECOND MURDERER

I'll not meddle with it. It makes a man a coward: a man
cannot steal but it accuseth him; a man cannot swear but it

125 checks him; a man cannot lie with his neighbor's wife but it
detects him. 'Tis a blushing, shamefaced spirit that
mutinies in a man's bosom. It fills a man full of obstacles. It
made me once restore a purse of gold that by chance I
found. It beggars any man that keeps it. It is turned out of

130 towns and cities for a dangerous thing, and every man that
means to live well endeavors to trust to himself and live
without it.

FIRST MURDERER

Zounds, 'tis even now at my elbow, persuading me
not to kill the duke.

SECOND MURDERER

135 Take the devil in thy mind, and believe him not. He would
insinuate with thee but to make thee sigh.

FIRST MURDERER

I am strong-framed. He cannot prevail with me.

FIRST MURDERER
Remember the reward we're getting when the deed's done.

SECOND MURDERER
Jesus, let's kill him! I forgot about the reward.

FIRST MURDERER
Where's your conscience now?

SECOND MURDERER
Oh, in the duke of Gloucester's wallet.

FIRST MURDERER
When he opens his wallet to give us our pay, your conscience will fly out?

SECOND MURDERER
It won't matter. Let it fly out. No one will listen to it.

FIRST MURDERER
And what will you do if it returns to you?

SECOND MURDERER
I won't bother with it. Conscience makes a man a coward. If he steals, it accuses him. If he wants to swear, it restrains him. If he sleeps with his neighbor's wife, it exposes him. It blushes, is easily embarrassed, and stages regular uprisings in a man's heart. It's just too much trouble. It once made me return a purse full of money that I found—it turns anyone who treats it decently into a beggar. It has been thrown out of all sorts of towns and cities it visits, and anyone who wants to live well should learn to trust only himself and live without it.

FIRST MURDERER
My God, now the thing is at *my* elbow, persuading me not to kill the duke.

SECOND MURDERER
Stop your conscience and don't listen to him. He wants to take over your thoughts and make you sad.

FIRST MURDERER
I'm strong-willed. He won't get the better of me.

SECOND MURDERER
> Spoke like a tall man that respects thy reputation. Come,
> shall we fall to work?

FIRST MURDERER
140   Take him on the costard with the hilts of thy sword, and
> then throw him into the malmsey butt in the next room.

SECOND MURDERER
> O excellent device— and make a sop of him.

FIRST MURDERER
> Soft, he wakes.

SECOND MURDERER
> Strike!

FIRST MURDERER
145   No, we'll reason with him.

CLARENCE *wakes*

CLARENCE
> Where art thou, keeper? Give me a cup of wine.

SECOND MURDERER
> You shall have wine enough, my lord, anon.

CLARENCE
> In God's name, what art thou?

FIRST MURDERER
>   A man, as you are.

CLARENCE
> But not, as I am, royal.

FIRST MURDERER
150   Nor you, as we are, loyal.

CLARENCE
> Thy voice is thunder, but thy looks are humble.

FIRST MURDERER
> My voice is now the king's, my looks mine own.

SECOND MURDERER

Spoken like a brave man who respects his reputation. Shall we get to work?

FIRST MURDERER

We'll hit him on the head with the handles of our swords, then throw him in the wine barrel in the next room.

SECOND MURDERER

What an excellent idea—he'll soak up the wine!

FIRST MURDERER

Wait a moment. He's waking up.

SECOND MURDERER

Strike!

FIRST MURDERER

No, first let's talk to him.

CLARENCE *wakes.*

CLARENCE

Where are you, keeper? Give me a cup of wine.

SECOND MURDERER

You'll have wine enough, my lord, soon.

CLARENCE

In God's name, who are you?

FIRST MURDERER

A man, like you.

CLARENCE

But not a member of the royal family, like me.

FIRST MURDERER

And you're not loyal, like us.

CLARENCE

Your voice is loud and commanding, but you look like a working man.

FIRST MURDERER

I'm speaking for the king, but I look like myself.

CLARENCE
How darkly and how deadly dost thou speak!
Your eyes do menace me. Why look you pale?
155   Who sent you hither? Wherefore do you come?

SECOND MURDERER
To, to, to—

CLARENCE
To murder me?

BOTH MURDERERS
Ay, ay.

CLARENCE
You scarcely have the hearts to tell me so,
160   And therefore cannot have the hearts to do it.
Wherein, my friends, have I offended you?

FIRST MURDERER
Offended us you have not, but the king.

CLARENCE
I shall be reconciled to him again.

SECOND MURDERER
Never, my lord. Therefore prepare to die.

CLARENCE
165   Are you drawn forth among a world of men
To slay the innocent? What is my offense?
Where is the evidence that doth accuse me?
What lawful quest have given their verdict up
Unto the frowning judge? Or who pronounced
170   The bitter sentence of poor Clarence' death
Before I be convict by course of law?
To threaten me with death is most unlawful.
I charge you, as you hope to have redemption,
By Christ's dear blood shed for our grievous sins,
175   That you depart, and lay no hands on me.
The deed you undertake is damnable.

FIRST MURDERER
What we will do, we do upon command.

CLARENCE

> The things you say scare me! Your eyes look threatening. And why are you so pale? Who sent you here? Why are you here?

SECOND MURDERER

> To, to, to—

CLARENCE

> To murder me?

BOTH MURDERERS

> Yes.

CLARENCE

> You barely have the heart to tell me, so you can't possibly have the nerve to do it. Besides, how have I offended you, my friends?

FIRST MURDERER

> You didn't offend us, you offended the king.

CLARENCE

> He and I will make up.

SECOND MURDERER

> Never, my lord. So prepare to die.

CLARENCE

> It's your job in life to kill the innocent? What did I do wrong? Where's the evidence against me? Where's the jury, the judge, the lawful proceedings, the verdict? Who pronounced this death sentence before a court of law could even convict me? For you to threaten to kill me is most unlawful. If you hope to have your sins forgiven by Christ's dear blood, which He shed for our terrible sins, you must leave and keep your hands off me. You'll go to Hell for the deed you're planning to do.

FIRST MURDERER

> What we do we have been commanded to do.

SECOND MURDERER
> And he that hath commanded is our king.

CLARENCE
> Erroneous vassals, the great King of kings
180 > Hath in the tables of His law commanded
> That thou shalt do no murder. Will thou then
> Spurn at His edict and fulfill a man's?
> Take heed, for He holds vengeance in His hand
> To hurl upon their heads that break His law.

SECOND MURDERER
185 > And that same vengeance doth He hurl on thee
> For false forswearing and for murder too.
> Thou didst receive the sacrament to fight
> In quarrel of the house of Lancaster.

FIRST MURDERER
> And, like a traitor to the name of God,
190 > Didst break that vow, and with thy treacherous blade
> Unrippedst the bowels of thy sovereign's son.

SECOND MURDERER
> Whom thou wert sworn to cherish and defend.

FIRST MURDERER
> How canst thou urge God's dreadful law to us
> When thou hast broke it in such dear degree?

CLARENCE
195 > Alas! For whose sake did I that ill deed?
> For Edward, for my brother, for his sake.
> He sends you not to murder me for this,
> For in that sin he is as deep as I.
> If God will be avengèd for this deed,
200 > O, know you yet He doth it publicly!
> Take not the quarrel from His powerful arm;
> He needs no indirect or lawless course
> To cut off those that have offended Him.

SECOND MURDERER

> And the one who commands us is our king.

CLARENCE

> Wrong-headed slaves, the King of kings says in his Ten Commandments, "Thou shalt not murder." Will you defy God and obey a man? Be careful. God takes revenge on those who break His laws.

SECOND MURDERER

> He does, and now he's taking revenge on you—for breaking promises and for murder, too. You took a holy oath to fight for King Henry VI.

FIRST MURDERER

> And like a traitor to God, you broke that oath and savagely murdered King Henry's young son.

SECOND MURDERER

> Whom you swore you would protect and defend.

FIRST MURDERER

> How dare you tell us about God's laws when you have broken them so savagely yourself?

CLARENCE

> But for whose sake did I do that sick deed? For my brother Edward's sake. He couldn't be sending you to murder me for that sin, because he's the one who asked me to commit it. He is as guilty as I am. If God will be revenged for this deed, he will do it publicly. God doesn't need to use indirect or illegal means to kill those who have offended him.

FIRST MURDERER
Who made thee then a bloody minister
205   When gallant-springing, brave Plantagenet,
That princely novice, was struck dead by thee?

CLARENCE
My brother's love, the devil, and my rage.

FIRST MURDERER
Thy brother's love, our duty, and thy faults
Provoke us hither now to slaughter thee.

CLARENCE
210   If you do love my brother, hate not me.
I am his brother, and I love him well.
If you are hired for meed, go back again,
And I will send you to my brother Gloucester,
Who shall reward you better for my life
215   Than Edward will for tidings of my death.

SECOND MURDERER
You are deceived. Your brother Gloucester hates you.

CLARENCE
O, no, he loves me, and he holds me dear.
Go you to him from me.

FIRST MURDERER
                                    Ay, so we will.

CLARENCE
Tell him, when that our princely father York
220   Blessed his three sons with his victorious arm,
He little thought of this divided friendship.
Bid Gloucester think of this, and he will weep.

FIRST MURDERER
Ay, millstones, as he lessoned us to weep.

CLARENCE
O, do not slander him, for he is kind.

FIRST MURDERER

> Then who were you working for when you killed brave, young Prince Edward?

CLARENCE

> My brother's love, the devil, and my own anger made me do it.

FIRST MURDERER

> Well, your brother's love, our duty, and your own crimes make us kill *you*.

CLARENCE

> If you love my brother, don't hate me. I am his brother, and I love him very much. If you're doing this for pay, go to my brother Richard. He will pay you more for saving my life than Edward will for killing me.

SECOND MURDERER

> You're mistaken. Richard, the duke of Gloucester, hates you.

CLARENCE

> No, he loves and cherishes me. Go to him from me.

FIRST MURDERER

> We will.

CLARENCE

> Tell him that when our noble father, the duke of York, gave his three sons his blessing, he never imagined that our friendship would come to this. Remind Richard of this, and he will weep.

FIRST MURDERER

> Yes, he'll weep stones, as he taught us to do.

CLARENCE

> Don't lie about my brother. He is kind.

FIRST MURDERER

225   Right, as snow in harvest. Come, you deceive yourself.
      'Tis he that sends us to destroy you here.

CLARENCE

      It cannot be, for he bewept my fortune,
      And hugged me in his arms, and swore with sobs
      That he would labor my delivery.

SECOND MURDERER

230   Why, so he doth, when he delivers you
      From this earth's thralldom to the joys of heaven.

FIRST MURDERER

      Make peace with God, for you must die, my lord.

CLARENCE

      Have you that holy feeling in your souls
      To counsel me to make my peace with God,
235   And art you yet to your own souls so blind
      That thou will war with God by murd'ring me?
      O sirs, consider: they that set you on
      To do this deed will hate you for the deed.

SECOND MURDERER

      (to **FIRST MURDERER***)* What shall we do?

CLARENCE

                              Relent, and save your souls.
240   Which of you—if you were a prince's son
      Being pent from liberty, as I am now—
      If two such murderers as yourselves came to you,
      Would not entreat for life? Ay, you would beg,
      Were you in my distress.

FIRST MURDERER

245   Relent? No. 'Tis cowardly and womanish.

FIRST MURDERER

Yes, as kind as snow to a harvest. Come on, you're fooling yourself. It's Richard who sent us here to slaughter you.

CLARENCE

It cannot be. When I left him, he hugged me in his arms and swore between sobs that he would work to set me free.

FIRST MURDERER

Well, that's what he's doing—making you free to enjoy heaven.

SECOND MURDERER

Make peace with God, for you must die, my lord.

CLARENCE

You have enough holy feeling to advise me to "make peace with God," but you're willing to go to war with God by murdering me? Oh sirs, consider this: those who sent you to do this deed will hate you for doing it.

SECOND MURDERER

(to FIRST MURDERER*)* What should we do?

CLARENCE

Relent, and save your souls. If either of you were a prince's son, and you were imprisoned as I am now, and two murderers like yourselves came to you—wouldn't you beg for your life? Yes, you would beg, if you were in my position.

FIRST MURDERER

Relent? No. That's cowardly and womanish.

CLARENCE

Not to relent is beastly, savage, devilish.
(to SECOND MURDERER*)*
My friend, I spy some pity in thy looks.
O, if thine eye be not a flatterer,
Come thou on my side and entreat for me.
250   A begging prince what beggar pities not?

SECOND MURDERER

Look behind you, my lord. — *Cowardly*

FIRST MURDERER

Take that, and that. *(stabs* CLARENCE*)*
If all this will not do,
I'll drown you in the malmsey butt within.

Exit with the body

SECOND MURDERER

255   A bloody deed, and desperately dispatched.
How fain, like Pilate, would I wash my hands
Of this most grievous murder.

Enter FIRST MURDERER

FIRST MURDERER

How now? What mean'st thou, that thou help'st me not?
By heavens, the duke shall know how slack you have been.

SECOND MURDERER

260   I would he knew that I had saved his brother.
Take thou the fee, and tell him what I say,
For I repent me that the duke is slain.

Exit

CLARENCE

> No, sticking to your plan is beastly, savage, devilish. *(to* SECOND MURDERER*)* My friend, I detect some pity in your eyes. Please, please take my side and argue for my life. What beggar wouldn't have sympathy for a prince reduced to begging?

SECOND MURDERER

> Look behind you, my lord.

FIRST MURDERER

> Take that, and that. *(he stabs* CLARENCE*)* If this won't do the job, I'll drown you in the wine barrel in the next room.

> *He exits with the body.*

SECOND MURDERER

Pontius Pilate was the Roman governor who ordered Jesus Christ to be crucified. As if to suggest that he was washing away his own guilt, Pilate washed his hands in public before the execution.

> A bloody deed, and desperately executed. I wish I could wash my hands of this terrible murder, like Pilate.

FIRST MURDERER *returns.*

FIRST MURDERER

> What's going on? What did you mean by not helping me? By God, I'm going to tell the duke how slack you've been.

SECOND MURDERER

> I wish you could tell him I saved his brother. Take the money yourself and tell him what I said. I'm sorry this duke was killed.

> *He exits.*

FIRST MURDERER
So do not I. Go, coward as thou art.
Well, I'll go hide the body in some hole
265   Till that the duke give order for his burial.
And when I have my meed, I will away,
For this will out, and then I must not stay.

Exit

FIRST MURDERER

I'm not. Go, coward that you are. Well, I'll go hide the body in some hole until the duke gives orders for his burial. And when I get my reward, I'll get out of here. The truth about this will come out, and I can't stick around then.

He exits.

ACT TWO
SCENE 1

Flourish. Enter KING EDWARD IV, *sick,* QUEEN ELIZABETH,
Lord Marquess DORSET, RIVERS, HASTINGS, BUCKINGHAM,
GREY, *and others*

KING EDWARD IV
    Why, so. Now have I done a good day's work.
    You peers, continue this united league.
    I every day expect an embassage
    From my Redeemer to redeem me hence,
5   And more in peace my soul shall part to heaven
    Since I have made my friends at peace on earth
    Rivers and Hastings, take each other's hand.
    Dissemble not your hatred. Swear your love.

RIVERS
    (taking HASTINGS*'s hand)* By heaven, my soul is purged
10   from grudging hate, And with my hand I seal my true
    heart's love.

HASTINGS
    So thrive I as I truly swear the like.

KING EDWARD IV
    Take heed you dally not before your king,
    Lest He that is the supreme King of kings
15   Confound your hidden falsehood, and award
    Either of you to be the other's end.

HASTINGS
    So prosper I as I swear perfect love.

RIVERS
    And I as I love Hastings with my heart.

ACT TWO
SCENE 1

Trumpets sound.
KING EDWARD IV *enters, sick, accompanied by* QUEEN
ELIZABETH, DORSET, RIVERS, HASTINGS,
BUCKINGHAM, GREY, *and others.*

KING EDWARD IV

Well. Now I've done a good day's work. You must all
keep up this united front. Every day I expect a message from God to bring me away from here. Now my
soul can depart for heaven peacefully, since my friends
have made peace here on earth. Rivers and Hastings,
take each other's hand. Don't simply hide your
hatred. Swear your love for each other.

RIVERS

(taking HASTINGS*'s hand)* I swear I have cleansed my
heart of all hate. With this handshake, I guarantee my
love.

HASTINGS

On my honor, I feel the same.

KING EDWARD IV

Make sure you mean what you say. Otherwise God,
the ultimate King, will uncover your lies and cause
you to be the death of each other.

HASTINGS

On my honor, I swear I love Rivers with all my heart.

RIVERS

And I love Hastings with all my heart.

KING EDWARD IV

(to QUEEN ELIZABETH*)*

Madam, yourself is not exempt in this,—

20 Nor you, son Dorset, —Buckingham, nor you.

You have been factious one against the other.—

Wife, love Lord Hastings. Let him kiss your hand,

And what you do, do it unfeignedly.

QUEEN ELIZABETH

There, Hastings, I will never more remember

25 Our former hatred, so thrive I and mine.

HASTINGS *kisses her hand*

KING EDWARD IV

Dorset, embrace him.—Hastings, love Lord Marquess.

DORSET

This interchange of love, I here protest,

Upon my part shall be inviolable.

HASTINGS

And so swear I.

They embrace

KING EDWARD IV

30 Now, princely Buckingham, seal thou this league

With thy embracements to my wife's allies

And make me happy in your unity.

KING EDWARD IV

> *(to* QUEEN ELIZABETH*)* Madam, you're not exempt from this—nor are you, Dorset— nor you, Buckingham. You have had too many separate factions among you. My dear wife, let Lord Hastings kiss your hand. And don't do it merely for appearance's sake.

QUEEN ELIZABETH

> Take my hand, Hastings. From now on, I'll forget the hatred I used to feel for you.

> HASTINGS *kisses her hand.*

KING EDWARD IV

> Dorset, embrace Hastings.—Hastings, express your affection for the marquess of Dorset.

DORSET

> I swear I will never break this promise of love.

HASTINGS

> And so do I, my lord.

> *They embrace.*

KING EDWARD IV

> Now, noble Buckingham, seal this alliance by embracing my wife's friends, and make me happy in your unity.

BUCKINGHAM
(*to* QUEEN ELIZABETH)
Whenever Buckingham doth turn his hate
Upon your Grace, but with all duteous love
35   Doth cherish you and yours, God punish me
When I have most need to employ a friend,
With hate in those where I expect most love.
And most assurèd that he is a friend,
Deep, hollow, treacherous, and full of guile
40   Be he unto me: this do I beg of God
When I am cold in love to you or yours.

They embrace

KING EDWARD IV
A pleasing cordial, princely Buckingham,
Is this thy vow unto my sickly heart.
There wanteth now our brother Gloucester here
45   To make the blessèd period of this peace.

BUCKINGHAM
And in good time,
Here comes Sir Richard Ratcliffe and the duke.

Enter RICHARD *and* RATCLIFFE

RICHARD
Good morrow to my sovereign king and queen,
And, princely peers, a happy time of day.

KING EDWARD IV
50   Happy indeed, as we have spent the day.
Gloucester, we have done deeds of charity,
Made peace of enmity, fair love of hate,
Between these swelling, wrong-incensèd peers.

BUCKINGHAM

(*to* QUEEN ELIZABETH) If I ever turn my hatred toward your majesty, and do not love and cherish you and yours, may God punish me. May I find hatred where I most expect love. When I most need a friend, and when I'm sure I have one, make him treacherous and deceitful to me. I beg God to do all this whenever I fail to show love to you or yours.

They embrace.

KING EDWARD IV

Noble Buckingham, your promise is like medicine to my ailing heart. All we need to put the final touches on this future peace is for Richard to appear.

BUCKINGHAM

And just in time, here he comes with Sir Richard Ratcliffe.

RICHARD *and* RATCLIFFE *enter.*

RICHARD

Good morning to my sovereign king and queen. Noble peers, how nice to see you.

KING EDWARD IV

Happy indeed, the way we have spent the day. Gloucester, we have done deeds of charity, turning enmity into peace and hate into love among these mistakenly angry nobles.

RICHARD
      A blessèd labor, my most sovereign lord.
55   Amongst this princely heap, if any here
      By false intelligence, or wrong surmise
      Hold me a foe,
      If I unwittingly, or in my rage,
      Have aught committed that is hardly borne
60   By any in this presence, I desire
      To reconcile me to his friendly peace.
      'Tis death to me to be at enmity;
      I hate it, and desire all good men's love.
      First, madam, I entreat true peace of you,
65   Which I will purchase with my duteous service;—
      Of you, my noble cousin Buckingham,
      If ever any grudge were lodged between us;—
      Of you and you, Lord Rivers and of Dorset,
      That all without desert have frowned on me;—
70   Of you, Lord Woodeville and Lord Scales;— of you,
      Dukes, earls, lords, gentlemen; indeed, of all.
      I do not know that Englishman alive
      With whom my soul is any jot at odds
      More than the infant that is born tonight.
75   I thank my God for my humility.

QUEEN ELIZABETH
      A holy day shall this be kept hereafter.
      I would to God all strifes were well compounded.
      My sovereign lord, I do beseech your Highness
      To take our brother Clarence to your grace.

RICHARD
80   Why, madam, have I offered love for this,
      To be so flouted in this royal presence?
      Who knows not that the gentle duke is dead?

They all start

      You do him injury to scorn his corse.

RICHARD

What blessed work, my king. If there's anyone among this princely group who mistakes me for an enemy— if by accident or in anger I have done anything to offend you—I want to join with you in peaceful friendship. It kills me to be enemies with you. I hate it and want all good men's love. *(to* QUEEN ELIZABETH*)* First, madam, I want there to be peace between you and me, which I will buy with my obedient service to you. And peace with you, my noble cousin Buckingham, if you ever felt any grudge against me; and with you, Lord Rivers, and, Lord Grey, with you. In fact, I want to get along with everyone who has frowned on me without good cause—dukes, earls, lords, gentlemen, everyone. There is not an Englishman alive with whom I'm at odds, anymore than a newborn baby would be. I thank God for my humbleness.

QUEEN ELIZABETH

Today shall always be remembered as a holy day. If only all struggles ended this well. One more thing, my dear majesty. Please pardon our brother Clarence.

RICHARD

Why, madam, have I offered you my love only to be flouted in front of the king? Who doesn't know that the good duke is dead?

They all start.

You do him wrong to laugh at his corpse.

KING EDWARD IV
Who knows not he is dead! Who knows he is?

QUEEN ELIZABETH
85   All-seeing heaven, what a world is this!

BUCKINGHAM
Look I so pale, Lord Dorset, as the rest?

DORSET
Ay, my good lord, and no one in the presence
But his red color hath forsook his cheeks.

KING EDWARD IV
Is Clarence dead? The order was reversed.

RICHARD
90   But he, poor man, by your first order died,
And that a wingèd Mercury did bear.
Some tardy cripple bear the countermand,
That came too lag to see him burièd.
God grant that some, less noble and less loyal,
95   Nearer in bloody thoughts, and not in blood,
Deserve not worse than wretched Clarence did,
And yet go current from suspicion.

Enter Lord STANLEY, *Earl of Derby*

STANLEY
(kneeling) A boon, my sovereign, for my service done.

KING EDWARD IV
I prithee, peace. My soul is full of sorrow.

STANLEY
100   I will not rise unless your Highness hear me.

KING EDWARD IV
Then say at once what is it thou requests.

STANLEY
The forfeit, sovereign, of my servant's life,
Who slew today a riotous gentleman
Lately attendant on the duke of Norfolk.

KING EDWARD IV

Who doesn't know he's dead? Who says he is?

QUEEN ELIZABETH

Oh my God, what a terrible world this is!

BUCKINGHAM

Do I look as pale as everyone else does, Lord Dorset?

DORSET

You do, my good lord. Everyone here has turned white.

KING EDWARD IV

Is Clarence dead? But I reversed the death sentence.

RICHARD

Well, the poor man died by your first order, which was carried by a winged messenger. Some tardy cripple must have taken the counter-order, who came after Clarence was already buried. It's clear that someone less noble, less loyal, more bloody-minded than Clarence but not a blood relation, deserves as bad an end as my brother, but he goes free.

Lord STANLEY, *Earl of Derby, enters.*

STANLEY

(kneeling) I ask a favor of you in return for the service I've done, my king.

KING EDWARD IV

Please be quiet. My soul is full of sorrow.

STANLEY

I will not rise until your Highness hears me.

KING EDWARD IV

Then hurry up and tell me what you want.

STANLEY

That you lift the death sentence on my servant, who killed a rowdy and belligerent former servant of the duke of Norfolk.

KING EDWARD IV

105   Have I a tongue to doom my brother's death,
    And shall the tongue give pardon to a slave?
    My brother killed no man; his fault was thought,
    And yet his punishment was bitter death.
    Who sued to me for him? Who, in my wrath,
110   Kneeled at my feet, and bade me be advised?
    Who spoke of brotherhood? Who spoke of love?
    Who told me how the poor soul did forsake
    The mighty Warwick and did fight for me?
    Who told me, in the field by Tewkesbury,
115   When Oxford had me down, he rescued me,
    And said "Dear brother, live, and be a king"?
    Who told me, when we both lay in the field
    Frozen almost to death, how he did lap me
    Even in his garments and did give himself,
120   All thin and naked, to the numb-cold night?
    All this from my remembrance brutish wrath
    Sinfully plucked, and not a man of you
    Had so much grace to put it in my mind.
    But when your carters or your waiting vassals
125   Have done a drunken slaughter and defaced
    The precious image of our dear Redeemer,
    You straight are on your knees for pardon, pardon,
    And I, unjustly too, must grant it you.
    Stanley rises
    But for my brother, not a man would speak,
130   Nor I, ungracious, speak unto myself
    For him, poor soul. The proudest of you all
    Have been beholding to him in his life,
    Yet none of you would once beg for his life.
    O God, I fear Thy justice will take hold
135   On me and you, and mine and yours for this!—
    Come, Hastings, help me to my closet.—
    Ah, poor Clarence.

KING EDWARD IV

I was willing to condemn my brother to death, but you want me to pardon a peasant? My brother didn't kill anyone. He was only to blame for some thoughts he had. But his punishment was bitter death. Who pleaded with me to pardon *his* life? Who, when I was in a rage, kneeled at my feet and told me to reconsider? Who talked about brotherhood? Who talked about love? Who told me how the poor man abandoned the mighty earl of Warwick to fight for me? Who told me how he rescued me in the field at Tewksbury, when Oxford had me down, saying, "Dear brother, live and be a king"? Who told me how, when we both lay in the field freezing to death, he wrapped me in his own clothes and spent a numbingly cold night naked? I forgot all of this in my brutish anger, and not one of you had the grace to remind me. But when your servants get drunk and kill someone, you go right down on your knees for "pardon, pardon." And, though he doesn't deserve it, I have to grant your request. But not one of you would speak up for my brother. And I didn't speak to myself on his behalf, either. The best of you owed something to him in his lifetime, but none of you would plead for his life. Oh God, I fear your justice will destroy me and all of these men, and their families and mine, because of this! Come, Hastings, help me to my room. Oh, poor Clarence.

Exeunt some with KING EDWARD IV *and* QUEEN ELIZABETH

RICHARD
This is the fruits of rashness. Marked you not
How that the guilty kindred of the queen
140   Looked pale when they did hear of Clarence' death?
O, they did urge it still unto the king.
God will revenge it. Come, lords, will you go
To comfort Edward with our company?

BUCKINGHAM
We wait upon your Grace.

Exeunt

> KING EDWARD IV *and* QUEEN ELIZABETH *exit*
> *with several others.*

RICHARD

> This is what happens when you act rashly. Did you
> notice how the queen's guilty relatives turned pale
> when they heard about Clarence's death? Oh, they
> continually urged the king to do it. God will revenge
> it. But come, lords, will you come with me to Edward's
> room to comfort him?

BUCKINGHAM

> We'll come with you, your Grace.

> *They all exit.*

ACT 2, SCENE 2

Enter the old DUCHESS *of York, with the two children of Clarence*

BOY

Good grandam, tell us, is our father dead?

DUCHESS

No, boy.

GIRL

Why do you weep so oft, and beat your breast,
And cry, "O Clarence, my unhappy son?"

BOY

5   Why do you look on us and shake your head,
And call us orphans, wretches, castaways,
If that our noble father were alive?

DUCHESS

My pretty cousins, you mistake me both.
I do lament the sickness of the king,
10   As loath to lose him, not your father's death.
It were lost sorrow to wail one that's lost.

BOY

Then, you conclude, my grandam, he is dead.
The king mine uncle is to blame for it.
God will revenge it, whom I will importune
15   With earnest prayers, all to that effect.

GIRL

And so will I.

DUCHESS

Peace, children, peace. The king doth love you well.
Incapable and shallow innocents,
You cannot guess who caused your father's death.

ACT 2, SCENE 2

The old DUCHESS OF YORK *enters with* CLARENCE'S *two children.*

BOY

Tell me, good grandmother, is our father dead?

DUCHESS

No, boy.

GIRL

Then why do you weep so often, and beat your breast, and cry, "Oh Clarence, my unlucky son"?

BOY

Why do you look at us and shake your head, and call us orphans, wretches, castaways, if our noble father is still alive?

DUCHESS

My pretty children, both of you misunderstand me. I'm lamenting the sickness of the king, because I'd hate to lose him—I'm not mourning your father's death. What would be the point of crying over someone who was already dead?

BOY

So you're admitting Clarence, my father, is dead. My uncle the king is to blame for this. God will take revenge. I will pray every day that he does.

GIRL

And so will I.

DUCHESS

Quiet, children, quiet. The king loves you very much. Innocent sweethearts, you have no idea who's responsible for your father's death.

BOY

20   Grandam, we can, for my good uncle Gloucester
      Told me the king, provoked to it by the queen,
      Devised impeachments to imprison him;
      And when my uncle told me so, he wept,
      And pitied me, and kindly kissed my cheek,
25   Bade me rely on him as on my father,
      And he would love me dearly as a child.

DUCHESS

      Ah, that deceit should steal such gentle shape,
      And with a virtuous visor hide deep vice.
      He is my son, ay, and therein my shame,
30   Yet from my dugs he drew not this deceit.

BOY

      Think you my uncle did dissemble, grandam?

DUCHESS

      Ay, boy.

BOY

      I cannot think it. Hark, what noise is this?

Enter QUEEN ELIZABETH, *with her hair about her ears,*
RIVERS *and* DORSET *after her*

QUEEN ELIZABETH

      Ah, who shall hinder me to wail and weep,
35   To chide my fortune and torment myself?
      I'll join with black despair against my soul
      And to myself become an enemy.

DUCHESS

      What means this scene of rude impatience?

QUEEN ELIZABETH

      To make an act of tragic violence.
40   Edward, my lord, thy son, our king, is dead.
      Why grow the branches when the root is gone?
      Why wither not the leaves that want their sap?

BOY

Yes we do, grandmother, because my good uncle Richard told me. He said the king was forced by the queen to make up charges against my father that would send him to prison. When my uncle explained this to me, he wept and hugged and kissed me. He told me I could rely on him as if he were my father, and he said he would love me as if I were his child.

DUCHESS

Ah, it's a shame that a liar can seem so nice, hiding his wicked intentions under a mask of goodness. He is my son, yes, and I'm ashamed of him. But he didn't get his deceitfulness from my breast.

BOY

You think my uncle was lying, grandmother?

DUCHESS

Yes, boy.

BOY

I can't believe that. Wait! What's that noise?

QUEEN ELIZABETH *enters with her hair undone.* RIVERS *and* DORSET *follow.*

QUEEN ELIZABETH

No one can stop me now from wailing and weeping about my terrible luck. I don't care if it kills me. I plan to fall into the blackest despair.

DUCHESS

Why are you making such a scene?

QUEEN ELIZABETH

I'm simply performing the violent tragedy that is my life: Edward—my husband, your son, our king—is dead. Why should we live now that our leader is dead? Why are the branches still living when the root is gone? Why aren't the leaves withering now that the sap is all dried up?

If you will live, lament. If die, be brief,
That our swift-wingèd souls may catch the king's,
45   Or, like obedient subjects, follow him
To his new kingdom of ne'er-changing night.

DUCHESS
Ah, so much interest have I in thy sorrow
As I had title in thy noble husband.
I have bewept a worthy husband's death
50   And lived with looking on his images;
But now two mirrors of his princely semblance
Are cracked in pieces by malignant death,
And I, for comfort, have but one false glass
That grieves me when I see my shame in him.
55   Thou art a widow, yet thou art a mother,
And hast the comfort of thy children left,
But death hath snatched my husband from mine arms
And plucked two crutches from my feeble hands,
Clarence and Edward. O, what cause have I,
60   Thine being but a moiety of my moan,
To overgo thy woes and drown thy cries!

BOY
(to QUEEN ELIZABETH*)* Ah, aunt, you wept not for our
        father's death.
How can we aid you with our kindred tears?

GIRL
Our fatherless distress was left unmoaned.
65   Your widow-dolor likewise be unwept!

QUEEN ELIZABETH
Give me no help in lamentation.
I am not barren to bring forth complaints.
All springs reduce their currents to mine eyes,
That I, being governed by the watery moon,
70   May send forth plenteous tears to drown the world.
Ah, for my husband, for my dear lord Edward!

If you do intend to live, then mourn. If you're going to die, be quick about it so you can catch the king's departing soul or follow him, like obedient subjects, to his new kingdom of endless night.

DUCHESS

As the king's mother, I have a large share in your grief. I have wept at my own good husband's death and only kept myself alive by looking at his sons, the mirror images of him. But now these two mirrors of their princely father have cracked to pieces: my sons are dead. And my only comfort is Richard, who is nothing like his father and only causes me shame. You may be a widow, but you're also a mother. You have your children as comfort. But death has snatched my husband from my arms and plucked my two crutches, Edward and Clarence, from my feeble hands. Since your woes are only a portion of mine, I have every reason to surpass your lamentations and drown out your cries with my own.

BOY

(to QUEEN ELIZABETH*)* Ah, Aunt, you didn't weep at our father's death. How can we help you by crying for your sorrow?

GIRL

You didn't sympathize with us when we became orphans; we won't cry for you!

QUEEN ELIZABETH

I don't need your help in grieving. I have my own sources of misery. In fact, all the world's springs and oceans flow from my weeping eyes. I could drown the world. My poor husband, my dear Edward!

CHILDREN
Ah, for our father, for our dear lord Clarence!

DUCHESS
Alas for both, both mine, Edward and Clarence!

QUEEN ELIZABETH
What stay had I but Edward? And he's gone.

CHILDREN
75   What stay had we but Clarence? And he's gone.

DUCHESS
What stays had I but they? And they are gone.

QUEEN ELIZABETH
Was never widow had so dear a loss.

CHILDREN
Were never orphans had so dear a loss.

DUCHESS
Was never mother had so dear a loss.
80   Alas, I am the mother of these griefs.
Their woes are parceled; mine are general.
She for an Edward weeps, and so do I;
I for a Clarence weep; so doth not she.
These babes for Clarence weep and so do I;
85   I for an Edward weep; so do not they.
Alas, you three, on me, threefold distressed,
Pour all your tears. I am your sorrow's nurse,
And I will pamper it with lamentations.

CHILDREN

Our poor father, Clarence!

DUCHESS

My sons Edward and Clarence!

QUEEN ELIZABETH

What support did I have other than Edward? And now he's gone.

CHILDREN

What support did we have besides our father? And now he's gone.

DUCHESS

What support did I have besides my two sons? And now they're both gone.

QUEEN ELIZABETH

There has never been a widow who suffered such loss as me.

CHILDREN

There have never been orphans who've suffered what we have.

DUCHESS

There was never a mother who suffered so much loss. Alas, I am the mother of all these others' griefs. Each of them has a single loss, while I share them all. She weeps for Edward and so do I, while she does not weep for Clarence, though I do. These young children cry for Clarence and so do I, though they don't cry for Edward, as I do. Alas, all of you can turn to me with your sorrow, because I feel all of it. I will comfort you by adding my own grief to your sorrow.

DORSET

    (to QUEEN ELIZABETH*)* Comfort, dear mother. God is
        much displeased

90   That you take with unthankfulness, his doing.
    In common worldly things, 'tis called ungrateful
    With dull unwillingness to repay a debt
    Which with a bounteous hand was kindly lent;
    Much more to be thus opposite with heaven,

95   For it requires the royal debt it lent you.

RIVERS

    Madam, bethink you, like a careful mother,
    Of the young prince your son. Send straight for him.
    Let him be crowned. In him your comfort lives.
    Drown desperate sorrow in dead Edward's grave

100   And plant your joys in living Edward's throne.

    Enter RICHARD, BUCKINGHAM, STANLEY, HASTINGS, *and*
    RATCLIFFE

RICHARD

    Sister, have comfort. All of us have cause
    To wail the dimming of our shining star,
    But none can help our harms by wailing them.—
    Madam, my mother, I do cry you mercy;

105   I did not see your Grace. Humbly on my knee
    I crave your blessing.

    He kneels

DUCHESS

    God bless thee, and put meekness in thy breast,
    Love, charity, obedience, and true duty.

RICHARD

    (standing) Amen. *(aside)* And make me die a good old man!

110   That is the butt end of a mother's blessing;
    I marvel that her Grace did leave it out.

DORSET

(to QUEEN ELIZABETH) Calm down, dear mother. God is unhappy that you've responded so unthankfully to his doings. In everyday life, when a person is unwilling to pay back a loan that was generously offered, he's considered ungrateful. How much worse it is when Heaven is the lender, as in your case?

RIVERS

Be a careful mother, madam, and think about your son, the young prince. Send for him right away and have him crowned. Your peace of mind depends on him. Bury your sorrows in dead Edward's grave and plant your hopes in Prince Edward's rise to the throne.

RICHARD, BUCKINGHAM, STANLEY, HASTINGS, and RATCLIFFE enter.

RICHARD

Sister, calm down. All of us have reason to mourn the dimming of our shining star the king. But no good comes from all this wailing. Oh, mother, forgive me. I didn't see you there. On my knee, I humbly ask your blessing.

He kneels.

DUCHESS

God bless you and make you obedient, loving, and kind.

RICHARD

(he stands) Amen. (to himself) And make me die a good old man! That should be the point of a mother's blessing. I'm surprised my mother forgot to make it.

BUCKINGHAM
You cloudy princes and heart-sorrowing peers
That bear this heavy mutual load of moan,
Now cheer each other in each other's love.
115 Though we have spent our harvest of this king,
We are to reap the harvest of his son.
The broken rancor of your high-swoll'n hates,
But lately splintered, knit, and joined together,
Must gently be preserved, cherished, and kept.
120 Meseemeth good that with some little train
Forthwith from Ludlow the young prince be fet
Hither to London, to be crowned our king.

RIVERS
Why "with some little train," my Lord of Buckingham?

BUCKINGHAM
Marry, my lord, lest by a multitude
125 The new-healed wound of malice should break out,
Which would be so much the more dangerous
By how much the estate is green and yet ungoverned.
Where every horse bears his commanding rein
And may direct his course as please himself,
130 As well the fear of harm as harm apparent,
In my opinion, ought to be prevented.

RICHARD
I hope the king made peace with all of us;
And the compact is firm and true in me.

RIVERS
And so in me, and so, I think, in all.
135 Yet since it is but green, it should be put
To no apparent likelihood of breach,
Which haply by much company might be urged.
Therefore I say with noble Buckingham
That it is meet so few should fetch the prince.

HASTINGS
140 And so say I.

BUCKINGHAM

You mournful princes and grieving gentlemen who have been sharing this burden of grief, now it's time to cheer each other up with love. Though we have lost a generous king, we are about to enjoy the benefits of a new king. We must preserve our goodwill toward each other and not break into factions again. I think a few members of the court should fetch the young prince from Wales and bring him to London to be crowned our king.

RIVERS

Why only a few courtiers, my lord of Buckingham?

BUCKINGHAM

Because if many of us go there, the hostility between us may break out again, which would be very dangerous with the young prince so newly crowned. When you have a situation where everyone seems free to take off on his or her own, it's important that the heads of state keep a low profile. We wouldn't want the prince or his new authority to be undermined by squabbling factions.

RICHARD

The king made peace among all of us. I, at least, intend to stick to our agreement to get along.

RIVERS

And so do I. I think we all do. But, since our agreement is a recent development, it shouldn't be put to the test, which could happen if the coronation turned into a huge ceremony. So, I agree with noble Buckingham—only a few should go to meet the prince.

HASTINGS

I think so too.

RICHARD
>   Then be it so, and go we to determine
>   Who they shall be that straight shall post to Ludlow.—
>   Madam, and you, my sister, will you go
>   To give your censures in this business?

Exeunt all but BUCKINGHAM *and* RICHARD

BUCKINGHAM
145
>   My lord, whoever journeys to the prince,
>   For God's sake let not us two at home.
>   For by the way I'll sort occasion,
>   As index to the story we late talked of,
>   To part the queen's proud kindred from the prince.

RICHARD
150
>   My other self, my council's consistory,
>   My oracle, my prophet, my dear cousin,
>   I, as a child, will go by thy direction
>   Toward Ludlow then, for we'll not stay behind.

Exeunt

RICHARD

> Then we're agreed. Now we need to figure out which of us will go to meet him. Madam and mother, will you go to offer your support to this weighty business?

Everyone but BUCKINGHAM *and* RICHARD *exits.*

BUCKINGHAM

> For God's sake, my lord, let's be sure to be part of the group that meets the prince. Along the way, I'll find an opportunity to separate him from the queen's proud relatives, as step one in the plan we've discussed.

RICHARD

> You are my other self, my oracle, my prophet, my dear brother! I plan to act like a child and do exactly what you say. To Wales then, for we will not be left out.

They exit.

ACT 2, SCENE 3

Enter one CITIZEN *at one door, and another at the other*

FIRST CITIZEN
Good morrow, neighbor, whither away so fast?

SECOND CITIZEN
I promise you I scarcely know myself.
Hear you the news abroad?

FIRST CITIZEN
Yes, that the king is dead.

SECOND CITIZEN
5   Ill news, by 'r Lady. Seldom comes the better.
I fear, I fear, 'twill prove a giddy world.

Enter THIRD CITIZEN

THIRD CITIZEN
Neighbors, God speed.

FIRST CITIZEN
                                    Give you good morrow, sir.

THIRD CITIZEN
Doth this news hold of good King Edward's
death?

SECOND CITIZEN
10   Ay, sir, it is too true, God help the while.

THIRD CITIZEN
Then, masters, look to see a troublous world.

FIRST CITIZEN
No, no, by God's good grace, his son shall reign.

THIRD CITIZEN
Woe to the land that's governed by a child.

SECOND CITIZEN
In him there is a hope of government,
15   Which, in his nonage, council under him,
And, in his full and ripened years, himself,
No doubt shall then, and till then, govern well.

ACT 2, SCENE 3

Two CITIZENS *enter through different doors.*

FIRST CITIZEN
Good day, neighbor. Where are you off to so fast?

SECOND CITIZEN
I'm telling you, I hardly know myself. Did you hear
the news that's going around?

FIRST CITIZEN
Yes, that the king is dead.

SECOND CITIZEN
Bad news, by God. The news is always bad. But this
news is bound to make the world go mad.

A THIRD CITIZEN *enters.*

THIRD CITIZEN
Neighbors, hello.

FIRST CITIZEN
Good day to you, sir.

THIRD CITIZEN
Is it true that good King Edward has died?

SECOND CITIZEN
Yes, sir, it's all too true, God help us.

THIRD CITIZEN
Then, gentlemen, we can count on trouble.

FIRST CITIZEN.
No, no, with God's help, his son will be king.

THIRD CITIZEN
It's bad news when a country is ruled by a child.

SECOND CITIZEN
His counselors will govern as long as he's a minor, and
then he'll take over. It shouldn't go so badly.

FIRST CITIZEN
So stood the state when Henry the Sixth
Was crowned in Paris but at nine months old.

THIRD CITIZEN
20   Stood the state so? No, no, good friends, God wot,
For then this land was famously enriched
With politic grave counsel; then the king
Had virtuous uncles to protect his Grace.

FIRST CITIZEN
Why, so hath this, both by the father and mother.

THIRD CITIZEN
25   Better it were they all came by his father,
Or by the father there were none at all,
For emulation who shall now be nearest
Will touch us all too near if God prevent not.
O, full of danger is the duke of Gloucester,
30   And the queen's sons and brothers haught and proud,
And were they to be ruled, and not to rule,
This sickly land might solace as before.

FIRST CITIZEN
Come, come, we fear the worst. All will be well.

THIRD CITIZEN
When clouds are seen, wise men put on their cloaks;
35   When great leaves fall, then winter is at hand;
When the sun sets, who doth not look for night?
Untimely storms make men expect a dearth.
All may be well; but if God sort it so,
'Tis more than we deserve or I expect.

SECOND CITIZEN
40   Truly, the hearts of men are full of fear.
Ye cannot reason almost with a man
That looks not heavily and full of dread.

FIRST CITIZEN

That's how it was with Henry the Sixth, who was crowned in Paris when he was only nine months old.

THIRD CITIZEN

Really? But at that point, the king had the benefit of excellent counselors. His uncles were good men and protected him.

FIRST CITIZEN

Well, this king has uncles too, on both his father and mother's side.

THIRD CITIZEN

It would be better if they were all on his father's side, or that there were none at all on his father's side. As it is, the rivalry between his father's and mother's relatives over who will be closest to the king is likely to endanger everyone, if we're not lucky. As it stands, there's a struggle between the two sides for the prince's attention. Richard, the duke of Gloucester, is very dangerous, and the queen's sons and brothers are haughty and proud—it would be better for this ailing country if they were subjects, not rulers.

FIRST CITIZEN

Come, come, we're worrying about the worst-case scenario. I'm sure everything will be fine.

THIRD CITIZEN

When the day turns cloudy, wise men put on their coats. When leaves fall from the trees, it means winter has arrived. When the sun sets, who's too stupid to recognize it's night? When storms arrive early, you can expect the harvest will be damaged. So, if all turns out fine, as you say, it's more than we deserve or I expect.

SECOND CITIZEN

It's true, people are really worried. It's hard to find a person who isn't.

THIRD CITIZEN
Before the days of change, still is it so.
By a divine instinct, men's minds mistrust
45   Ensuing dangers, as by proof we see
The water swell before a boist'rous storm.
But leave it all to God. Whither away?

SECOND CITIZEN
Marry, we were sent for to the justices.

THIRD CITIZEN
And so was I. I'll bear you company.

Exeunt

THIRD CITIZEN

> It's always like this in times of change. By some sort of deep instinct, we always know when danger is approaching, just as we know that a storm is coming when the sea swells. But leave it all to God. Where are you all off to?

SECOND CITIZEN

> The court has sent for us.

THIRD CITIZEN

> For me, too. I'll go with you.

> *They all exit.*

ACT 2, SCENE 4

Enter the ARCHBISHOP *of York, the young duke of* YORK,
QUEEN ELIZABETH, *and the old* DUCHESS *of York*

ARCHBISHOP
Last night, I hear, they lay at Stony Stratford,
And at Northampton they do rest tonight.
Tomorrow or next day they will be here.

DUCHESS
I long with all my heart to see the prince.
5   I hope he is much grown since last I saw him.

QUEEN ELIZABETH
But I hear no; they say my son of York
Has almost overta'en him in his growth.

YORK
Ay, mother, but I would not have it so.

DUCHESS
Why, my young cousin? It is good to grow.

YORK
10   Grandam, one night as we did sit at supper,
My uncle Rivers talked how I did grow
More than my brother: "Ay," quoth my uncle Gloucester,
"Small herbs have grace; great weeds do grow apace."
And since, methinks I would not grow so fast
15   Because sweet flowers are slow and weeds make haste.

DUCHESS
Good faith, good faith, the saying did not hold
In him that did object the same to thee!
He was the wretched'st thing when he was young,
So long a-growing and so leisurely,
20   That if this rule were true, he should be gracious.

YORK
And so no doubt he is, my gracious madam.

ACT 2, SCENE 4

The ARCHBISHOP *of York,* QUEEN ELIZABETH, *her son, the young duke of* YORK, *and the* DUCHESS *of York enter.*

ARCHBISHOP

Last night, I hear, they stayed in Stony Stratford. Tonight they will rest in Northhampton. They'll be here tomorrow or the next day.

DUCHESS

I'm dying to see the prince. I hope he's grown a lot since I last saw him.

QUEEN ELIZABETH

But I hear he hasn't. They say my son York has almost passed him in height.

YORK

Yes, mother, but I wish I hadn't.

DUCHESS

Why, dear child? It's good to grow.

YORK

Grandmother, one night when we were eating dinner, my uncle Rivers mentioned that I had grown more than my brother. "Yes," said my uncle Gloucester, "Small plants are graceful, while ugly weeds grow fast." And since then, I've wished I wouldn't grow so fast, because sweet flowers are slow while the weeds grow in a hurry.

DUCHESS

Well, it certainly wasn't true for Richard! As a child, he took such a long time to grow up that, according to his rule, he should have grown up into a gracious adult.

YORK

And no doubt he is, gracious madam.

DUCHESS
I hope he is, but yet let mothers doubt.

YORK
Now, by my troth, if I had been remembered,
I could have given my uncle's grace a flout
25   To touch his growth nearer than he touched mine.

DUCHESS
How, my pretty York? I prithee let me hear it.

YORK
Marry, they say my uncle grew so fast
That he could gnaw a crust at two hours old.
'Twas full two years ere I could get a tooth.
30   Grandam, this would have been a biting jest.

DUCHESS
I prithee, pretty York, who told thee this?

YORK
Grandam, his nurse.

DUCHESS
His nurse? Why, she was dead ere thou wast born.

YORK
If 'twere not she, I cannot tell who told me.

QUEEN ELIZABETH
35   A parlous boy! Go to, you are too shrewd.

DUCHESS
Good madam, be not angry with the child.

QUEEN ELIZABETH
Pitchers have ears.

Enter a MESSENGER

ARCHBISHOP
Here comes a messenger. —What news?

MESSENGER
Such news, my lord, as grieves me to report.

DUCHESS

I hope he is, but mothers get to have their doubts.

YORK

Hey, if I'd remembered something about him, I could have had a good comeback for my uncle, touching on his growth worse than he touched on mine.

DUCHESS

What would you have said, my young York? Do tell.

YORK

Indeed, they say my uncle grew so fast that he could gnaw on a crust of bread when he was two hours old. It took me two years before I had a single tooth. Grandmother, this would have been a biting joke.

DUCHESS

Pretty York, who told you about his teeth?

YORK

His nurse, grandmother.

DUCHESS

His nurse? Why, she was dead before you were even born.

YORK

Well, if it wasn't her, I don't know.

QUEEN ELIZABETH

A mischievous child. Come, come, you are too clever for your own good.

DUCHESS

Good lady, don't be angry with the child.

QUEEN ELIZABETH

Little pitchers have big ears.

A MESSENGER *enters.*

ARCHBISHOP

Here comes a messenger. What's the news?

MESSENGER

My lord, it's news I wish I didn't have to report.

QUEEN ELIZABETH
40   How doth the prince?

MESSENGER
Well, madam, and in health.

DUCHESS
What is thy news then?

MESSENGER
Lord Rivers and Lord Grey are sent to Pomfret,
And, with them, Sir Thomas Vaughan, prisoners.

DUCHESS
45   Who hath committed them?

MESSENGER
The mighty dukes, Gloucester and Buckingham.

ARCHBISHOP
For what offence?

MESSENGER
The sum of all I can, I have disclosed.
Why, or for what, the nobles were committed
50   Is all unknown to me, my gracious lord.

QUEEN ELIZABETH
Ay me! I see the ruin of my house.
The tiger now hath seized the gentle hind.
Insulting tyranny begins to jut
Upon the innocent and aweless throne.
55   Welcome, destruction, blood, and massacre.
I see, as in a map, the end of all.

QUEEN ELIZABETH

How's the prince?

MESSENGER

He's fine and healthy, madam.

DUCHESS

What is your news?

MESSENGER

Lord Rivers and Lord Grey have been imprisoned in Pomfret. So has Sir Thomas Vaughan.

Pomfret was a castle in northern England used for political executions; Richard II was killed there. Sir Thomas Vaughan was a chief member of Prince Edward's court.

DUCHESS

Who sent them there?

MESSENGER

The powerful dukes Gloucester and Buckingham.

ARCHBISHOP

What did they do wrong?

MESSENGER

I've told you everything I know. Why the nobles were imprisoned, and on what charges, I don't know, my gracious lord.

QUEEN ELIZABETH

Oh no! I see the downfall of my family. The tiger has seized the gentle deer: a tyrant has begun to attack the weak, innocent king. Welcome, destruction, blood, and massacre! I can see how all this will end as clearly as if I was looking at a map.

DUCHESS
Accursèd and unquiet wrangling days,
How many of you have mine eyes beheld?
My husband lost his life to get the crown,
60   And often up and down my sons were tossed
For me to joy, and weep, their gain and loss.
And being seated, and domestic broils
Clean overblown, themselves the conquerors
Make war upon themselves, brother to brother,
65   Blood to blood, self against self. O, preposterous
And frantic outrage, end thy damnèd spleen,
Or let me die, to look on death no more.

QUEEN ELIZABETH
(to YORK*)* Come, come, my boy. We will to sanctuary.
Madam, farewell.

DUCHESS
                    Stay, I will go with you

QUEEN ELIZABETH
70   You have no cause.

ARCHBISHOP
(to QUEEN ELIZABETH*)*
My gracious lady, go,
And thither bear your treasure and your goods.
For my part, I'll resign unto your Grace
The seal I keep; and so betide to me
75   As well I tender you and all of yours.
Go. I'll conduct you to the sanctuary.

                                        Exeunt

DUCHESS

How many times have I had to live through cursed times of violent struggle? My husband lost his life to get the crown, and my sons' fortunes have been tossed up and down, leaving me to rejoice over their victories and weep over their losses. And once one of them achieved the throne and had taken care of domestic quarrels, they made war among themselves. It's a pre-posterous outrage. Let it end, or let me die so I won't have to watch any more of it.

QUEEN ELIZABETH

Taking "sanctuary" meant going into a church, where for a certain length of time people could be free from civil authority.

(to YORK*)* Come, my boy, let's go to sanctuary. Madam, farewell.

DUCHESS

Wait, I'll go with you.

QUEEN ELIZABETH

You have no reason to.

ARCHBISHOP

The archbishop had both religious and civic duties. By assigning the Seal to the queen, he's suggesting that he will treat her, not her son (or her brother-in-law Richard), as the lawful monarch. It's not really the Arch-bishop's role, though, to reas-sign the Seal. Only the king can do that.

(to QUEEN ELIZABETH*)* My gracious lady, go, and take your money and belongings with you. For my part, I'll reassign the Great Seal of England to you and will take it upon myself to protect you. Come, I'll conduct you to the sanctuary.

They all exit.

ACT THREE

SCENE 1

The trumpets sound. Enter the young PRINCE *Edward,*
RICHARD, BUCKINGHAM, *the* CARDINAL, CATESBY, *and others*

BUCKINGHAM
  Welcome, sweet prince, to London, to your chamber.

RICHARD
  (to PRINCE*)* Welcome, dear cousin, my thoughts' sovereign.
  The weary way hath made you melancholy.

PRINCE
  No, uncle, but our crosses on the way
5 Have made it tedious, wearisome, and heavy.
  I want more uncles here to welcome me.

RICHARD
  ⟨Sweet prince, the untainted virtue of your years
  Hath not yet dived into the world's deceit;
  Nor more can you distinguish of a man
10 Than of his outward show, which, God He knows,
  Seldom or never jumpeth with the heart.⟩
  Those uncles which you want were dangerous.
  Your Grace attended to their sugared words
  But looked not on the poison of their hearts.
15 God keep you from them, and from such false friends.

PRINCE
  God keep me from false friends, but they were none.

RICHARD
  My lord, the mayor of London comes to greet you.

  Enter the LORD MAYOR *and his train*

ACT THREE
SCENE 1

The trumpets sound. The young PRINCE *Edward,*
RICHARD, BUCKINGHAM, *the* CARDINAL, CATESBY, *and*
others enter.

BUCKINGHAM

Welcome, sweet prince, to London, the capital of the
king.

RICHARD

Welcome, dear nephew, king of all my thoughts. The
tiring journey seems to have made you gloomy.

PRINCE

It wasn't the journey itself, uncle, but the troubles we
encountered that made it wearisome and dull. I want
more uncles here to welcome me.

RICHARD

Sweet prince, you're just an innocent child. You don't
really understand how capable people are of trickery.
All you know is what a man shows you, which has little to do with what he's really thinking. Those uncles
that you wish were here were dangerous. Your Grace
heard their saccharine words, but didn't take note of
their poisonous intentions. God protect you from
them and from other false friends!

PRINCE

God should keep me from false friends, but they
weren't false.

RICHARD

My lord, the mayor of London is here to greet you.

The LORD MAYOR *and his train enter.*

LORD MAYOR
God bless your Grace with health and happy days.

PRINCE
I thank you, good my lord, and thank you all.—
20   I thought my mother and my brother York
Would long ere this have met us on the way.
Fie, what a slug is Hastings that he comes not
To tell us whether they will come or no!

Enter HASTINGS

BUCKINGHAM
And in good time here comes the sweating lord.

PRINCE
25   Welcome, my lord. What, will our mother come?

HASTINGS
On what occasion God He knows, not I,
The queen your mother and your brother York
Have taken sanctuary. The tender prince
Would fain have come with me to meet your Grace,
30   But by his mother was perforce withheld.

BUCKINGHAM
Fie, what an indirect and peevish course
Is this of hers! —Lord Cardinal, will your Grace
Persuade the queen to send the duke of York
Unto his princely brother presently?—
35   If she deny, Lord Hastings, go with him,
And from her jealous arms pluck him perforce.

CARDINAL
My Lord of Buckingham, if my weak oratory
Can from his mother win the duke of York,
Anon expect him here; but if she be obdurate
40   To mild entreaties, God in heaven forbid
We should infringe the holy privilege
Of blessèd sanctuary! Not for all this land
Would I be guilty of so deep a sin.

LORD MAYOR

God bless your Grace with health and happy days.

PRINCE

Thank you, my good lord, thank you all. I thought my mother and my brother, York, would have met us on our way here long before now. And what a slug Hastings is that he hasn't even arrived to tell us whether they're coming!

HASTINGS *enters.*

BUCKINGHAM

And, just in time, here comes the sweaty lord.

PRINCE

Welcome, my lord. What, isn't my mother coming?

HASTINGS

God knows why, but your mother and your brother have taken sanctuary in Westminster Abbey. Your sweet brother wanted to come meet you, but his mother wouldn't let him.

BUCKINGHAM

Damn, what a sneaky and spiteful course your mother is taking!—Lord Cardinal, will you please persuade the queen to hurry and send the duke of York here?— Go with him, Lord Hastings, and if she refuses, take the boy from her by force.

CARDINAL

My Lord of Buckingham, if my weak skills of persuasion convince his mother to part with the duke of York, you can expect him here shortly. But if she resists my mild pleas, let God in heaven forbid us from disobeying the holy laws of the sanctuary and taking the child from her. I wouldn't commit so serious a crime for anything.

BUCKINGHAM
You are too senseless obstinate, my lord,
45   Too ceremonious and traditional.
Weigh it but with the grossness of this age,
You break not sanctuary in seizing him.
The benefit thereof is always granted
To those whose dealings have deserved the place
50   And those who have the wit to claim the place.
This prince hath neither claimed it nor deserved it
And therefore, in mine opinion, cannot have it.
Then taking him from thence that is not there,
You break no privilege nor charter there.
55   Oft have I heard of sanctuary men,
But sanctuary children, ne'er till now.

CARDINAL
My lord, you shall o'errule my mind for once.—
Come on, Lord Hastings, will you go with me?

HASTINGS
I go, my lord.

PRINCE
60   Good lords, make all the speedy haste you may.

Exeunt CARDINAL *and* HASTINGS
Say, uncle Gloucester, if our brother come,
Where shall we sojourn till our coronation?

RICHARD
Where it seems best unto your royal self.
If I may counsel you, some day or two
65   Your Highness shall repose you at the Tower;
Then where you please and shall be thought most fit
For your best health and recreation.

PRINCE
I do not like the Tower, of any place.—
Did Julius Caesar build that place, my lord?

BUCKINGHAM

> You are too inexplicably stubborn, my lord, too stuck on ceremony. In these less dainty times, you're not breaking the laws of sanctuary to seize him. It's only a sanctuary for those who really need protection or those who are smart enough to claim they do. The prince has done neither; therefore, in my opinion, he isn't really protected by sanctuary. You're not breaking any holy laws to take him away. Often I have heard of "sanctuary men," but until now I've never heard of "sanctuary children."

CARDINAL

> My lord, you've won me over this time. Lord Hastings, will you go with me?

HASTINGS

> I'm coming, my lord.

PRINCE

> Go as fast as you can.

> > CARDINAL *and* HASTINGS *exit.*

> Say, uncle Richard, if my brother comes, where will I stay till my coronation?

RICHARD

> Whatever seems best to you. If I can give you some advice, if I were you, I would stay in the Tower for a day or two. Then you can stay wherever best suits your health and entertainment needs.

PRINCE

> Of all places, I don't like the Tower. Didn't Julius Caesar build it, my lord?

Julius Caesar conquered Britain, which then became a part of the Roman Empire.

BUCKINGHAM

70   He did, my gracious lord, begin that place,
        Which, since, succeeding ages have re-edified.

PRINCE

        Is it upon record, or else reported
        Successively from age to age, he built it?

BUCKINGHAM

        Upon record, my gracious lord.

PRINCE

75   But say, my lord, it were not registered,
        Methinks the truth should live from age to age,
        As 'twere retailed to all posterity,
        Even to the general all-ending day.

RICHARD

        (aside) So wise so young, they say, do never live long.

PRINCE

80   What say you, uncle?

RICHARD

        I say, without characters fame lives long.
        (aside) Thus, like the formal Vice, Iniquity,
        I moralize two meanings in one word.

PRINCE

        That Julius Caesar was a famous man.
85   With what his valor did enrich his wit,
        His wit set down to make his valor live.
        Death makes no conquest of this conqueror,
        For now he lives in fame, though not in life.
        I'll tell you what, my cousin Buckingham—

BUCKINGHAM

He started it, my noble lord, and succeeding generations rebuilt it.

PRINCE

Is it on record that he built it, or is it just word of mouth?

BUCKINGHAM

On record, my gracious lord.

PRINCE

Well, I think that even if it weren't on record, the truth would be remembered from one generation to the next—all the way to Doomsday.

RICHARD

(to himself) As the saying goes, "Those that are this wise when they're this young won't live long."

PRINCE

What did you say, uncle?

RICHARD

I said, "When there are no written records, a person's fame lasts for a long time." *(to himself)* Like Injustice, I get two meanings out of one word.

Iniquity, or injustice/wickedness, was a common figure in medieval morality plays, which often personified the Seven Deadly Sins. Like Richard, Iniquity favors double talk to serve his own wicked purposes.

PRINCE

That Julius Caesar was a famous man. His courage helped his cleverness, and his cleverness made sure that his reputation for being courageous outlived him. Death didn't conquer *this* conqueror, for he lives on in his fame, even though he's dead. I'll tell you what, my cousin Buckingham—

BUCKINGHAM

90   What, my gracious lord?

PRINCE

           An if I live until I be a man,
           I'll win our ancient right in France again
           Or die a soldier, as I lived a king.

RICHARD

           (aside) Short summers lightly have a forward spring.

           Enter young YORK, HASTINGS, *and the* CARDINAL

BUCKINGHAM

95   Now in good time here comes the duke of York.

PRINCE

           Richard of York, how fares our loving brother?

YORK

           Well, my dread lord—so must I call you now.

PRINCE

           Ay, brother, to our grief, as it is yours.
           Too late he died that might have kept that title,
100   Which by his death hath lost much majesty.

RICHARD

           How fares our cousin, noble Lord of York?

YORK

           I thank you, gentle uncle. O, my lord,
           You said that idle weeds are fast in growth.
           The prince my brother hath outgrown me far.

RICHARD

105   He hath, my lord.

YORK

                           And therefore is he idle?

BUCKINGHAM

What, my dear lord?

PRINCE

If I live to be a man, I'll win France again or die a soldier, as honorably as I lived as a king.

In the Hundred Years War (1337–1453), the English invaded France in an attempt to make good on hereditary claims to the French throne.

RICHARD

(to himself) As the saying goes, "Short summers often have an early spring." This smarty-pants won't live long.

Young YORK, HASTINGS, *and the* CARDINAL *enter.*

BUCKINGHAM

Making good time, here's the duke of York.

PRINCE

Richard of York, how are you doing, my loving brother?

YORK

Very well, my supreme lord—that's what I have to call you now.

PRINCE

Yes, brother, I feel bad about that, too. The man who might have kept that title died too soon, and now it isn't worth nearly as much.

RICHARD

How's my nephew doing, noble lord of York?

YORK

Thank you for asking, uncle. Oh, my lord, you once said that lazy weeds grow fast. The prince has far outgrown me.

RICHARD

He has, my lord.

YORK

Does that mean he's lazy?

RICHARD
O, my fair cousin, I must not say so.

YORK
Then is he more beholding to you than I.

RICHARD
He may command me as my sovereign,
But you have power in me as in a kinsman.

YORK
110 I pray you, uncle, give me this dagger.

RICHARD
My dagger, little cousin? With all my heart.

PRINCE
A beggar, brother?

YORK
Of my kind uncle, that I know will give,
And being but a toy, which is no grief to give.

RICHARD
115 A greater gift than that I'll give my cousin.

YORK
A greater gift? O, that's the sword to it.

RICHARD
Ay, gentle cousin, were it light enough.

YORK
O, then I see you will part but with light gifts.
In weightier things you'll say a beggar nay.

RICHARD
120 It is too heavy for your Grace to wear.

YORK
I weigh it lightly, were it heavier.

RICHARD
What, would you have my weapon, little lord?

YORK
I would, that I might thank you as you call me.

RICHARD
How?

RICHARD

Oh, my handsome nephew, I must not say that.

YORK

In that case, he's more obliged to you than I am.

RICHARD

He may command me as my king, but you still have power over me as a relative.

YORK

Uncle, please give me your dagger.

RICHARD

My dagger, little nephew? With all my heart.

PRINCE

Are you begging, brother?

YORK

From my kind uncle, who I know will give it to me, especially as it's not worth much.

RICHARD

I'll give you a greater gift than that, nephew.

YORK

A greater gift? That must mean a sword.

RICHARD

Yes, gentle cousin, if it were light enough for you.

YORK

Oh, I see, you will only part with lightweight presents. For more important things, you'll say no.

RICHARD

A sword's too heavy for you to wear.

YORK

I wouldn't think much of it even if it were heavier.

RICHARD

What, do you want to wear *my* weapon, little lord?

YORK

I do, so I can thank you for what you called me.

RICHARD

What's that?

YORK

125   Little.

PRINCE

My lord of York will still be cross in talk.
Uncle, your Grace knows how to bear with him.

YORK

You mean, to bear me, not to bear with me.—
Uncle, my brother mocks both you and me.
130   Because that I am little, like an ape,
He thinks that you should bear me on your shoulders.

BUCKINGHAM

(aside) With what a sharp-provided wit he reasons!
To mitigate the scorn he gives his uncle,
He prettily and aptly taunts himself.
135   So cunning and so young is wonderful.

RICHARD

(to PRINCE*)* My lord, will 't please you pass along?
Myself and my good cousin Buckingham
Will to your mother, to entreat of her
To meet you at the Tower and welcome you.

YORK

140   *(to* PRINCE*)* What, will you go unto the Tower, my lord?

PRINCE

My lord protector needs will have it so.

YORK

I shall not sleep in quiet at the Tower.

RICHARD

Why, what should you fear?

YORK

Marry, my uncle Clarence' angry ghost.
145   My grandam told me he was murdered there.

YORK

"Little."

PRINCE

The lord of York is always a bit perverse in his chatter. But, uncle, you know how to bear with him.

YORK

You mean, to bear me, not to bear *with* me. Uncle, my brother makes fun of both of us. Because I'm little, like an ape, he thinks you should bear me on your shoulders, like a fool.

Professional jesters often carried apes on their shoulders. York may also be suggesting that Richard's humpback would provide a perfect spot for an ape to perch.

BUCKINGHAM

(to himself) What a sharp mind this boy has! To make up for his scorn toward his uncle, he makes fun of himself as well. It's amazing that he's so cunning at his age.

RICHARD

(to PRINCE) My lord, will you please continue on your way to the Tower? My good cousin Buckingham and I will go to your mother and ask her to meet you there.

YORK

(to PRINCE) What, you're going to the Tower, my lord?

PRINCE

My protector, Richard, insists on it.

YORK

I can't sleep quietly in the Tower.

RICHARD

Why, what are you afraid of?

YORK

My uncle Clarence's angry ghost. My grandmother told me he was murdered there.

PRINCE
    I fear no uncles dead.

RICHARD
    Nor none that live, I hope.

PRINCE
    An if they live, I hope I need not fear.
    (to YORK*)* But come, my lord. With a heavy heart,
150   Thinking on them, go I unto the Tower.

A sennet. Exeunt all but RICHARD, BUCKINGHAM, *and*
CATESBY

BUCKINGHAM
    (to RICHARD*)* Think you, my lord, this little prating York
    Was not incensèd by his subtle mother
    To taunt and scorn you thus opprobriously?

RICHARD
    No doubt, no doubt. O, 'tis a parlous boy,
155   Bold, quick, ingenious, forward, capable.
    He is all the mother's, from the top to toe.

BUCKINGHAM
    Well, let them rest.—Come hither, Catesby.
    Thou art sworn as deeply to effect what we intend
    As closely to conceal what we impart.
160   Thou knowest our reasons, urged upon the way.
    What thinkest thou? Is it not an easy matter
    To make William Lord Hastings of our mind
    For the installment of this noble duke
    In the seat royal of this famous isle?

CATESBY
165   He, for his father's sake, so loves the prince
    That he will not be won to aught against him.

BUCKINGHAM
    What think'st thou then of Stanley? Will not he?

PRINCE

I'm not afraid of dead uncles.

RICHARD

Nor living ones, I hope.

PRINCE

Well, I hope not. *(to* YORK*)* But come, my lord. With a heavy heart, thinking about my dead uncles, I will go to the Tower.

A trumpet sounds. Everyone except RICHARD, BUCKINGHAM, *and* CATESBY *exits.*

BUCKINGHAM

Richard, don't you think this chattering little York was encouraged to taunt you by his sneaky mother in that outrageous way?

RICHARD

No doubt, no doubt. Oh, he's a dangerously clever boy—bold, quick-witted, capable. He's his mother's child from head to toe.

BUCKINGHAM

Well, enough about them.—Come here, Catesby. You've sworn to participate in our plot and to keep it a secret. What do you think: wouldn't it be easy to convince Lord Hastings to join us in installing Richard as king of England?

CATESBY

Hastings loved the prince's father so much that we won't be able to persuade him to do anything against the prince.

BUCKINGHAM

What about Stanley? Won't he join us?

CATESBY
He will do all in all as Hastings doth.

BUCKINGHAM
Well then, no more but this: go, gentle Catesby,
170   And, as it were far off, sound thou Lord Hastings
How he doth stand affected to our purpose
And summon him tomorrow to the Tower
To sit about the coronation.
If thou dost find him tractable to us,
175   Encourage him and show him all our reasons.
If he be leaden, icy, cold, unwilling,
Be thou so too, and so break off the talk,
And give us notice of his inclination;
For we tomorrow hold divided councils,
180   Wherein thyself shalt highly be employed.

RICHARD
Commend me to Lord William. Tell him, Catesby,
His ancient knot of dangerous adversaries
Tomorrow are let blood at Pomfret castle,
And bid my lord, for joy of this good news,
185   Give mistress Shore one gentle kiss the more.

BUCKINGHAM
Good Catesby, go effect this business soundly.

CATESBY
My good lords both, with all the heed I can.

RICHARD
Shall we hear from you, Catesby, ere we sleep?

CATESBY
You shall, my lord.

RICHARD
190   At Crosby Place, there shall you find us both.

Exit CATESBY

BUCKINGHAM
Now, my lord, what shall we do, if we perceive
Lord Hastings will not yield to our complots?

CATESBY

> He'll do whatever Hastings does.

BUCKINGHAM

> Okay, just do this, noble Catesby: sound out Lord Hastings, but make it seem as if you're just mulling over the idea, that it hasn't been firmed up yet. Invite him to come to the Tower tomorrow for the coronation ceremony. If he seems game to our plan, encourage him to join us and explain all our reasons. But if he's resistant and chilly, then be like that too and break off the conversation. Let us know how he responds. Tomorrow we're going to hold two separate meetings, one for those who are with us and one for those who aren't. You'll have a lot to do in these meetings.

RICHARD

> Give my regards to Hastings, Catesby. Tell him the nest of dangerous enemies that plagued him for years will die tomorrow at Pomfret. And tell him to give Mistress Shore one extra kiss to celebrate this good news.

After King Edward died, Mistress Shore became Hastings's mistress.

BUCKINGHAM

> Good Catesby, do your work well.

CATESBY

> My good lords, I plan to.

RICHARD

> Will we hear from you before bedtime, Catesby?

CATESBY

> You will, my lord.

RICHARD

> You'll find us both at Crosby Place.

CATESBY exits.

BUCKINGHAM

> Now, my lord, what are we going to do if we find that Lord Hastings won't go along with our plans?

RICHARD
  Chop off his head. Something we will determine.
  And look when I am king, claim thou of me
195 The earldom of Hereford, and all the moveables
  Whereof the king my brother was possessed.

BUCKINGHAM
  I'll claim that promise at your Grace's hands.

RICHARD
  And look to have it yielded with all kindness.
  Come, let us sup betimes, that afterwards
200 We may digest our complots in some form.

Exeunt

RICHARD

> Chop off his head. Whatever we decide to do. And when I'm king, remember to ask me for the earldom of Hereford and all the possessions that go with it, which my brother the king used to own.

BUCKINGHAM

> I look forward to that present.

RICHARD

> You'll find I'll give it to you very willingly. Come, let's have an early dinner so that we have time to work out our plans.

> *They exit.*

ACT 3, SCENE 2

Enter a MESSENGER *at door of* HASTINGS

MESSENGER
> *(knocking)* My lord, my lord.

HASTINGS
> *(within)* Who knocks?

MESSENGER
> One from the Lord Stanley.

HASTINGS
> *(within)* What is 't o'clock?

MESSENGER
5 Upon the stroke of four.

Enter HASTINGS

HASTINGS
> Cannot my Lord Stanley sleep these tedious nights?

MESSENGER
> So it appears by that I have to say.
> First, he commends him to your noble self.

HASTINGS
> What then?

MESSENGER
10 Then certifies your Lordship that this night
> He dreamt the boar had razèd his helm.
> Besides, he says there are two councils kept,
> And that may be determined at the one
> Which may make you and him to rue at th' other.
15 Therefore he sends to know your Lordship's pleasure,
> If you will presently take horse with him
> And with all speed post with him toward the north
> To shun the danger that his soul divines.

ACT 3, SCENE 2

A MESSENGER *enters and goes to Hastings's door.*

MESSENGER

(*knocking*) My lord, my lord.

HASTINGS

(*offstage*) Who's knocking?

MESSENGER

A messenger from Lord Stanley.

HASTINGS

(*offstage*) What time is it?

MESSENGER

Four o'clock in the morning.

HASTINGS *enters.*

HASTINGS

Can't Lord Stanley sleep?

MESSENGER

I guess not—for good reason, as you'll soon hear. First, he sends his regards.

HASTINGS

And then?

MESSENGER

And then he said to tell you that tonight he dreamed the duke of Gloucester cut off his helmet—that is, his head. Besides that, he says that two meetings are going to be held tomorrow, and something may be decided at one of them that may make you and him, who are at the other, sorry. He wants to know if instead of going to the meeting, you'll get on your horse and ride north with him to get out of harm's way.

HASTINGS
    Go, fellow, go. Return unto thy lord.
20   Bid him not fear the separated council.
    His Honor and myself are at the one,
    And at the other is my good friend Catesby,
    Where nothing can proceed that toucheth us
    Whereof I shall not have intelligence.
25   Tell him his fears are shallow, without instance.
    And for his dreams, I wonder he's so simple
    To trust the mock'ry of unquiet slumbers.
    To fly the boar before the boar pursues
    Were to incense the boar to follow us
30   And make pursuit where he did mean no chase.
    Go, bid thy master rise and come to me,
    And we will both together to the Tower,
    Where he shall see, the boar will use us kindly.

MESSENGER
    I'll go, my lord, and tell him what you say.

Exit

Enter CATESBY

CATESBY
35   Many good morrows to my noble lord.

HASTINGS
    Good morrow, Catesby. You are early stirring.
    What news, what news in this our tott'ring state?

CATESBY
    It is a reeling world indeed, my lord,
    And I believe will never stand upright
40   Till Richard wear the garland of the realm.

HASTINGS
    How "wear the garland"? Dost thou mean the crown?

HASTINGS

> Go, man, return to your lord and tell him not to worry about the separate meetings. While he and I are at one, my loyal servant Catesby will be at the other, so nothing will happen that we won't find out about. Tell your master there is no sound basis for his worries. And as for his dreams, I'm surprised he's so foolish as to trust the fantasies of a restless night. If we flee from the boar before the boar even pursues us, we'll only make the boar angry and suspicious, causing him to chase us when he never intended to. Tell your master to get up and come here, and we'll go together to the Tower to meet the boar, who will treat us well, as he'll see.

"The boar" refers to Richard, whose heraldic emblem, worn on his armor to indicate his noble lineage, was the boar.

MESSENGER

> I'll go, my lord, and tell him what you say.

He exits.

CATESBY *enters.*

CATESBY

> Good morning, my noble lord.

HASTINGS

> Good day, Catesby. You're up early. What news can you tell me in this fast-moving, unsteady state of ours?

CATESBY

> Our world sure is spinning fast, my lord. I believe it won't stop moving and stand upright till Richard wears the wreath of the realm.

HASTINGS

> What do you mean, "wears the wreath"? Are you talking about the crown?

CATESBY
    Ay, my good lord.

HASTINGS
    I'll have this crown of mine cut from my shoulders
    Before I'll see the crown so foul misplaced.
45   But canst thou guess that he doth aim at it?

CATESBY
    Ay, on my life, and hopes to find you forward
    Upon his party for the gain thereof;
    And thereupon he sends you this good news,
    That this same very day your enemies,
50   The kindred of the queen, must die at Pomfret.

HASTINGS
    Indeed, I am no mourner for that news,
    Because they have been still my adversaries.
    But that I'll give my voice on Richard's side
    To bar my master's heirs in true descent,
55   God knows I will not do it, to the death.

CATESBY
    God keep your Lordship in that gracious mind.

HASTINGS
    But I shall laugh at this a twelve-month hence,
    That they which brought me in my master's hate,
    I live to look upon their tragedy.
60   Well, Catesby, ere a fortnight make me older
    I'll send some packing that yet think not on 't.

CATESBY
    'Tis a vile thing to die, my gracious lord,
    When men are unprepared and look not for it.

HASTINGS
    O monstrous, monstrous! And so falls it out
65   With Rivers, Vaughan, Grey; and so 'twill do
    With some men else that think themselves as safe
    As thou and I, who, as thou know'st, are dear
    To princely Richard and to Buckingham.

CATESBY

Yes, my good lord.

HASTINGS

I'll have my head cut from my shoulders before I'll see the crown so misplaced. But do you think that's what he's aiming for?

CATESBY

Yes, I swear, and he hopes you'll join his party to help. For that reason he sends you this good news—that this very day your enemies, the queen's relatives, will die at Pomfret.

HASTINGS

Well, I'm not sorry to hear that, because they have always been my enemies. But the idea that I'd give my support to Richard and keep my master King Edward IV's true heirs from the crown—never. God knows I'd die before I'd do that.

CATESBY

Well, let's hope you stay in that noble frame of mind.

HASTINGS

In a year, when things have calmed down, I'll laugh about how those who got King Edward IV to hate me are now brought low. But as for now—before two weeks have gone by, I'm going to send some people packing. They have no idea what's coming.

CATESBY

It's a horrible thing to die when you're not prepared for it, my gracious lord.

HASTINGS

Yes, monstrous, monstrous! That's how it will be for Rivers, Vaughan, and Grey. That's how it will be for some other men, too, who think they're as safe as you and I, who are well-loved by noble Richard and Buckingham.

CATESBY
>The princes both make high account of you—
70 >*(aside)* For they account his head upon the Bridge.

HASTINGS
>I know they do, and I have well deserved it.

>*Enter* STANLEY

>Come on, come on. Where is your boar-spear, man?
>Fear you the boar, and go so unprovided?

STANLEY
>My lord, good morrow. —Good morrow, Catesby.—
75 >You may jest on, but, by the Holy Rood,
>I do not like these several councils, I.

HASTINGS
>My lord, I hold my life as dear as you do yours,
>And never in my days, I do protest,
>Was it so precious to me as 'tis now.
80 >Think you but that I know our state secure,
>I would be so triumphant as I am?

STANLEY
>The lords at Pomfret, when they rode from London,
>Were jocund and supposed their states were sure,
>And they indeed had no cause to mistrust;
85 >But yet you see how soon the day o'ercast.
>This sudden stab of rancor I misdoubt.
>Pray God, I say, I prove a needless coward!
>What, shall we toward the Tower? The day is spent.

CATESBY

Richard and Buckingham have a high opinion of you. (*to himself*) So high they'll stick your head on the Bridge.

London Bridge, where heads of traitors were displayed on poles to serve as warnings to the general populace.

HASTINGS

I know they do, and I certainly deserve it.

STANLEY *enters.*

Come on, come on, where is your spear for the boar, man? You're afraid of the boar but you go around without your spear?

STANLEY

My lord, good morning. Good morning, Catesby. Go ahead and laugh at me, but by Jesus, I don't like these separate meetings—I really don't.

HASTINGS

My lord, my life is as important to me as yours is to you, and it was never as precious to me as it is now. Do you think I would be feeling as triumphant as I am if I didn't know that our situation was secure?

STANLEY

When the lords who are imprisoned at Pomfret left London, they also were in a good mood and supposed their situation was secure. And they also had no reason to worry. But you see how soon the day got cloudy for them. Richard's sudden, hateful attack on them makes me worry. I hope to God I'm proven wrong! Well, should we head to the Tower? The day is well on its way.

HASTINGS
Come, come. Have with you. Wot you what, my lord?
90 Today the lords you talked of are beheaded.

LORD STANLEY
They, for their truth, might better wear their heads
Than some that have accused them wear their hats.
But come, my lord, let's away.

Enter a **PURSUIVANT**

HASTINGS
Go on before. I'll talk with this good fellow.

Exeunt **STANLEY** *and* **CATESBY**
95 How now, sirrah! How goes the world with thee?

PURSUIVANT
The better that your Lordship please to ask.

HASTINGS
I tell thee, man, 'tis better with me now
Than when thou met'st me last where now we meet.
Then was I going prisoner to the Tower
100 By the suggestion of the queen's allies.
But now, I tell thee—keep it to thyself—
This day those enemies are put to death,
And I in better state than e'er I was.

PURSUIVANT
God hold it, to your Honor's good content!

HASTINGS
105 Gramercy, fellow. There, drink that for me.

Throws him his purse

PURSUIVANT
I thank your Honor.

Exit

HASTINGS

Come on, let's get going. You know what, my lord?
Those men you just mentioned will be beheaded today.

LORD STANLEY

They deserved to keep their heads more than some
people who have managed to keep their positions. But
come, my lord, let's go.

A **PURSUIVANT** *enters.*

pursuivant =
junior officer

Go on ahead. I'll talk with this good man.

STANLEY *and* **CATESBY** *exit.*

What's up, man? How's it going?

PURSUIVANT

Better, since your lordship was nice enough to ask.

HASTINGS

I tell you, man, it's better for me, too, than the last time
we met here. Then I was on my way to the Tower, where
I was going to be locked up thanks to the false charges
of the queen's allies. But now, I tell you—keep it to
yourself, though—those enemies of mine are being put
to death today, and I'm better than I've ever been.

PURSUIVANT

Well, let's hope your good fortune continues!

HASTINGS

Thanks a lot, mister. Here, drink to me.

He throws the **PURSUIVANT** *some money.*

PURSUIVANT

God be good to you!

He exits.

Enter a PRIEST

PRIEST
Well met, my lord. I am glad to see your Honor.

HASTINGS
I thank thee, good Sir John, with all my heart.
I am in your debt for your last exercise.
110   Come the next sabbath, and I will content you.

PRIEST
I'll wait upon your Lordship.

HASTINGS *whispers in his ear.*

Exit PRIEST.

Enter BUCKINGHAM

BUCKINGHAM
What, talking with a priest, Lord Chamberlain?
Your friends at Pomfret, they do need the priest;
Your Honor hath no shriving work in hand.

HASTINGS
115   Good faith, and when I met this holy man,
The men you talk of came into my mind.
What, go you toward the Tower?

BUCKINGHAM
I do, my lord, but long I shall not stay there.
I shall return before your Lordship thence.

HASTINGS
120   Nay, like enough, for I stay dinner there.

BUCKINGHAM
(aside) And supper too, although thou know'st it not.—
Come, will you go?

HASTINGS
I'll wait upon your Lordship.

Exeunt

A PRIEST *enters.*

PRIEST

A nice coincidence, my lord. I'm glad to see you.

HASTINGS

I thank you, Sir John, with all my heart. I am indebted to you for your last sermon. By next week, I'll be able to pay you.

PRIEST

I'll come to you, your Lordship.

HASTINGS *whispers in his ear.*

The PRIEST *exits.*

BUCKINGHAM *enters.*

BUCKINGHAM

What, talking with a priest, Hastings? Your friends at Pomfret, they're the ones who need a priest. You, on the other hand, don't have any confessions you have to make.

HASTINGS

When I ran into this holy man, those men you mentioned did come to mind, in fact. Are you headed to the Tower?

BUCKINGHAM

I am, my lord. But I won't be there for long. I'll be off before you are.

HASTINGS

Yes, probably, because I'm staying for lunch.

BUCKINGHAM

(to himself) And for dinner, too, though you don't know it. *(to* HASTINGS*)* Come, are you going?

HASTINGS

I'll follow you, my lord.

They exit.

ACT 3, SCENE 3

Enter Sir Richard RATCLIFFE, *with halberds, carrying*
RIVERS, GREY, *and* VAUGHAN *to death at Pomfret.*

RIVERS
Sir Richard Ratcliffe, let me tell thee this:
Today shalt thou behold a subject die
For truth, for duty, and for loyalty.

GREY
(to RATCLIFFE*)*
God bless the prince from all the pack of you!
5   A knot you are of damnèd bloodsuckers.

VAUGHAN
(to RATCLIFFE*)* You live that shall cry woe for this hereafter.

RATCLIFFE
Dispatch. The limit of your lives is out.

RIVERS
O Pomfret, Pomfret! O thou bloody prison,
Fatal and ominous to noble peers!
10   Within the guilty closure of thy walls,
Richard the Second here was hacked to death,
And, for more slander to thy dismal seat,
We give thee up our guiltless blood to drink.

GREY
Now Margaret's curse is fall'n upon our heads,
15   When she exclaimed on Hastings, you, and I,
For standing by when Richard stabbed her son.

RIVERS
Then cursed she Richard, then cursed she Buckingham.
Then cursed she Hastings. O, remember, God,
To hear her prayer for them, as now for us!
20   And for my sister and her princely sons,
Be satisfied, dear God, with our true blood,
Which, as thou know'st, unjustly must be spilt.

ACT 3, SCENE 3

RATCLIFFE *enters with armed guards. He leads* RIVERS, GREY, *and* VAUGHAN *to their deaths at Pomfret.*

RIVERS

Sir Richard Ratcliffe, let me tell you this. Today you will witness a person die for truth, duty, and loyalty.

GREY

(to RATCLIFFE*)* God protect the prince from all of you. You're a group of damned bloodsuckers!

VAUGHAN

(to RATCLIFFE*)* You'll live to regret this.

RATCLIFFE

Hurry up. Your lives are over.

RIVERS

Oh, Pomfret, Pomfret! Oh, you bloody prison, fatal and threatening to noble lords! Within these guilty walls, Richard II was hacked to death. And now, to add more blood to its name, we're losing our innocent lives here.

GREY

Now Margaret's curse has fallen on our heads, for standing by and doing nothing when Richard stabbed her son.

RIVERS

She cursed Richard then. She cursed Buckingham then. She cursed Hastings then. Oh God, remember to hear her prayer for them, just as for us! But don't kill my sister and her royal sons, be satisfied, dear God, with our blood, which is being spilled unjustly, as you know.

RATCLIFFE
Make haste. The hour of death is expiate.

RIVERS
Come, Grey. Come, Vaughan. Let us all embrace.

They embrace

25   Farewell until we meet in heaven.

Exeunt

NO FEAR SHAKESPEARE

RATCLIFFE

Hurry up. The hour of death is approaching.

RIVERS

Come, Grey. Come, Vaughan. Let's embrace
(they embrace) and say goodbye until we meet again in
heaven.

They all exit.

ACT 3, SCENE 4

Enter BUCKINGHAM, STANLEY, HASTINGS, *the bishop of* ELY,
RATCLIFFE, LOVELL, *with others, at a table*

HASTINGS
Now, noble peers. the cause why we are met
Is to determine of the coronation.
In God's name, speak. When is the royal day?

BUCKINGHAM
Is all things ready for the royal time?

STANLEY
5   It is, and wants but nomination.

ELY
Tomorrow, then, I judge a happy day.

BUCKINGHAM
Who knows the Lord Protector's mind herein?
Who is most inward with the noble duke?

ELY
Your Grace, we think, should soonest know his mind.

BUCKINGHAM
10   We know each other's faces; for our hearts,
He knows no more of mine than I of yours,
Or I of his, my lord, than you of mine.—
Lord Hastings, you and he are near in love.

HASTINGS
I thank his Grace. I know he loves me well.
15   But for his purpose in the coronation,
I have not sounded him, nor he delivered
His gracious pleasure any way therein.
But you, my honorable lords, may name the time,
And in the duke's behalf I'll give my voice,
20   Which I presume he'll take in gentle part.

Enter RICHARD

ACT 3, SCENE 4

BUCKINGHAM, STANLEY, HASTINGS, *the bishop of* ELY, RATCLIFFE, *and* LOVELL *enter with others and take their seats at a table.*

HASTINGS

Now, noble lords, the reason we're meeting is to determine the day the prince will be crowned. In God's name, speak. When should the royal day be?

BUCKINGHAM

Is everything ready for that event?

STANLEY

It is. All we have to do is name the day.

ELY

Tomorrow's a good day.

BUCKINGHAM

Who knows what the Lord Protector thinks? Who's closest to him?

ELY

You, I think, would best know what he's thinking.

BUCKINGHAM

We know each other's faces, but as for our thoughts, he doesn't know any more about my thinking than I do about yours or his—or you do about mine. Lord Hastings, you and he are close.

HASTINGS

Thank you. I know he holds me dear, but I haven't asked him about the coronation, and he hasn't told me. But you, my noble lords, may name a time, and I'll second it on the duke's behalf, which I don't think he'll mind.

RICHARD *enters.*

ELY
  In happy time here comes the duke himself.

RICHARD
  My noble lords and cousins all, good morrow.
  I have been long a sleeper; but I trust
  My absence doth neglect no great design
25 Which by my presence might have been concluded.

BUCKINGHAM
  Had you not come upon your cue, my lord,
  William Lord Hastings had pronounced your part—
  I mean your voice for crowning of the king.

RICHARD
  Than my Lord Hastings no man might be bolder.
30 His Lordship knows me well, and loves me well.—
  My lord of Ely, when I was last in Holborn
  I saw good strawberries in your garden there;
  I do beseech you, send for some of them.

ELY
  Marry and will, my lord, with all my heart.

                                                      Exit

RICHARD
35 Cousin of Buckingham, a word with you.
  They move aside
  Catesby hath sounded Hastings in our business
  And finds the testy gentleman so hot
  As he will lose his head ere give consent
  His master's child, as worshipfully he terms it,
40 Shall lose the royalty of England's throne.

BUCKINGHAM
  Withdraw yourself awhile. I'll go with you.

                    Exeunt RICHARD *and* BUCKINGHAM

ELY

Right on cue, here's the duke himself.

RICHARD

My noble lords and relatives, good morning. I slept in. But I hope I didn't delay any important decisions.

BUCKINGHAM

If you hadn't shown up on cue, my lord, Lord Hastings was going to take your part—I mean, he was going to speak for you—in the crowning of the king.

RICHARD

No one may be bolder than my Lord Hastings. He knows me well and loves me well.—Ely, when I was last at your palace, I saw some great strawberries in your garden. I beg you, send someone to bring some of them.

ELY

Yes, my lord. With pleasure.

He exits.

RICHARD

Buckingham, I need to have a word with you. *(drawing him aside)* Catesby has sounded Hastings out and found the prickly gentleman so opposed to our plan that he actually said he would die before he'd agree to have his "master's son," as he put it so devotedly, lose the crown.

BUCKINGHAM

Move to the other room, my lord. I'll come soon.

RICHARD *exits, with* BUCKINGHAM *following him.*

STANLEY
> We have not yet set down this day of triumph.
> Tomorrow, in my judgement, is too sudden,
> For I myself am not so well provided
45 > As else I would be, were the day prolonged.

Enter Bishop of ELY

ELY
> Where is my lord the duke of Gloucester?
> I have sent for these strawberries.

HASTINGS
> His grace looks cheerfully and smooth this morning.
> There's some conceit or other likes him well
50 > When that he bids good morrow with such spirit.
> I think there's never a man in Christendom
> Can lesser hide his love or hate than he,
> For by his face straight shall you know his heart.

STANLEY
> What of his heart perceive you in his face
55 > By any livelihood he showed today?

HASTINGS
> Marry, that with no man here he is offended,
> For were he, he had shown it in his looks.

STANLEY
> I pray God he be not, I say.

Enter RICHARD *and* BUCKINGHAM

RICHARD
> I pray you all, tell me what they deserve
60 > That do conspire my death with devilish plots
> Of damnèd witchcraft, and that have prevailed
> Upon my body with their hellish charms?

STANLEY

We have not yet set the coronation day. Tomorrow, in my opinion, is too soon. I myself am not as well-equipped as I would be if the day were put off a bit.

ELY *returns.*

ELY

Where is my lord, the duke of Gloucester? I have sent for the strawberries.

HASTINGS

Richard is looking cheerful today. You always know he's got some plan that pleases him when he says good morning with such gusto. I don't think there's a man under the sun who's worse at hiding his love or hate than Richard. You know his feelings immediately just by looking at his face.

STANLEY

And what feelings did you see in his face today?

HASTINGS

That he's not angry with anyone here. If he were, he would have shown it.

STANLEY

I pray to God he isn't.

RICHARD *and* BUCKINGHAM *return.*

RICHARD

Tell me, all of you, what punishment does a person deserve who conspires to kill me with witchcraft and who has already plagued my body with black magic?

HASTINGS

The tender love I bear your Grace, my lord,
Makes me most forward in this princely presence
65   To doom th' offenders, whosoe'er they be.
I say, my lord, they have deservèd death.

RICHARD

Then be your eyes the witness of their evil.
(shows his arm)
Look how I am bewitched! Behold mine arm
Is like a blasted sapling withered up;
70   And this is Edward's wife, that monstrous witch,
Consorted with that harlot, strumpet Shore,
That by their witchcraft thus have markèd me.

HASTINGS

If they have done this deed, my noble lord—

RICHARD

If? Thou protector of this damnèd strumpet,
75   Talk'st thou to me of "ifs"? Thou art a traitor—
Off with his head. Now by Saint Paul I swear
I will not dine until I see the same.—
Lovell and Ratcliffe, look that it be done.—
The rest that love me, rise and follow me.

The need for Love

Exeunt all but HASTINGS, RATCLIFFE, *and* LOVELL

HASTINGS

80   Woe, woe for England! Not a whit for me,
For I, too fond, might have prevented this.
Stanley did dream the boar did raze his helm,
And I did scorn it and disdain to fly.
Three times today my foot-cloth horse did stumble,
85   And started when he looked upon the Tower,
As loath to bear me to the slaughterhouse.
O, now I need the priest that spake to me!

HASTINGS

> Because I love your Grace, I say that whoever the offenders are deserve to die.

RICHARD

> Then see the evidence of their evil with your own eyes. *(he shows his arm)* Look how I've been bewitched! See how my arm has become like a withered tree-branch? This is the work of Edward's wife, that monstrous witch, who is in league with that tramp Shore. They have used witchcraft to harm me.

HASTINGS

> If they have done this thing, my noble lord—

RICHARD

> If? You lover of that damned whore, you're talking to me of "ifs"? You're a traitor.—Off with his head. By Saint Paul, I swear I won't eat lunch until I see him beheaded. Lovell and Ratcliffe, make sure it gets done. The rest of you who love me, come with me.

Everyone but HASTINGS, RATCLIFFE, *and* LOVELL *exits.*

HASTINGS

> I pity England, but not myself. I was too foolish. I might have prevented this. Stanley dreamed the boar beheaded him, and I laughed and refused to flee with him. Three times today my horse stumbled and started when he looked in the direction of the Tower, as if he hated to carry me to this slaughterhouse. Oh, now I really need that priest who spoke to me today!

The Curse

I now repent I told the pursuivant,
As too triumphing, how mine enemies
90 Today at Pomfret bloodily were butchered,
And I myself secure in grace and favor.
O Margaret, Margaret, now thy heavy curse
Is lighted on poor Hastings' wretched head.

RATCLIFFE
Come, come, dispatch. The duke would be at dinner.
95 Make a short shrift. He longs to see your head.

HASTINGS
O momentary grace of mortal men,
Which we more hunt for than the grace of God!
Who builds his hopes in air of your good looks
Lives like a drunken sailor on a mast,
100 Ready with every nod to tumble down
Into the fatal bowels of the deep.

LOVELL
Come, come, dispatch. 'Tis bootless to exclaim.

HASTINGS
O bloody Richard! Miserable England,
I prophesy the fearfull'st time to thee
105 That ever wretched age hath looked upon.—
Come, lead me to the block. Bear him my head.
They smile at me that shortly shall be dead.

Exeunt

And I regret having bragged to the messenger about how my enemies were being butchered at Pomfret while I, as I said, was in good standing with Richard. Oh Margaret, Margaret, your heavy curse has now landed on poor Hastings's miserable head!

RATCLIFFE

Hurry up—the duke wants to eat his dinner. Make your confession short. He's eager to see your head.

HASTINGS

We spend more time seeking out the fleeting glories of this temporary world than looking to the permanent grace of God! Anyone who builds his hopes on air lives like a drunken sailor hanging on a mast, ready with every dizzy nod of his head to tumble to the bottom of the sea. The things we worry about, like good looks and possessions, aren't lasting, and they don't matter.

LOVELL

Come, come, hurry up. It's pointless to talk now.

HASTINGS

Oh bloody Richard! Miserable England, I foresee for you the most frightening time you have ever experienced.—Come, lead me to the block. Bring him my head. Those who smile at it will soon be dead themselves.

They all exit.

ACT 3, SCENE 5

Enter RICHARD *and* BUCKINGHAM, *in rotten armor,*
marvelous ill-favored

RICHARD
Come, cousin, canst thou quake and change thy color,
Murder thy breath in the middle of a word,
And then begin again, and stop again,
As if thou wert distraught and mad with terror?

BUCKINGHAM
5   Tut, I can counterfeit the deep tragedian,
Speak, and look back, and pry on every side,
Tremble and start at wagging of a straw,
Intending deep suspicion. Ghastly looks
Are at my service, like enforcèd smiles,
10   And both are ready in their offices,
At any time to grace my stratagems.
But what, is Catesby gone?

RICHARD
He is; and see, he brings the mayor along.

Enter the LORD MAYOR *and* CATESBY

BUCKINGHAM
Lord Mayor—

RICHARD
15   Look to the drawbridge there!

BUCKINGHAM
Hark, a drum!

RICHARD
Catesby, o'erlook the walls.

Exit CATESBY

ACT 3, SCENE 5

RICHARD *and* BUCKINGHAM *enter wearing rusty,*
hideous-looking armor.

RICHARD

Tell me, cousin, I need to know if you can shake like
you've got a fever, turn pale all of a sudden, and stop
speaking in the middle of a word—as if you were
driven crazy with fear.

BUCKINGHAM

Oh please, I can imitate the best tragic actor around.
I can speak and then look all around, and tremble, and
start at a mere piece of straw as if I were paranoid.
Frightening looks are also at my service, as are fake
smiles. Anytime I need them, they're waiting to do
my bidding. But has Catesby gone?

RICHARD

He has. But here he is, back with the mayor.

The LORD MAYOR *and* CATESBY *enter.*

BUCKINGHAM

Lord Mayor—

RICHARD

Richard and
Buckingham are
pretending they
are under attack.

Watch out for the drawbridge over there!

BUCKINGHAM

Listen! A drum!

RICHARD

Catesby, look over the top of these walls to see if anyone's there.

CATESBY *exits.*

BUCKINGHAM
Lord Mayor, the reason we have sent—

RICHARD
Look back! Defend thee! Here are enemies.

BUCKINGHAM
20 God and our innocence defend and guard us!

Enter LOVELL *and* RATCLIFFE, *with* HASTINGS's *head*

RICHARD
Be patient. They are friends, Ratcliffe and Lovell.

LOVELL
Here is the head of that ignoble traitor,
The dangerous and unsuspected Hastings.

RICHARD
So dear I loved the man that I must weep.
25 I took him for the plainest harmless creature
That breathed upon this earth a Christian;
Made him my book, wherein my soul recorded
The history of all her secret thoughts.
So smooth he daubed his vice with show of virtue
30 That, his apparent open guilt omitted—
I mean his conversation with Shore's wife—
He lived from all attainder of suspects.

BUCKINGHAM
Well, well, he was the covert'st sheltered traitor
That ever lived.—
35 Would you imagine, or almost believe,
Were 't not that by great preservation
We live to tell it, that subtle traitor
This day had plotted, in the council house
To murder me and my good Lord of Gloucester?

LORD MAYOR
40 Had he done so?

BUCKINGHAM

Lord Mayor, the reason we have sent—

RICHARD

Look behind you! Defend yourself! There are enemies here.

BUCKINGHAM

God defend and guard us innocents against them!

LOVELL *and* RATCLIFFE *enter with* HASTINGS's *head.*

RICHARD

Stay calm. They're friends—Ratcliffe and Lovell.

LOVELL

Here's the head of that notorious traitor, the dangerous and unsuspected Hastings.

RICHARD

I loved this man so much it makes me weep. I took him to be the plainest, most harmless Christian on earth. He was the book in which I recorded all of my most secret thoughts. He was so slick in covering over his plans that if it hadn't been for his love affair with Shore's wife, I would never have suspected him.

BUCKINGHAM

Well, well, he was the most covert traitor who ever lived. Would you believe, if we hadn't caught him, this subtle traitor would have murdered the Lord of Gloucester and me in the council room today?

LORD MAYOR

He would have?

RICHARD
What, think you we are Turks or infidels?
Or that we would, against the form of law,
Proceed thus rashly in the villain's death,
But that the extreme peril of the case,
45 The peace of England and our persons' safety
Enforced us to this execution?

LORD MAYOR
Now fair befall you! He deserved his death,
And your good Graces both have well proceeded
To warn false traitors from the like attempts.

BUCKINGHAM
50 I never looked for better at his hands
After he once fell in with Mistress Shore. *Adultery*
Yet had we not determined he should die
Until your Lordship came to see his end
(Which now the loving haste of these our friends,
55 Something against our meaning, have prevented),
Because, my lord, I would have had you heard
The traitor speak, and timorously confess
The manner and the purpose of his treasons,
That you might well have signified the same
60 Unto the citizens, who haply may
Misconstrue us in him, and wail his death.

LORD MAYOR
But, my good lord, your Graces' words shall serve
As well as I had seen and heard him speak;
And do not doubt, right noble princes both,
65 But I'll acquaint our duteous citizens
With all your just proceedings in this case.

RICHARD
And to that end we wished your Lordship here
T' avoid the censures of the carping world.

RICHARD

> What, do you think we're Turks or savages, instead of Christians? You think we would have disobeyed the law and proceeded to kill this villain if England's peace and our own lives hadn't been at stake?

LORD MAYOR

> I hope nothing else like this ever happens to you! This man deserved his death. And you, my good lords, were right to warn other traitors from trying the same.

BUCKINGHAM

> I didn't expect any better from him once he got involved with Mistress Shore. But we had decided that he shouldn't die until you were able to come witness his execution. (Which was prevented by the haste of our friends, Lovell and Ratcliffe here, who went against what we intended somewhat in their hurry to protect us). If you could have heard the traitor speak for himself and confess the exact way he planned to murder us, you could have told the citizens what terrible intentions he had, though now they're likely to misconstrue what we did and wail over his death.

LORD MAYOR

> But, my good lord, the words of you and Lord Buckingham are as trustworthy to me as if I had seen and heard him speak myself. And do not doubt, you honest, noble princes, that I'll let our citizens know how fairly you proceeded in this case.

RICHARD

> That is exactly why we wanted you here, your lordship—to avoid the public carping and complaints.

BUCKINGHAM
>Which since you come too late of our intent,
>70   Yet witness what you hear we did intend.
>And so, my good Lord Mayor, we bid farewell.

Exit LORD MAYOR

RICHARD
>Go, after, after, cousin Buckingham.
>The mayor towards Guildhall hies him in all post.
>There, at your meetest vantage of the time,
>75   Infer the bastardy of Edward's children.
>Tell them how Edward put to death a citizen
>Only for saying he would make his son
>Heir to the Crown—meaning indeed his house,
>Which, by the sign thereof, was termèd so.
>80   Moreover, urge his hateful luxury,
>And bestial appetite in change of lust,
>Which stretched to their servants, daughters, wives,
>Even where his raging eye or savage heart,
>Without control, lusted to make his prey.
>85   Nay, for a need, thus far come near my person:
>Tell them when that my mother went with child
>Of that insatiate Edward, noble York
>My princely father then had wars in France,
>And, by true computation of the time,
>90   Found that the issue was not his begot,
>Which well appearèd in his lineaments,
>Being nothing like the noble duke my father.
>Yet touch this sparingly, as 'twere far off,
>Because, my lord, you know my mother lives.

BUCKINGHAM

> But since you've come too late to see the execution as
> we intended, at least let people know what you *hear* we
> intended. And so, good Lord Mayor, we bid you
> goodbye.

> *The* LORD MAYOR *exits.*

RICHARD

> Follow him, Buckingham. He's traveling at a gallop to
> the London meeting hall. There, as soon as you have
> a chance, drop the hint that Edward's children are
> bastards. Tell the citizens how Edward put to death a
> citizen just because the citizen said he was going to
> make his own son "heir to the crown"—when all the
> citizen meant was that he owned a tavern called "the
> Crown" and was going to leave it to his son. And then
> point out what a lech Edward was and what a bestial
> appetite he had for women, which touched even the
> citizens' own servants, daughters, and wives. There
> was no limit to what his lustful eye and savage heart
> would prey on. And, if you need to, approach the sub-
> ject of me: tell them that when my mother became
> pregnant with the insatiable Edward, my noble father
> was fighting in France. With a little calculating, it's
> obvious that Edward is not in fact my father's child—
> not a surprising revelation if you consider how my
> father the noble duke looked nothing like this man.
> But only hint at this vaguely, because, as you know,
> my mother's still alive.

BUCKINGHAM

95   Doubt not, my lord. I'll play the orator
As if the golden fee for which I plead
Were for myself. And so, my lord, adieu.

RICHARD

If you thrive well, bring them to Baynard's Castle,
Where you shall find me well accompanied
100   With reverend fathers and well-learnèd bishops.

BUCKINGHAM

I go; and towards three or four o'clock
Look for the news that the Guildhall affords.

Exit

RICHARD

Go, Lovell, with all speed to Doctor Shaw.
(to RATCLIFFE*)* Go thou to Friar Penker. Bid them both
105   Meet me within this hour at Baynard's Castle.

Exit LOVELL *and* RATCLIFFE

Now will I go to take some privy order
To draw the brats of Clarence out of sight,
And to give order that no manner of person
Have any time recourse unto the princes.

Exit

BUCKINGHAM

Don't worry, my lord, I'll be as eloquent as if the golden crown I'm pleading for were for myself. Goodbye, my lord.

RICHARD

Baynard's Castle was another of Richard's London estates.

If things go well, bring the crowd to Baynard's Castle, where I'll be surrounded by priests and learned bishops.

BUCKINGHAM

I'm off. Around three or four o'clock, look for news from the meeting hall.

BUCKINGHAM exits.

RICHARD

Lovell, go as fast as you can to Doctor Shaw. *(to RATCLIFFE)* Go to Friar Penker. Both of you, tell these men to meet me in less than an hour at Baynard's Castle.

LOWELL and RADCLIFFE exits.

Now I'll go inside and write out a secret order to keep Clarence's brats out of sight and to forbid anyone whatsoever from seeing King Edward's sons.

He exits.

ACT 3, SCENE 6

Enter a SCRIVENER, *with paper*

SCRIVENER
This is the indictment of the good Lord Hastings,
Which in a set hand fairly is engrossed,
That it may be today read o'er in Paul's.
And mark how well the sequel hangs together:
5 Eleven hours I have spent to write it over,
For yesternight by Catesby was it sent me;
The precedent was full as long a-doing,
And yet within these five hours Hastings lived,
Untainted, unexamined, free, at liberty.
10 Here's a good world the while. Who is so gross
That cannot see this palpable device?
Yet who so bold but says he sees it not?
Bad is the world, and all will come to naught
When such ill dealing must be seen in thought.

Exit

ACT 3, SCENE 6

A SCRIVENER *enters with a paper in his hand.*

Scrivener = professional copier

SCRIVENER
Here's the indictment of the good Lord Hastings, which has been written out in a clear hand, like any legal document, so it can be read aloud in public outside St. Paul's Cathedral. And look how well this sequence of events holds together: after Catesby brought the indictment to me last night, I spent eleven hours copying it. The original took just as long to write out. So that's twenty-two hours. And yet five hours ago, Lord Hastings was alive, untouched, free, at liberty. What a backward world we live in! Why, who's so stupid that he can't see through this fraud? But who's so blind to the consequences of speaking out that he'll admit what he knows? The world is a bad place, where you can't speak what you know.

He exits.

ACT 3, SCENE 7

Enter RICHARD *and* BUCKINGHAM, *at several doors*

RICHARD
15   How now, how now? What say the citizens?

BUCKINGHAM
        Now, by the holy mother of our Lord,
        The citizens are mum, say not a word.

RICHARD
        Touched you the bastardy of Edward's children?

BUCKINGHAM
        I did; with his contract with Lady Lucy
20   And his contract by deputy in France;
        Th' unsatiate greediness of his desire
        And his enforcement of the city wives;
        His tyranny for trifles; his own bastardy,
        As being got, your father then in France,
25   His resemblance being not like the duke.
        Withal, I did infer your lineaments,
        Being the right idea of your father,
        Both in your form and nobleness of mind;
        Laid open all your victories in Scotland,
30   Your discipline in war, wisdom in peace,
        Your bounty, virtue, fair humility;
        Indeed, left nothing fitting for your purpose
        Untouched or slightly handled in discourse.
        And when mine oratory grew toward end,
35   I bid them that did love their country's good
        Cry "God save Richard, England's royal king!"

RICHARD
        And did they so?

ACT 3, SCENE 7

RICHARD *and* BUCKINGHAM *enter through different doors.*

RICHARD

So what did the citizens say?

BUCKINGHAM

It's incredible—they didn't say a word.

RICHARD

Did you mention that Edward's children are bastards?

BUCKINGHAM

Edward IV was engaged to Elizabeth Lucy and had a child with her before he married Elizabeth Grey.

Edward sent Warwick to secure this French marriage and then backed out of it.

I did. I talked about how he was engaged to Lady Lucy, and how he was engaged to Lady Bona through the help of the earl of Warwick. I spoke of the unquenchable greediness of Edward's desires and the way he forced himself on the wives of Londoners. I mentioned the way he punished people harshly for minor offenses. I said he was not the son of the noble duke of York, because your father was in France when he was conceived, which explains why he doesn't have anything in common with his father. And then I suggested that you were the spitting image of your father, both in the way you look and in the nobleness of your character. I went into all your victories in Scotland, your skill as a warrior, your wisdom in peacetime, your generosity, your goodness, and your exceptional modesty. Indeed, I left nothing out. And when my oration came to a close, I asked those who loved their country to cry, "God save Richard, England's royal king!"

RICHARD

And did they?

BUCKINGHAM

No. So God help me, they spake not a word
But, like dumb statues or breathing stones,
40 Stared each on other and looked deadly pale;
Which when I saw, I reprehended them
And asked the mayor what meant this willful silence.
His answer was, the people were not used
To be spoke to but by the recorder.
45 Then he was urged to tell my tale again:
"Thus saith the duke. Thus hath the duke inferred"—
But nothing spoke in warrant from himself.
When he had done, some followers of mine own,
At the lower end of the hall, hurled up their caps,
50 And some ten voices cried "God save King Richard!"
And thus I took the vantage of those few.
"Thanks, gentle citizens and friends," quoth I.
"This general applause and cheerful shout
Argues your wisdoms and your love to Richard"—
55 And even here brake off, and came away.

RICHARD

What tongueless blocks were they! Would not they speak?
Will not the mayor then and his brethren come?

BUCKINGHAM

The mayor is here at hand. Intend some fear;
Be not you spoke with but by mighty suit.
60 And look you get a prayer book in your hand
And stand between two churchmen, good my lord,
For on that ground I'll make a holy descant.
And be not easily won to our requests.
Play the maid's part: still answer "nay," and take it.

RICHARD

65 I go. An if you plead as well for them
As I can say "nay" to thee for myself,
No doubt we bring it to a happy issue.

Knocking within

BUCKINGHAM

No, God help me, they didn't say a word. Like silent statues or stones that breathed, they just gazed at each other and turned as pale as the dead. When I saw this, I scolded them and asked the mayor what this stubborn silence meant. He said that the people weren't used to being spoken to except by the Recorder. So I urged the Recorder to repeat my tale—you know, "The duke of Buckingham said this, Buckingham meant that," but nothing on his own authority. When he was done, a few followers of my own at the far end of the hall hurled their caps in the air. Some ten voices cried, "God save King Richard!" I jumped on this slender opportunity and said, "Thank you, noble citizens and friends. This widespread applause and enthusiastic shouts make clear you stand behind Richard." And then I broke off and quickly came away.

*Recorder =
a legal official*

RICHARD

What blocks of wood! They wouldn't say anything? Aren't the mayor and his fellow citizens coming?

BUCKINGHAM

The mayor is here at hand. Pretend you're afraid, my lord, and don't speak until you're pleaded with. And make sure to carry a prayer book in your hand and to stand between two priests, okay? Then I'll have the grounds to build a holy sermon about why you should be king. But don't be easily won over. Act like a virgin, always answering "No," but taking it in the end.

RICHARD

I'm going now. If you're as good at pleading to them as I am at saying no to you, this will definitely come to a happy end.

A sound of knocking from offstage.

BUCKINGHAM
Go, go, up to the leads. The Lord Mayor knocks.

Exit RICHARD

Enter the LORD MAYOR *and* CITIZENS

Welcome, my lord. I dance attendance here.
70   I think the duke will not be spoke withal.

Enter CATESBY

Now, Catesby, what says your lord to my request?

CATESBY
He doth entreat your Grace, my noble lord,
To visit him tomorrow or next day.
He is within, with two right reverend fathers,
75   Divinely bent to meditation,
And in no worldly suits would he be moved
To draw him from his holy exercise.

BUCKINGHAM
Return, good Catesby, to the gracious duke.
Tell him myself, the mayor, and aldermen,
80   No less importing than our general good,
In deep designs, and matters of great moment
Are come to have some conference with his grace.

CATESBY
I'll signify so much unto him straight.

Exit

BUCKINGHAM

> Hurry, go up to the roof. The Lord Mayor is knocking.

> *RICHARD exits.*

> *The* LORD MAYOR *and* CITIZENS *enter.*

> Welcome, my lord. I'm twiddling my thumbs waiting for the duke to show up. I don't think he wants to be disturbed.

> CATESBY *enters.*

> Here comes his servant. Now, Catesby, what does your lord say to my request?

CATESBY

> My lord, he asks that you please visit him tomorrow or the next day. He's inside in prayer, with two reverend fathers. He doesn't want to be disturbed in his holy work by any worldly requests.

BUCKINGHAM

> Return to the gracious duke, good Catesby. Tell him that the mayor, some citizens, and I have come to confer with his grace in matters of great importance concerning the general good.

CATESBY

> I'll tell him right away, my lord.

> *He exits.*

BUCKINGHAM
Ah, ha, my lord, this prince is not an Edward!
85 He is not lolling on a lewd love bed,
But on his knees at meditation;
Not dallying with a brace of courtesans,
But meditating with two deep divines;
Not sleeping, to engross his idle body,
90 But praying, to enrich his watchful soul.
Happy were England would this virtuous prince
Take on his grave the sovereignty thereof.
But sure I fear we shall not win him to it.

LORD MAYOR
Marry, God defend his grace should say us nay!

BUCKINGHAM
95 I fear he will. Here Catesby comes again.

Enter CATESBY

Now, Catesby, what says his grace?

CATESBY
He wonders to what end you have assembled
Such troops of citizens to come to him,
His grace not being warned thereof before.
100 He fears, my lord, you mean no good to him.

BUCKINGHAM
Sorry I am my noble cousin should
Suspect me that I mean no good to him.
By heaven, we come to him in perfect love,
And so once more return and tell his grace.

Exit CATESBY

105 When holy and devout religious men
Are at their beads, 'tis much to draw them thence,
So sweet is zealous contemplation.

BUCKINGHAM

Ah, my lord, this prince is nothing like Edward! He is not lolling in bed but on his knees in prayer. He's not enjoying himself with a couple of prostitutes but studying with two learned priests. He's not sleeping to fatten up his lazy body, but praying, to nourish his attentive soul. England would be lucky to have this virtuous prince as king. But I'm afraid we'll never get him to agree to be king.

LORD MAYOR

But God forbid he says no to us!

BUCKINGHAM

I'm afraid he will. Here comes Catesby again.

CATESBY *returns.*

What's up, Catesby, what does your master say?

CATESBY

My lord, he wonders why you have assembled such troops of citizens to speak with him, since he had no idea they were coming. My lord, he's afraid you mean him harm.

BUCKINGHAM

I'm sorry my noble brother is suspicious of me. By God, I'm here because I love him. Return and tell him so.

CATESBY *exits.*

When devoutly religious men are praying, it's hard to draw them out of it, because they get lost in the wonder of their contemplation.

Enter RICHARD *aloft, between two bishops*
CATESBY *returns*

LORD MAYOR
See where his Grace stands, 'tween two clergymen.

BUCKINGHAM
Two props of virtue for a Christian prince,
110   To stay him from the fall of vanity;
And, see, a book of prayer in his hand,
True ornaments to know a holy man.—
Famous Plantagenet, most gracious prince,
Lend favorable ears to our requests,
115   And pardon us the interruption
Of thy devotion and right Christian zeal.

RICHARD
My lord, there needs no such apology.
I do beseech your Grace pardon me,
Who, earnest in the service of my God,
120   Deferred the visitation of my friends.
But, leaving this, what is your Grace's pleasure?

BUCKINGHAM
Even that, I hope, which pleaseth God above
And all good men of this ungoverned isle.

RICHARD
I do suspect I have done some offense
125   That seems disgracious in the city's eye,
And that you come to reprehend my ignorance.

BUCKINGHAM
You have, my lord. Would it might please your Grace,
On our entreaties, to amend your fault.

RICHARD
Else wherefore breathe I in a Christian land?

RICHARD *enters overhead, between two bishops.*
CATESBY *returns.*

LORD MAYOR

> See how he stands between two clergymen!

BUCKINGHAM

> Two props of virtue for a Christian prince, to prevent
> him from ever becoming vain. And, see, he has a
> prayer book in each hand, the signs of a holy man.
> Most gracious prince of the famous house of Plan-
> tagenet, pardon us for interrupting your righteous,
> Christian prayer. Please listen favorably to our
> request.

RICHARD

> My lord, you don't need to apologize. I beg you to par-
> don me. I've been so intent on serving God that I've
> kept my friends waiting. In any case, what would you
> like?

BUCKINGHAM

> Only what, I hope, will please God above and all good
> men on this island, which currently has no king.

RICHARD

> I suspect that I have committed some offence to the
> city and you have come to reprimand me for not
> knowing better.

BUCKINGHAM

> You have, my lord. I hope you'll make up for it!

RICHARD

> Why else would I live in a Christian country, if I can't
> ask forgiveness for my faults?

BUCKINGHAM

130   Know, then, it is your fault that you resign
    The supreme seat, the throne majestical,
    The sceptered office of your ancestors,
    Your state of fortune, and your due of birth,
    The lineal glory of your royal house,
135   To the corruption of a blemished stock,
    Whiles in the mildness of your sleepy thoughts,
    Which here we waken to our country's good,
    The noble isle doth want her proper limbs—
    Her face defaced with scars of infamy,
140   Her royal stock graft with ignoble plants,
    And almost shouldered in the swallowing gulf
    Of dark forgetfulness and deep oblivion;
    Which to recure, we heartily solicit
    Your gracious self to take on you the charge
145   And kingly government of this your land,
    Not as Protector, steward, substitute,
    Or lowly factor for another's gain,
    But as successively, from blood to blood,
    Your right of birth, your empery, your own.
150   For this, consorted with the citizens,
    Your very worshipful and loving friends,
    And by their vehement instigation,
    In this just suit come I to move your Grace.

RICHARD

    I cannot tell if to depart in silence
155   Or bitterly to speak in your reproof
    Best fitteth my degree or your condition.
    If not to answer, you might haply think
    Tongue-tied ambition, not replying, yielded
    To bear the golden yoke of sovereignty,
160   Which fondly you would here impose on me.
    If to reprove you for this suit of yours,
    So seasoned with your faithful love to me,
    Then on the other side I checked my friends.

BUCKINGHAM

Then you should know that we take fault with your resigning the supreme seat, the majestic throne, the sceptered office, of your ancestors—the power and greatness that destiny and your noble birth have handed you—to the wrong person. You aren't respecting the lineage of your royal family. You're lost in sleepy thoughts, and we have come to wake you to our country's needs. This noble island has been compromised. She is scarred by the infamous deeds of King Edward IV. Her royal stock has been corrupted and nearly lost. We want that royalty remembered again. We heartily beg you, in all your goodness, to take upon yourself the responsibility and rule of this land, not merely as a servant, substitute, or other lowly agent of the king, but as the king himself. It is your birthright to be king. It's for this reason that we are here—the citizens of England and your devoted friends. We strongly urge you on.

RICHARD

I can't tell which is the better course of action, to leave in silence or to scold you. If I don't answer, perhaps you'll think I'm accepting the heavy responsibility you foolishly want to impose on me. But if I do speak and refuse your request, then I'm guilty of reprimanding my friends, who have been faithful and loving toward me.

Therefore, to speak, and to avoid the first,
165   And then, in speaking, not to incur the last,
Definitively thus I answer you:
Your love deserves my thanks, but my desert
Unmeritable shuns your high request.
First, if all obstacles were cut away
170   And that my path were even to the crown
As the ripe revenue and due of birth,
Yet so much is my poverty of spirit,
So mighty and so many my defects,
That I would rather hide me from my greatness,
175   Being a bark to brook no mighty sea,
Than in my greatness covet to be hid
And in the vapor of my glory smothered.
But, God be thanked, there is no need of me,
And much I need to help you, were there need.
180   The royal tree hath left us royal fruit,
Which, mellowed by the stealing hours of time,
Will well become the seat of majesty,
And make, no doubt, us happy by his reign.
On him I lay what you would lay on me,
185   The right and fortune of his happy stars,
Which God defend that I should wring from him.

BUCKINGHAM

My lord, this argues conscience in your Grace,
But the respects thereof are nice and trivial,
All circumstances well considerèd.
190   You say that Edward is your brother's son;
So say we too, but not by Edward's wife.
For first was he contract to Lady Lucy—
Your mother lives a witness to that vow—
And afterward by substitute betrothed
195   To Bona, sister to the king of France.
These both put off, a poor petitioner,
A care-crazed mother to a many sons,
A beauty-waning and distressèd widow,

So, I'll speak to make clear I don't want the crown but also that I am grateful to you. Here is my definitive answer: thank you for your love, but I'm going to have to turn down your weighty request because I don't deserve to be king. First of all, even if all the obstacles were eliminated and my path led straight to the crown—if it were truly my birthright—I would rather hide from my greatness than hide inside the greatness of the position itself and be smothered by it. My spirit is poor, and I have so many terrible defects that as king I would be like a little boat tossed about on a mighty sea. So, thank God, there is no real need for me, as I wouldn't be able to help you much. The royal tree has left us other fruit, which, with time, will do just fine on the throne and make us all happy as king, I'm sure. Someone other than I has the right and the good fortune to be made king. God forbid that I snatch the crown from him.

BUCKINGHAM

My lord, what you've said makes clear you have a conscience, but your objections are trivial, given the circumstances. You say that Prince Edward is your brother's son. We agree, but not by your brother's wife. King Edward was going to marry Lady Lucy—your mother can vouch for that—and then he was betrothed to Bona, the King of France's sister-in-law. But both of these were put off by Elizabeth Grey, a careworn mother of many children who had once been a beauty but was now a stressed-out widow

Even in the afternoon of her best days,
200   Made prize and purchase of his wanton eye,
Seduced the pitch and height of his degree
To base declension and loathed bigamy.
By her in his unlawful bed he got
This Edward, whom our manners term "the Prince."
205   More bitterly could I expostulate,
Save that, for reverence to some alive,
I give a sparing limit to my tongue.
Then, good my lord, take to your royal self
This proffered benefit of dignity,
210   If not to bless us and the land withal,
Yet to draw forth your noble ancestry
From the corruption of abusing times
Unto a lineal, true-derivèd course.

LORD MAYOR
Do, good my lord. Your citizens entreat you.

BUCKINGHAM
215   Refuse not, mighty lord, this proffered love.

CATESBY
O, make them joyful. Grant their lawful suit.

RICHARD
Alas, why would you heap this care on me?
I am unfit for state and majesty.
I do beseech you, take it not amiss;
220   I cannot, nor I will not, yield to you.

BUCKINGHAM
If you refuse it, as in love and zeal
Loath to depose the child, your brother's son—
As well we know your tenderness of heart
And gentle, kind, effeminate remorse,
225   Which we have noted in you to your kindred
And equally indeed to all estates—

long past her prime. Nevertheless, under pretence of
asking a favor of him, she attracted his lustful eye and
seduced him so thoroughly that he completely
debased himself, committing adultery with her. It
resulted in this Edward, whom we're polite enough to
call "Prince." Out of respect for the living, I'll restrain
myself from telling you everything. But, my good
lord, if you don't care about this country, at least use
your own pure lineage to rescue us from the current
corruption of the royal line.

LORD MAYOR

Yes, my good lord, your citizens beg you.

BUCKINGHAM

Don't refuse the love we offer you.

CATESBY

Oh, make them joyful! Grant their law-abiding
request!

RICHARD

Alas, why would you heap all these responsibilities on
me? I am unfit to rule and to be king. Please, don't take
it badly, but I cannot and will not give in to you.

BUCKINGHAM

Perhaps you refuse our request out of love for your
brother's son. You don't want to depose the child. We
know how tender your heart is and what gentle, kind,
womanly feelings you have for your relatives, as well
as for people from all walks of life.

Yet know whe'er you accept our suit or no,
Your brother's son shall never reign our king,
But we will plant some other in the throne,
230   To the disgrace and downfall of your house.
And in this resolution here we leave you.—
Come, citizens. Zounds, I'll entreat no more.

RICHARD
O, do not swear, my lord of Buckingham!

Exit BUCKINGHAM *and some others*

CATESBY
Call them again, sweet prince. Accept their suit.
235   If you deny them, all the land will rue it.

RICHARD
Will you enforce me to a world of cares?
Call them again. I am not made of stones,
But penetrable to your kind entreaties,
Albeit against my conscience and my soul.

Enter BUCKINGHAM *and the rest*

240   Cousin of Buckingham and sage, grave men,
Since you will buckle fortune on my back,
To bear her burden, whe'er I will or no,
I must have patience to endure the load;
But if black scandal or foul-faced reproach
245   Attend the sequel of your imposition,
Your mere enforcement shall acquittance me
From all the impure blots and stains thereof,
For God doth know, and you may partly see,
How far I am from the desire of this.

LORD MAYOR
250   God bless your Grace! We see it and will say it.

RICHARD
In saying so, you shall but say the truth.

But listen, if *you* won't become king, we'll just get someone else, to the disgrace and ruin of your family. We will not have your brother's son as king. On this note, we're leaving. Come, citizens. Damn it, I'm not going to beg anymore!

RICHARD

Oh, please don't swear, my lord of Buckingham.

BUCKINGHAM *exits with* CITIZENS *and* LORD MAYOR.

CATESBY

Call them back, my lord, and accept their request. If you refuse it, the whole country will regret it.

RICHARD

Would you tie me to a whole world of worries? Well, call them back again. I am not made of stone; I am affected by all these kind pleas, though it goes against my conscience and my soul.

BUCKINGHAM *and the rest return.*

Buckingham, my brother, and you wise, serious men, since you intend to force me to take responsibility for these changing times, whether I want to or not, I'm going to have to be brave and endure the load. But if this imposition you've put on me happens to result in dark scandal or ugly reproach, the fact that you forced me to accept this should clear me from blame. God knows, and you may have noticed, I'm not to eager to take on this job.

LORD MAYOR

God bless your Grace! We understand you're just doing it for us, and we'll be sure to say so.

RICHARD

If you say that, you'll only be telling the truth.

BUCKINGHAM

Then I salute you with this royal title:
Long live Richard, England's worthy king!

ALL

Amen.

BUCKINGHAM

255   Tomorrow will it please you to be crowned?

RICHARD

Even when you please, since you will have it so.

BUCKINGHAM

Tomorrow, then, we will attend your Grace,
And so most joyfully we take our leave.

RICHARD

(to the bishops) Come, let us to our holy task again.—
260   Farewell, my cousin. Farewell, gentle friends.

Exeunt

BUCKINGHAM

Then I salute you with this royal title: long live Richard, England's worthy king!

ALL

Amen.

BUCKINGHAM

Will you be crowned tomorrow?

RICHARD

Whenever you want, since you're the one who wants it.

BUCKINGHAM

Tomorrow, then, we will wait on your Grace. Now we'll take our leave—joyfully.

RICHARD

(to the bishops) Come, let us get back to praying.— Farewell, my cousin; farewell, noble friends.

They all exit.

ACT FOUR
SCENE 1

Enter QUEEN ELIZABETH, DUCHESS *of York, and* DORSET *at one door;* ANNE, *duchess of Gloucester with* CLARENCE'*s young daughter at another door*

DUCHESS
Who meets us here? My niece Plantagenet
Led in the hand of her kind aunt of Gloucester?
Now, for my life, she's wandering to the Tower,
On pure heart's love, to greet the tender prince.—
5   Daughter, well met.

ANNE
                                        God give your Graces both
A happy and a joyful time of day.

QUEEN ELIZABETH
As much to you, good sister. Whither away?

ANNE
No farther than the Tower, and, as I guess,
10   Upon the like devotion as yourselves,
To gratulate the gentle princes there.

QUEEN ELIZABETH
Kind sister, thanks. We'll enter all together.

Enter BRAKENBURY

And in good time here the lieutenant comes.—
Master Lieutenant, pray you, by your leave,
15   How doth the prince and my young son of York?

BRAKENBURY
Right well, dear madam. By your patience,
I may not suffer you to visit them.
The king hath strictly charged the contrary.

ACT FOUR

SCENE 1

QUEEN ELIZABETH, DUCHESS *of York, and* DORSET *enter on one side, and* ANNE, *the duchess of Gloucester, enters on the other, leading Clarence's young daughter, Lady Margaret Plantagenet.*

DUCHESS

Who's this? My granddaughter, with her kind aunt, the duchess of Gloucester, leading her by the hand? Now, on my life, the young child must be headed to the Tower to greet the young princes, whom she adores. Daughter, how nice to see you.

ANNE

Good afternoon!

QUEEN ELIZABETH

The same to you, good sister. Where are you going?

ANNE

Just to the Tower—I'm guessing, for the same reason you are: to salute the noble princes who are staying there.

QUEEN ELIZABETH

Yes, kind sister. We can all go together.

BRAKENBURY *enters.*

And here comes the warden, just in time. Officer, please tell us, if you will, how are the prince and my little son, York?

BRAKENBURY

They're just fine, my dear madam. But I'm sorry— I'm not allowed to let you visit them. The king has strictly forbidden it.

QUEEN ELIZABETH
The king? Who's that?

BRAKENBURY
                                    I mean, the Lord Protector.

QUEEN ELIZABETH
20   The Lord protect him from that kingly title!
Hath he set bounds between their love and me?
I am their mother. Who shall bar me from them?

DUCHESS
I am their father's mother. I will see them.

ANNE
Their aunt I am in law, in love their mother.
25   Then bring me to their sights. I'll bear thy blame
And take thy office from thee, on my peril.

BRAKENBURY
No, madam, no. I may not leave it so.
I am bound by oath, and therefore pardon me.

                                                        Exit

Enter Lord STANLEY, *earl of Derby*

STANLEY
Let me but meet you ladies one hour hence,
30.   And I'll salute your Grace of York as mother
And reverend looker-on, of two fair queens.
(to ANNE*)*
Come, madam, you must straight to Westminster,
There to be crownèd Richard's royal queen.

QUEEN ELIZABETH
Ah, cut my lace asunder,
35   That my pent heart may have some scope to beat,
Or else I swoon with this dead-killing news!

ANNE
Despiteful tidings! O, unpleasing news!

DORSET
(to QUEEN ELIZABETH*)* Be of good cheer, mother. How fares
your Grace?

QUEEN ELIZABETH

> The king? Who's that?

BRAKENBURY

> I meant to say the Lord Protector.

QUEEN ELIZABETH

> The Lord keep him from the title of king! Richard has set boundaries between my love and theirs? I am their mother. Who's going to keep me from them?

DUCHESS

> I am their father's mother. I will see them.

ANNE

> I am their aunt, and I love them like a mother. So take me to see them. Officer, I'll take the responsibility from you, and the blame too.

BRAKENBURY

> No, madam, no. I can't do this. I am bound by oath, so please forgive me.

> > *He exits.*

Lord STANLEY, *earl of Derby, enters.*

STANLEY

> In just an hour from now, Duchess of York, I'll be saluting you as the mother of two beautiful queens. *(to* ANNE*)* Come, madam, you must go straight to Westminster Abbey, where you will be crowned Richard's queen.

QUEEN ELIZABETH

> Oh, cut my bodice-staps so that my pent-up heart can have some room to breathe, or I'll faint from this deadly news!

ANNE

> Cruel, cruel news!

DORSET

> *(to* QUEEN ELIZABETH*)* Cheer up, mother. How are you feeling?

QUEEN ELIZABETH

    O Dorset, speak not to me. Get thee gone.

40   Death and destruction dogs thee at thy heels.

    Thy mother's name is ominous to children.

    If thou wilt outstrip death, go, cross the seas,

    And live with Richmond, from the reach of hell.

    Go, hie thee, hie thee from this slaughterhouse,

45   Lest thou increase the number of the dead

    And make me die the thrall of Margaret's curse,

    Nor mother, wife, nor England's counted queen.

STANLEY

    Full of wise care is this your counsel, madam.

    (to DORSET*)* Take all the swift advantage of the hours.

50   You shall have letters from me to my son

    In your behalf, to meet you on the way.

    Be not ta'en tardy by unwise delay.

DUCHESS

    O ill-dispersing wind of misery!

    O my accursèd womb, the bed of death!

55   A cockatrice hast thou hatched to the world,

    Whose unavoided eye is murderous.

STANLEY

    (to ANNE*)* Come, madam, come. I in all haste was sent.

ANNE

    And I in all unwillingness will go.

    O, would to God that the inclusive verge

60   Of golden metal that must round my brow

    Were red-hot steel to sear me to the brains!

    Anointed let me be with deadly venom,

    And die ere men can say, "God save the Queen."

QUEEN ELIZABETH

    Go, go, poor soul, I envy not thy glory.

65   To feed my humor, wish thyself no harm.

QUEEN ELIZABETH

Oh, Dorset, don't waste your time talking to me. Leave. Death and destruction are following at your heels. Your mother's name has become a threat to her own children. If you want to outrun death, go cross the sea to France and stay with Richmond, out of the reach of hell. Go, get out of here, get out of this slaughterhouse. Otherwise you'll just increase the number of the dead, and make me die the slave of Margaret's curse, no longer a mother, a wife, or England's queen.

Henry Tudor, the earl of Richmond, later to succeed Richard as King Henry VII.

STANLEY

Madam, your advice is wise and caring.—Dorset, take advantage of the time you have. I'll write to my stepson Richmond on your behalf, so that he'll meet you on the way. But don't delay.

DUCHESS

O, this evil wind that spreads nothing but misery. O, my cursed womb—it's a deathbed, really, since Richard came out of it. It has hatched a cockatrice, whose gaze kills whatever it lands on.

The cockatrice was a mythical being that could kill with its gaze.

STANLEY

(to ANNE*)* Come, madam, come. I was sent in a hurry.

ANNE

I go unwillingly. I wish to God that the golden crown that I'll have to wear were red-hot steel and burned me straight through to the brain! I wish I could be anointed queen with deadly venom, not oil, and that I would die before anyone even had a chance to say, "God save the Queen!"

QUEEN ELIZABETH

Go, go, poor soul. I don't envy your position. If you want to make me happy, don't wish yourself harm.

ANNE

No? Why? When he that is my husband now
Came to me, as I followed Henry's corse,
When scarce the blood was well washed from his hands
Which issued from my other angel husband
70   And that dear saint which then I weeping followed—
O, when, I say, I looked on Richard's face,
This was my wish: be thou, quoth I, accursed
For making me, so young, so old a widow;
And, when thou wedd'st, let sorrow haunt thy bed;
75   And be thy wife, if any be so mad,
More miserable by the life of thee
Than thou hast made me by my dear lord's death.
Lo, ere I can repeat this curse again,
Within so small a time my woman's heart
80   Grossly grew captive to his honey words
And proved the subject of mine own soul's curse,
Which hitherto hath held my eyes from rest,
For never yet one hour in his bed
Did I enjoyed the golden dew of sleep,
85   But with his timorous dreams was still awaked.
Besides, he hates me for my father Warwick,
And will, no doubt, shortly be rid of me.

QUEEN ELIZABETH

Poor heart, adieu. I pity thy complaining.

ANNE

No more than from my soul I mourn for yours.

DORSET

90   Farewell, thou woeful welcomer of glory.

ANNE

Adieu, poor soul that tak'st thy leave of it.

ANNE

No? Why? The man I'm married to now came to me when he'd barely washed the blood off his hands from killing my first husband, that angel, as well as my husband's sainted father, whose corpse I was following to burial. I'm telling you, when I looked at Richard's face, this is what I wished: "I want you to be cursed for making me a widow so young. And when you get married, let sorrow haunt your bed. And I hope your wife—if any woman is crazy enough to marry you—is more miserable about the fact that you're alive as you have made me by killing my husband!" And then what? Before I even had time to repeat the curse, my woman's heart was taken captive by his sweet, slick words. I became the victim of my own curse. Since I married him, I have not had one hour's sleep in his bed. Every night I'm awakened by his terrified dreams. It doesn't matter if I sleep, though. He hates me because of who my father is. He will, no doubt, get rid of me soon.

Anne's father, the earl of Warwick, fought on the opposite side from Richard and the other Yorkists in the wars between the Lancasters and Yorks.

QUEEN ELIZABETH

Poor dear, goodbye. I pity your situation.

ANNE

No more than I do yours.

DORSET

Goodbye. I know you're unhappy with the glory of becoming queen.

ANNE

(to ELIZABETH*)* And goodbye to you, the poor soul who has to leave that glory behind.

DUCHESS

(to DORSET*)*

Go thou to Richmond, and good fortune guide thee.

(to ANNE*)* Go thou to Richard, and good angels tend thee.

(to QUEEN ELIZABETH*)*

Go thou to sanctuary, and good thoughts possess thee.

95 I to my grave, where peace and rest lie with me.

Eighty-odd years of sorrow have I seen,

And each hour's joy wracked with a week of teen.

QUEEN ELIZABETH

Stay, yet look back with me unto the Tower.—

Pity, you ancient stones, those tender babes

100 Whom envy hath immured within your walls—

Rough cradle for such little pretty ones.

Rude ragged nurse, old sullen playfellow

For tender princes, use my babies well.

So foolish sorrows bids your stones farewell.

Exeunt

DUCHESS

(to DORSET*)* Go to Richmond, and good luck. *(to* ANNE*)* You go to Richard. I hope good angels will protect you. *(to* QUEEN ELIZABETH*)* You take sanctuary in the Abbey and think good thoughts for us. I will go to my grave, where I can look forward to peace and rest. I have witnessed eighty-odd years of sorrow; for each hour of joy I've experienced, I've suffered a full week of misery.

QUEEN ELIZABETH

Wait. Look back at the Tower with me. Please, you ancient building, take pity on those tender babes locked inside your walls by envious rivals! You are such a rough cradle for such little pretty ones. You are a rude, ragged nurse and an old, sullen playmate for such tender princes. Please treat my babies well. I know I must look foolish saying goodbye to a building, but I'm aching with sorrow.

They all exit.

ACT 4, SCENE 2

Sound a sennet. Enter RICHARD *in pomp;* BUCKINGHAM,
CATESBY, RATCLIFFE, LOVELL, *a page, and others*

RICHARD
Stand all apart. —Cousin of Buckingham.

Others move aside

BUCKINGHAM
My gracious sovereign.

RICHARD
Give me thy hand.
Here he ascendeth the throne. Sound trumpets
Thus high, by thy advice
5   And thy assistance is King Richard seated.
But shall we wear these glories for a day,
Or shall they last and we rejoice in them?

BUCKINGHAM
Still live they, and forever let them last.

RICHARD
Ah, Buckingham, now do I play the touch,
10   To try if thou be current gold indeed.
Young Edward lives; think now what I would speak.

BUCKINGHAM
Say on, my loving lord.

RICHARD
Why, Buckingham, I say I would be king,

BUCKINGHAM
Why so you are, my thrice-renownèd lord.

RICHARD
15   Ha! Am I king? 'Tis so—but Edward lives.

BUCKINGHAM
True, noble prince.

ACT 4, SCENE 2

Trumpets play. RICHARD *enters, already crowned and dressed as a king.* BUCKINGHAM, CATESBY, *a* PAGE, *and others enter with him.*

RICHARD

Everyone stand aside.—Cousin Buckingham.

Everyone moves aside.

BUCKINGHAM

My gracious king.

RICHARD

Give me your hand.
RICHARD *ascends the throne with* BUCKINGHAM *at his side.*
Because of your advice and your help, I have a high position now. But will I wear these honors for only a day or will I enjoy them for a long time?

BUCKINGHAM

Let them last forever.

RICHARD

Oh Buckingham, now I'm going to test to see if you're truly made of gold. Young Prince Edward is still alive—what do you think I'm going to say next?

BUCKINGHAM

Go on, my loving lord.

RICHARD

Why, Buckingham, I say I want to be king.

BUCKINGHAM

Why, you are king, your highness.

RICHARD

Ha! Am I king? I guess I am. But Edward is still alive.

BUCKINGHAM

True, noble prince.

RICHARD
                    O bitter consequence
          That Edward still should live "true noble prince"!
          Cousin, thou wast not wont to be so dull.
          Shall I be plain? I wish the bastards dead,
20   And I would have it suddenly performed.
          What sayest thou now? Speak suddenly. Be brief.

BUCKINGHAM
          Your Grace may do your pleasure.

RICHARD
          Tut, tut, thou art all ice; thy kindness freezes.
          Say, have I thy consent that they shall die?

BUCKINGHAM
25   Give me some little breath, some pause, dear lord,
          Before I positively speak in this.
          I will resolve you herein presently.

                                                              Exit

CATESBY
          (aside to the other attendants)
          The king is angry. See, he gnaws his lip.

RICHARD
          (aside) I will converse with iron-witted fools
30   And unrespective boys. None are for me
          That look into me with considerate eyes.
          High-reaching Buckingham grows circumspect.—
          Boy!

PAGE
          (coming forward) My lord?

RICHARD
35   Know'st thou not any whom corrupting gold
          Will tempt unto a close exploit of death?

RICHARD

Oh, how bitter it is that Edward—the real "true, noble prince"—should still be alive! Cousin, you didn't used to be so thickheaded. Shall I put it plainly? I want the bastards dead. And I want it done right away. What do you say? Speak now and to the point.

BUCKINGHAM

Your Grace can do whatever he wants.

RICHARD

Tut, tut, you've become rather icy. Your friendliness toward me seems to be freezing over. Tell me, do I have your consent to kill them?

BUCKINGHAM

Give me a little breathing space, my lord, a little pause to think. I'll let you know my answer shortly.

He exits.

CATESBY

(so only the attendant nearest him can hear) The king is angry. See, he bites his lip.

RICHARD

(to himself) I only want to deal with stupid fools and careless boys. I have no use for people who look at me insightfully. Ambitious Buckingham grows much too circumspect. Boy!

PAGE

My lord?

RICHARD

Do you know anyone who would kill someone for money?

PAGE
> I know a discontented gentleman
> Whose humble means match not his haughty spirit.
> Gold were as good as twenty orators,
40 > And will, no doubt, tempt him to anything.

RICHARD
> What is his name?

PAGE
> His name, my lord, is Tyrrel.

RICHARD
> I partly know the man. Go, call him hither, boy

Exit **PAGE**

> *(aside)* The deep-revolving witty Buckingham
> No more shall be the neighbor to my counsels
45 > Hath he so long held out with me, untired,
> And stops he now for breath? Well, be it so.
> *Enter* **STANLEY**
> How now, Lord Stanley, what's the news?

STANLEY
> Know, my long lord,
> The marquess Dorset, as I hear, is fled
50 > To Richmond, in the parts where he abides.
> *He walks aside*

RICHARD
> Come hither, Catesby. Rumor it abroad
> That Anne my wife is very grievous sick.
> I will take order for her keeping close.
> Inquire me out some mean poor gentleman,
55 > Whom I will marry straight to Clarence' daughter.
> The boy is foolish, and I fear not him.
> Look how thou dream'st! I say again, give out
> That Anne my queen is sick and like to die.
> About it, for it stands me much upon
60 > To stop all hopes whose growth may damage me.

PAGE

My lord, I know one unhappy gentleman who has more pride than money. Money talks, and would very likely get him to do anything.

RICHARD

What's his name?

PAGE

His name is Tyrrel, my lord.

RICHARD

I know the man a bit. Go, bring him here, boy.

The PAGE exits.

(to himself) The thoughtful, witty Buckingham will no longer be privy to my innermost thoughts. Has he held out for me for so long and without a moment's doubt only to suddenly need some "breathing room"? Well, so be it.

STANLEY *enters.*

Look who's here! What's the news with you?

STANLEY

You should know, my loving lord, I've heard that the marquess Dorset has fled to Brittany, to the earl of Richmond.

He stands aside.

RICHARD

Come here, Catesby. Spread the rumor abroad that Anne, my wife, is very sick. I will make sure she's kept out of view. And find a poverty stricken gentleman who I can marry straightaway to Clarence's daughter. Clarence's son is dull-witted, so I'm not worried about him. Look at you, standing there in a stupor! I repeat, spread the rumor that Anne, my wife, is sick and likely to die. Hurry up because it's absolutely crucial that I destroy anything that may damage my position.

Exit CATESBY

(aside) I must be married to my brother's daughter,
Or else my kingdom stands on brittle glass.
Murder her brothers, and then marry her—
Uncertain way of gain. But I am in
65   So far in blood that sin will pluck on sin.
Tear-falling pity dwells not in this eye.

Enter PAGE *with* TYRREL

Is thy name Tyrrel?

TYRREL
James Tyrrel, and your most obedient subject.

RICHARD
Art thou indeed?

TYRREL
                              Prove me, my gracious sovereign.

RICHARD
70   Dar'st thou resolve to kill a friend of mine?

TYRREL
Please you. But I had rather kill two enemies.

RICHARD
Why then, thou hast it. Two deep enemies,
Foes to my rest, and my sweet sleep's disturbers,
Are they that I would have thee deal upon.
75   Tyrrel, I mean those bastards in the Tower.

TYRREL
Let me have open means to come to them,
And soon I'll rid you from the fear of them.

RICHARD
Thou sing'st sweet music. Hark, come hither, Tyrrel.

TYRREL *approaches* RICHARD *and kneels*

Go, by this token. Rise, and lend thine ear.

CATESBY *exits.*

(to himself) I must get married to my brother's daughter. Otherwise, my kingdom stands on glass. Murdering her brothers and then marrying her isn't the most foolproof way to secure my position. But I'm steeped so deep in blood by now that one sin has to follow the next. I have no tears of pity for anyone.

Elizabeth of York, daughter of Queen Elizabeth and King Edward. She later married Henry Tudor, earl of Richmond. She was the grandmother of Elizabeth I and considered by Elizabethans to mark the start of the Tudor reign.

The PAGE *returns with* TYRREL.

Are you Tyrrel?

TYRREL
James Tyrrel—and your most obedient subject.

RICHARD
Are you indeed?

TYRREL
Test me, my blessed king.

RICHARD
Do you dare kill a friend of mine?

TYRREL
Yes, my lord, but I'd rather kill two enemies.

RICHARD
Well, that's what you get to do. Two great enemies, in fact, enemies to my peace of mind. Tyrrel, I mean those bastards in the Tower.

TYRREL
Give me access to them, and soon you won't have to worry about them anymore.

RICHARD
That's music to my ears. Come here, Tyrrel.

TYRREL *approaches* RICHARD *and kneels.*

By this token, you'll be admitted to their cell. Get up and listen to me.

He whispers

80   There is no more but so. Say it is done,
      And I will love thee and prefer thee for it.

TYRREL
      I will dispatch it straight.

                                                    Exit

Enter BUCKINGHAM

BUCKINGHAM
      My lord, I have considered in my mind
      The late request that you did sound me in.

RICHARD
85   Well, let that rest. Dorset is fled to Richmond.

BUCKINGHAM
      I hear the news, my lord.

RICHARD
      Stanley, he is your wife's son. Well, look unto it.

BUCKINGHAM
      My lord, I claim the gift, my due by promise,
      For which your honor and your faith is pawned—
90   Th' earldom of Hereford and the movables
      Which you promisèd I shall possess.

RICHARD
      Stanley, look to your wife. If she convey
      Letters to Richmond, you shall answer it.

BUCKINGHAM
      What says your Highness to my just request?

RICHARD *whispers to* TYRREL.

That's all there is to it. As soon as the deed is done, you will be in my favor and I will promote you.

TYRREL

I'll do it right away.

He exits.

BUCKINGHAM *returns.*

BUCKINGHAM

My lord, I have thought over the request you just made of me.

RICHARD

Well, it doesn't matter anymore. Dorset has fled to the earl of Richmond.

BUCKINGHAM

I heard the news, my lord.

RICHARD

Stanley, Richmond is your wife's son. Get information from her.

BUCKINGHAM

My lord, I'd want to have the gift you promised me on your honor: the earldom of Hereford and all the possessions that go with it.

RICHARD

Stanley, pay attention to your wife's doings. If she sends any letters to Richmond, you will be accountable to me for it.

BUCKINGHAM

What do you say, your Highness, about my just request?

RICHARD

95   I do remember me, Henry the Sixth
Did prophesy that Richmond should be king,
When Richmond was a little peevish boy.
A king, perhaps—

BUCKINGHAM
My lord—

RICHARD

100   How chance the prophet could not at that time
Have told me, I being by, that I should kill him?

BUCKINGHAM
My lord, your promise for the earldom—

RICHARD
Richmond! When last I was at Exeter,
The mayor in courtesy showed me the castle

105   And called it Rougemont, at which name I started,
Because a bard of Ireland told me once
I should not live long after I saw Richmond.

BUCKINGHAM
My Lord—

RICHARD
Ay, what's o'clock?

BUCKINGHAM

110   I am thus bold to put your Grace in mind
Of what you promised me.

RICHARD
Well, but what's o'clock?

BUCKINGHAM
Upon the stroke of ten.

RICHARD
Well, let it strike.

BUCKINGHAM

115   Why let it strike?

RICHARD

As I remember, Henry the Sixth prophesied that Richmond would be king when Richmond was only a foolish little boy. A king, perhaps—

BUCKINGHAM

My lord—

RICHARD

How is it that the prophet didn't tell me at the time that I would kill him?

BUCKINGHAM

My lord, your promise of the earldom—

RICHARD

Richmond! The last time I was in Exeter, the mayor kindly showed me the castle there and called it "Rougemont." The name startled me because an Irish poet once told me that I would die soon after seeing "Richmond."

The words "Rougemont" and "Richmond" were pronounced similarly, and both mean "red hill."

BUCKINGHAM

My lord!

RICHARD

Yes, what time is it?

BUCKINGHAM

I'm reminding your grace what you promised me.

RICHARD

Well, but what time is it?

BUCKINGHAM

It's almost ten o'clock.

RICHARD

Well, let it strike ten then.

BUCKINGHAM

Why "let it strike"?

RICHARD
>Because that, like a jack, thou keep'st the stroke
>Betwixt thy begging and my meditation.
>I am not in the giving vein today.

BUCKINGHAM
>Why then, resolve me whether you will or no.

RICHARD
120   Thou troublest me; I am not in the vein.

Exeunt all but BUCKINGHAM

BUCKINGHAM
>And is it thus? Repays he my deep service
>With such deep contempt? Made I him king for this?
>O, let me think on Hastings and be gone
>To Brecknock, while my fearful head is on!

Exit

RICHARD

> Because you're like the lowborn fellow who strikes the bell—you keep interrupting my thoughts. I am not in the giving mood today.

BUCKINGHAM

> Well, then, let me know whether you will give me the earldom some other time.

RICHARD

> You're bothering me. I'm not in the mood.

Everyone except BUCKINGHAM *exits.*

BUCKINGHAM

> Is this really happening? Does he reward my dedicated service with such deep contempt? Did I work to make him king for this? Oh, let me remember what happened to Hastings and hurry to Brecknock while I still have my head on my shoulders!

Brecknock was Buckingham's family estate in southeast Wales.

He exits.

ACT 4, SCENE 3

Enter TYRREL

TYRREL
The tyrannous and bloody act is done,
The most arch deed of piteous massacre
That ever yet this land was guilty of.
Dighton and Forrest, whom I did suborn
To do this piece of ruthless butchery,
Albeit they were fleshed villains, bloody dogs,
Melted with tenderness and mild compassion,
Wept like two children in their deaths' sad story.
"O thus" quoth Dighton, "lay those gentle babes."
"Thus, thus," quoth Forrest, "girdling one another
Within their alabaster innocent arms.
Their lips were four red roses on a stalk,
And in their summer beauty kissed each other.
A book of prayers on their pillow lay,
Which once," quoth Forrest, "almost changed my mind,
But O, the devil—"There the villain stopped;
When Dighton thus told on: "We smotherèd
The most replenishèd sweet work of nature
That from the prime creation e'er she framed."
Hence both are gone with conscience and remorse;
They could not speak; and so I left them both
To bear this tidings to the bloody king.

Enter RICHARD

And here he comes.—All health, my sovereign lord.

RICHARD
Kind Tyrrel, am I happy in thy news?

ACT 4, SCENE 3

TYRREL *enters.*

TYRREL

The tyrant's bloody request has been met. It was the most ruthless massacre this country has ever been guilty of. Dighton and Forrest, whom I hired to perform the butchery, are used to killing people, the bloody dogs. But they melted with tenderness and human compassion, weeping like children, when they described what they'd done. "The tender babes lay like this," said Dighton. "Like this," said Forrest, "with their innocent white arms around each other. Their lips, like four red roses on a stalk, touched. A prayer book lay on their pillow, which" said Forrest, "almost made me change my mind. But, oh, the devil"—there he stopped talking and Dighton took up where he left off: "We smothered the perfect, most sweet work of nature." The two men were both destroyed by remorse. They couldn't speak. So I left them to bring the news to the murderous king. And here he comes.

RICHARD *enters.*

Here he comes.—Health to you, my king.

RICHARD

Kind Tyrrel, will your news make me happy?

TYRREL

25   If to have done the thing you gave in charge
         Beget your happiness, be happy then,
         For it is done.

RICHARD

                              But did'st thou see them dead?

TYRREL

         I did, my lord.

RICHARD

                              And buried, gentle Tyrrel?

TYRREL

         The chaplain of the Tower hath buried them,
30   But where, to say the truth, I do not know.

RICHARD

         Come to me, Tyrrel, soon at after-supper,
         When thou shalt tell the process of their death.
         Meantime, but think how I may do thee good,
         And be inheritor of thy desire.
35   Farewell till then.

TYRREL

                              I humbly take my leave.

Exit TYRREL

RICHARD

         The son of Clarence have I pent up close,
         His daughter meanly have I matched in marriage,
         The sons of Edward sleep in Abraham's bosom,
         And Anne my wife hath bid this world goodnight.
40   Now, for I know the Breton Richmond aims
         At young Elizabeth, my brother's daughter,
         And by that knot looks proudly on the crown,
         To her go I, a jolly thriving wooer.

Enter RATCLIFFE

TYRREL

If my doing what you told me to makes you happy, then be happy, because I did it.

RICHARD

But did you see them dead?

TYRREL

I did, my lord.

RICHARD

And buried, noble Tyrrel?

TYRREL

The Tower's chaplain has buried them, but to tell you the truth, I don't know where.

RICHARD

Tyrrel, come back shortly after dinner and tell me the details of their deaths. In the meantime, think about how I can do you good and give you what you want. See you soon.

TYRELL

I humbly say goodbye.

TYRREL exits.

RICHARD

I've locked up Clarence's son and matched his daughter with a poor fellow. Edward's sons have been carried off by the angels and Anne, my wife, has bid good night to the world. Now I go, a jolly, thriving wooer, to marry my brother Edward's young daughter, Elizabeth, because I know Richmond has his eye on her. He wants to win the crown by way of marrying her.

RATCLIFFE enters.

RATCLIFFE
My lord!

RICHARD
45   Good or bad news, that thou com'st in so bluntly?

RATCLIFFE
Bad news, my lord. Morton is fled to Richmond,
And Buckingham, backed with the hardy Welshmen,
Is in the field, and still his power increaseth.

RICHARD
Ely with Richmond troubles me more near
50   Than Buckingham and his rash-levied strength.
Come, I have learned that fearful commenting
Is leaden servitor to dull delay;
Delay leads impotent and snail-paced beggary;
Then fiery expedition be my wing,
55   Jove's Mercury, and herald for a king.
Go, muster men. My counsel is my shield.
We must be brief when traitors brave the field.

Exeunt

RATCLIFFE

My lord!

RICHARD

Is the news good or bad that you enter without knocking?

RATCLIFFE

Bad news, my lord. The Bishop of Ely has fled to Richmond, and Buckingham, backed by a hardy Welsh army, is on the march. His army is growing.

RICHARD

Ely joining Richmond troubles me more than Buckingham and his quickly assembled army. Come, I've heard that frightened analysis only serves to delay action, and delay can lead to ruin. So my method is going to be to move as quickly as fire. Come, let's gather an army. The best strategy is to head right to the battlefield. When traitors challenge us to fight, it's best to act fast.

They exit.

ACT 4, SCENE 4

Enter old QUEEN MARGARET

QUEEN MARGARET
So now prosperity begins to mellow
And drop into the rotten mouth of death.
Here in these confines slyly have I lurked
To watch the waning of mine enemies.
5   A dire induction am I witness to,
And will to France, hoping the consequence
Will prove as bitter, black, and tragical.
Withdraw thee, wretched Margaret. Who comes here?
She steps aside
Enter QUEEN ELIZABETH *and the* DUCHESS *of York*

QUEEN ELIZABETH
Ah, my poor princes! Ah, my tender babes,
10   My unblown flowers, new-appearing sweets,
If yet your gentle souls fly in the air
And be not fixed in doom perpetual,
Hover about me with your airy wings
And hear your mother's lamentation.

QUEEN MARGARET
15   Hover about her; say that right for right
Hath dimmed your infant morn to agèd night.

DUCHESS
So many miseries have crazed my voice
That my woe-wearied tongue is still and mute.
Edward Plantagenet, why art thou dead?

QUEEN MARGARET
20   *(aside)* Plantagenet doth quit Plantagenet;
Edward for Edward pays a dying debt.

ACT 4, SCENE 4

Old QUEEN MARGARET *enters.*

QUEEN MARGARET

So now the good times have ripened and grown rotten. I've lurked in the shadows here to watch the downfall of my enemies. I've been watching the terrible prologue to a scene that I hope will prove dark and tragic. I'll head to France soon. It's time to hide, wretched Margaret. Who's coming?

QUEEN ELIZABETH *and the* DUCHESS *of York enter.*

QUEEN ELIZABETH

Ah, my poor princes! Ah, my tender babes, my flowers who didn't even get a chance to bloom. If your gentle souls are still flying in the air and have not yet landed where they will remain forever, hover around me with your airy wings and hear your mother's lament.

QUEEN MARGARET

Hover about her and tell her she got what she deserved, with her children dead before their time.

DUCHESS

I've been crazed with so many miseries that my tongue has tired of lamenting and gone mute. Edward Plantagenet, why are you dead?

QUEEN MARGARET

(to herself) One Plantagenet pays for the other. One Edward dies to pay a debt for the other Edward who died.

QUEEN ELIZABETH
Wilt thou, O God, fly from such gentle lambs
And throw them in the entrails of the wolf?
When didst thou sleep when such a deed was done?

QUEEN MARGARET
25   *(aside)* When holy Harry died, and my sweet son.

DUCHESS
(sitting down)
Dead life, blind sight, poor mortal living ghost,
Woe's scene, world's shame, grave's due by life usurped,
Brief abstract and record of tedious days,
Rest thy unrest on England's lawful earth,
30   Unlawfully made drunk with innocent blood.

QUEEN ELIZABETH
(sitting down beside her)
Ah, that thou wouldst as soon afford a grave
As thou canst yield a melancholy seat,
Then would I hide my bones, not rest them here.
O, who hath any cause to mourn but we?

QUEEN MARGARET
35   *(joining them)* If ancient sorrow be most reverend,
Give mine the benefit of seigniory,
And let my griefs frown on the upper hand.
If sorrow can admit society,
Tell o'er your woes again by viewing mine.
40   I had an Edward till a Richard killed him;
I had a husband till a Richard killed him.
Thou hadst an Edward till a Richard killed him;
Thou hadst a Richard till a Richard killed him.

DUCHESS
I had a Richard too, and thou did'st kill him;
45   I had a Rutland too; thou holp'st to kill him.

QUEEN ELIZABETH

Will you abandon such gentle lambs, God, and throw them to the wolves? Have you ever slept before while such a terrible deed was done?

QUEEN MARGARET

Harry = Henry VI

(to herself) Sure—when my husband, holy Harry, died and when my sweet son died.

DUCHESS

(sitting down) Sight has gone blind, life is as dead as a ghost. This is a mournful scene—it's a shame to the world, when someone like me, who should have died long ago, still lives. As a short summary and record of an unbearable life, I'll settle my restless bones on England's lawful ground *(sitting down)*, which broke the law when it got drunk on the blood of the innocent!

QUEEN ELIZABETH

(sitting down beside her) Oh, if only the earth would offer me not just a seat for mourning but a grave. Then I would bury myself, not just rest my bones. Oh, who has any reason to mourn except us?

QUEEN MARGARET

If the oldest grief is the most revered, then mine should have the most weight here. Let my sorrow have the upper hand. If you can allow for comparison *(sitting down with them)*, consider your losses next to mine. I had an Edward till a Richard killed him, and I had a Harry till a Richard killed him. On your side, you had an Edward till a Richard killed him, and you had the young Richard, York, till a Richard killed him. So, I guess we're equal.

DUCHESS

I had a Richard too—namely, my husband—and you killed him. I had my son Rutland, and you helped kill him.

QUEEN MARGARET
Thou hadst a Clarence too, and Richard killed him
Then forth the kennel of thy womb hath crept
A hellhound that doth hunt us all to death—
That dog, that had his teeth before his eyes,
50   To worry lambs and lap their gentle blood;
That excellent grand tyrant of the earth,
That reigns in gallèd eyes of weeping souls;
That foul defacer of God's handiwork
Thy womb let loose to chase us to our graves.
55   O upright, just, and true-disposing God,
How do I thank thee that this carnal cur
Preys on the issue of his mother's body
And makes her pew-fellow with others' moan!

DUCHESS
O Harry's wife, triumph not in my woes!
60   God witness with me, I have wept for thine.

QUEEN MARGARET
Bear with me, I am hungry for revenge,
And now I cloy me with beholding it.
Thy Edward he is dead, that killed my Edward,
Thy other Edward dead, to quit my Edward;
65   Young York, he is but boot, because both they
Matched not the high perfection of my loss.
Thy Clarence he is dead that stabbed my Edward,
And the beholders of this frantic play,
Th' adulterate Hastings, Rivers, Vaughan, Grey,
70   Untimely smothered in their dusky graves.
Richard yet lives, hell's black intelligencer,
Only reserved their factor to buy souls
And send them thither. But at hand, at hand
Ensues his piteous and unpitied end.
75   Earth gapes, hell burns, fiends roar, saints pray,
To have him suddenly conveyed from hence.
Cancel his bond of life, dear God I pray,
That I may live to say, "The dog is dead."

QUEEN MARGARET

You had a Clarence, too, and Richard killed him. Your womb let loose a hellhound that hunts us all to death. That dog, who was born with sharp teeth for lapping up the blood of lambs, who had teeth before he even had eyes, is the world's worst tyrant, making the eyes of a whole kingdom red with weeping. He destroys God's handiwork and will send us to our graves. Oh righteous God, how can I thank you enough that this meat-eating mutt preys on his mother's children and forces her to join others in their grief!

DUCHESS

O Harry's wife, do not triumph in my sorrow! With God as my witness, I swear I have wept for yours.

QUEEN MARGARET

Bear with me. I am hungry for revenge, and now I plan to gorge myself on it. Your son Edward, who stabbed my son Edward, is dead. To even the balance, your grandson Edward is also dead, with young York thrown in because both your grandsons aren't equal to my one son. Your Clarence, who stabbed my Edward, is also dead. And the audience to this insane play—the adulterer Hastings, as well as Rivers, Vaughan, and Grey—have been sent early to their graves. Richard, a fiendish spy for hell itself, still lives, but only long enough to buy souls to send below. Soon, very soon, he will meet his ghastly and well deserved end.

When he dies, the earth will gape open, hell will burn hotter, devils will roar, and saints will pray to get him out of here fast. I pray that God ends his life before I die, so I can say, "The dog is dead!"

QUEEN ELIZABETH
O, thou didst prophesy the time would come
80   That I should wish for thee to help me curse
That bottled spider, that foul bunch-backed toad!

QUEEN MARGARET
I called thee then "vain flourish of my fortune."
I called thee then poor shadow, "painted queen,"
The presentation of but what I was,
85   The flattering index of a direful pageant,
One heaved a-high, to be hurled down below,
A mother only mocked with two fair babes,
A dream of what thou wast, a garish flag
To be the aim of every dangerous shot,
90   A sign of dignity, a breath, a bubble,
A queen in jest, only to fill the scene.
Where is thy husband now? Where be thy brothers?
Where are thy two sons? Wherein dost thou joy?
Who sues and kneels and says "God save the queen?"
95   Where be the bending peers that flattered thee?
Where be the thronging troops that followed thee?
Decline all this, and see what now thou art:
For happy wife, a most distressèd widow;
For joyful mother, one that wails the name;
100   For queen, a very caitiff crowned with care;
For she that scorned at me, now scorned of me;
For she being feared of all, now fearing one;
For she commanding all, obeyed of none.
Thus hath the course of justice whirled about
105   And left thee but a very prey to time,
Having no more but thought of what thou wast
To torture thee the more, being what thou art.
Thou didst usurp my place, and dost thou not
Usurp the just proportion of my sorrow?
110   Now thy proud neck bears half my burdened yoke,
From which even here I slip my weary head
And leave the burthen of it all on thee.

QUEEN ELIZABETH

Oh, you prophesied that the time would come when I would want your help in cursing that humpbacked spider, that hideous toad!

QUEEN MARGARET

Back then, I called you "a poor, imitation queen," a badly reproduced copy of what I was, a pretty prologue for the tragedy that was about to follow, a woman who was lifted high only to be hurled down to hell, a mother only teased with two beautiful children, who would soon die. I said you were a mere shadow of what a queen once was, a garish target to be aimed at again and again, an empty symbol of dignity without any substance, a mockery of a queen only there to fill in a role. And I was right, because where's your husband now? Your brothers? Your two sons? Your source of joy? Who kneels at your feet now and says, "God save the Queen?" What noblemen are bowing and scraping to flatter you now? And where is your throng of followers? Once you've laid out all of these losses, it's clear what's left. In place of a happy wife, there's a miserable widow. Instead of a joyful mother, here's a woman who cries at the mention of her children. For one who bestows favors on others, here's one who has to beg for favors. Instead of a queen, we have a poor woman with a crown of worries. She who mocked me now is mocked by me. She who once ordered everyone about is now obeyed by no one. Your fortune has fallen. Now you have only the memory of what you were, which tortures you when you consider what you've become.

You once stole my position; now you get to have the grief that goes with it. Now like an ox, you carry half my heavy burden of grief—here, I'll give you the rest. Farewell, York's wife. Goodbye, queen of tragic mis-

Farewell, York's wife, and queen of sad mischance.
These English woes will make me smile in France.

QUEEN ELIZABETH

115   O, thou well-skilled in curses, stay awhile,
And teach me how to curse mine enemies.

QUEEN MARGARET

Forbear to sleep the nights, and fast the days;
Compare dead happiness with living woe;
Think that thy babes were sweeter than they were,
120   And he that slew them fouler than he is.
Bettering thy loss makes the bad causer worse.
Revolving this will teach thee how to curse.

QUEEN ELIZABETH

My words are dull. O, quicken them with thine!

QUEEN MARGARET

Thy woes will make them sharp and pierce like mine.

Exit

DUCHESS

125   Why should calamity be full of words?

QUEEN ELIZABETH

Windy attorneys to their clients' woes,
Airy succeeders of intestate joys,
Poor breathing orators of miseries,
Let them have scope, though what they will impart
130   Help nothing else, yet do they ease the heart.

DUCHESS

If so, then be not tongue-tied. Go with me,
And in the breath of bitter words let's smother
My damnèd son that thy two sweet sons smothered.

A trumpet sounds

The trumpet sounds. Be copious in exclaims.

fortune. Your English sorrows will make me smile in France.

QUEEN ELIZABETH

You who are so skilled in cursing, stay awhile and teach me how to curse my enemies.

QUEEN MARGARET

Don't sleep at night, and don't eat during the day. Compare what you've lost with what you suffer now. Remember your children as being sweeter than they actually were, and think of the man who killed them as worse than he is. Making your loss greater makes the person who caused it worse. Think like this all day, and you'll learn how to curse.

QUEEN ELIZABETH

My words are dull. Enliven them with yours!

QUEEN MARGARET

Your misery will make them sharp and piercing like mine.

She exits.

DUCHESS

What good does it do to respond to catastrophe with a lot of words?

QUEEN ELIZABETH

Words are a lot of useless breath, like lawyers who won't stop arguing for their sad clients, like a worthless inheritance, or like poor speech-makers who won't stop speaking. But give words a chance. Though they won't help in any other way, at least they make us feel better.

DUCHESS

If that's true, then don't be tongue-tied. Come with me, and let's smother my fiendish son—who smothered your two sweet sons—in bitter words.

A trumpet plays.

I hear his battle drums. Don't stint on your words.

They rise

Enter King RICHARD *and his train, including* CATESBY

RICHARD

135   Who intercepts my expedition?

DUCHESS

        O, she that might have intercepted thee,
        By strangling thee in her accursèd womb,
        From all the slaughters, wretch, that thou hast done.

QUEEN ELIZABETH

        Hid'st thou that forehead with a golden crown
140   Where should be branded, if that right were right,
        The slaughter of the prince that owed that crown
        And the dire death of my poor sons and brothers?
        Tell me, thou villain-slave, where are my children?

DUCHESS

        Thou toad, thou toad, where is thy brother Clarence?
145   And little Ned Plantagenet his son?

QUEEN ELIZABETH

        Where is gentle Rivers, Vaughan, Grey?

DUCHESS

        Where is kind Hastings?

RICHARD

        A flourish, trumpets! Strike alarum, drums!
        Let not the heavens hear these telltale women
150   Rail on the Lord's anointed. Strike, I say!
        Flourish. Alarums

        Either be patient and entreat me fair,
        Or with the clamorous report of war
        Thus will I drown your exclamations.

DUCHESS

        Art thou my son?

They rise.

King RICHARD *enters, with his followers, including* CASTEBY.

RICHARD

Who's blocking the way?

DUCHESS

The woman who might have blocked you from all the murders you've committed by strangling you in her cursed womb.

QUEEN ELIZABETH

Are you hiding your forehead with a golden crown, when, if there was any justice in this world, it should be branded with the murders you committed—your slaughter of the prince who held that crown, and of my sons and my brothers? Tell me, you villainous lowlife, where are my children?

DUCHESS

You toad, where is your brother Clarence and his son, little Ned Plantagenet?

QUEEN ELIZABETH

Where are the noble Hastings, Rivers, Vaughan, Grey?

DUCHESS

Where is kind Hastings?

RICHARD

Play, trumpets! A call to arms, drums! Don't let the heavens hear these chattery women abuse the Lord's anointed king. Play, I say!
Trumpet and drums play military music.
Either be calm and polite or I'll drown you out with the music of war.

DUCHESS

Are you my son?

RICHARD

155   Ay, I thank God, my father, and yourself.

DUCHESS

Then patiently hear my impatience.

RICHARD

Madam, I have a touch of your condition,
Which cannot brook the accent of reproof.

DUCHESS

O, let me speak!

RICHARD

Do then, but I'll not hear.

DUCHESS

160   I will be mild and gentle in my words.

RICHARD

And brief, good mother, for I am in haste.

DUCHESS

Art thou so hasty? I have stayed for thee,
God knows, in torment and in agony.

RICHARD

And came I not at last to comfort you?

DUCHESS

165   No, by the Holy Rood, thou know'st it well.
Thou cam'st on earth to make the earth my hell.
A grievous burden was thy birth to me;
Tetchy and wayward was thy infancy;
Thy school days frightful, desp'rate, wild, and furious;
170   Thy prime of manhood daring, bold, and venturous;
Thy age confirmed, proud, subtle, sly, and bloody,
More mild, but yet more harmful, kind in hatred.
What comfortable hour canst thou name,
That ever graced me in thy company?

RICHARD

Yes, I thank God, my father, and yourself.

DUCHESS

Then patiently listen to my impatience.

RICHARD

Madam, I'm a bit like you in that I can't tolerate a tone of disapproval.

DUCHESS

Oh, let me speak!

RICHARD

Go ahead, but I won't listen.

DUCHESS

I'll be gentle and mild.

RICHARD

And brief, good mother—I'm in a hurry.

DUCHESS

Are you that impatient? God knows I waited for you in anguish, pain, and agony when I gave birth to you.

RICHARD

And didn't I finally arrive to comfort you?

DUCHESS

No, by God, you know perfectly well you arrived on earth to make it my hell. Your birth was incredibly painful; you were a fussy and difficult baby; as a schoolboy, you were frightening, wild, furious, and caused me despair; as a young man, you were daring, bold, and enterprising, and in your maturity, you have been haughty, bloody, and treacherous—both more mild and more harmful than before. So, what hour of comfort have I ever had in your company? Name one.

RICHARD
175 Faith, none but Humfrey Hower, that called your Grace
To breakfast once, forth of my company.
If I be so disgracious in your eye,
Let me march on and not offend you, madam.—
Strike up the drum.

DUCHESS
                                   I prithee, hear me speak.

RICHARD
180 You speak too bitterly.

DUCHESS
                                   Hear me a word,
For I shall never speak to thee again.

RICHARD
So.

DUCHESS
Either thou wilt die by God's just ordinance
Ere from this war thou turn a conqueror,
185 Or I with grief and extreme age shall perish
And nevermore behold thy face again.
Therefore take with thee my most grievous curse,
Which in the day of battle tire thee more
Than all the complete armor that thou wear'st.
190 My prayers on the adverse party fight,
And there the little souls of Edward's children
Whisper the spirits of thine enemies
And promise them success and victory.
Bloody thou art; bloody will be thy end.
195 Shame serves thy life and doth thy death attend.

RICAHRD

> *Humphrey Hour is an obscure reference, though Shakespeare is probably playing off the expression, "to dine with Duke Humphrey," which meant, "to go hungry." Richard is saying, in effect, "The only comfort you ever had was an hour you had without me, at breakfast time when you were hungry."*

I guess none except Humphrey Hour, who once invited you to have breakfast without me. If I be such a disgrace in your eyes, let me march on and not offend you. Strike up the band!

DUCHESS

Please, listen to me.

RICHARD

You're too bitter.

DUCHESS

Just listen this once. I'll never speak to you again.

RICHARD

So be it.

DUCHESS

Either you will die as you should, before you've had a chance to win this battle, or *I* will die from grief and age and never look upon your face again. So, take with you my heaviest curse, which I hope wears you out in battle even more than your heavy suit of armor will. I pray that the little souls of Edward's children will whisper to your enemies and promise them success and victory. You are violent, and your end will be violent. Your life was shameful, and let your death be, too.

Exit

QUEEN ELIZABETH
> Though far more cause, yet much less spirit to curse
> Abides in me. I say amen to her.

RICHARD
> Stay, madam. I must talk a word with you.

QUEEN ELIZABETH
> I have no more sons of the royal blood
> For thee to slaughter. For my daughters, Richard,
> They shall be praying nuns, not weeping queens,
> And therefore level not to hit their lives.

RICHARD
> You have a daughter called Elizabeth,
> Virtuous and fair, royal and gracious.

QUEEN ELIZABETH
> And must she die for this? O, let her live,
> And I'll corrupt her manners, stain her beauty,
> Slander myself as false to Edward's bed,
> Throw over her the veil of infamy.
> So she may live unscarred of bleeding slaughter,
> I will confess she was not Edward's daughter.

RICHARD
> Wrong not her birth. She is a royal princess.

QUEEN ELIZABETH
> To save her life, I'll say she is not so.

RICHARD
> Her life is safest only in her birth.

QUEEN ELIZABETH
> And only in that safety died her brothers.

RICHARD
> Lo, at their births good stars were opposite.

QUEEN ELIZABETH
> No, to their lives ill friends were contrary.

RICHARD
> All unavoided is the doom of destiny.

200
205
210
215

She exits.

QUEEN ELIZABETH

> Though I have far more reason, I don't have as much energy to curse you. But I say amen to everything she said.

RICHARD

> Wait, madam. I need to speak a word with you.

QUEEN ELIZABETH

> I have no more royal sons for you to murder. As for my daughters, Richard, they will become praying nuns, not weeping queens. So don't aim at them.

RICHARD

> You have a daughter named Elizabeth, who is virtuous and beautiful, aristocratic and full of grace.

QUEEN ELIZABETH

> And does she have to die for this? Oh, let her live, and I'll ruin her manners and her beauty. So that she may live, I'll say I cheated on Edward and that she is not really his child.

RICHARD

> Don't wrong her birth. She has royal blood.

QUEEN ELIZABETH

> To save her life, I'll say she doesn't.

RICHARD

> Her life is only safe if she's really of royal blood.

QUEEN ELIZABETH

> Yes, as safe as her brothers' lives were.

RICHARD

> They were born under unlucky stars.

QUEEN ELIZABETH

> The stars weren't the problem. Bad friends were.

RICHARD

> You can't escape a bad destiny.

QUEEN ELIZABETH
True, when avoided grace makes destiny.
My babes were destined to a fairer death
220   If grace had blessed thee with a fairer life.

RICHARD
You speak as if that I had slain my cousins.

QUEEN ELIZABETH
Cousins, indeed, and by their uncle cozened
Of comfort, kingdom, kindred, freedom, life.
Whose hand soever launched their tender hearts,
225   Thy head, all indirectly, gave direction.
No doubt the murd'rous knife was dull and blunt
Till it was whetted on thy stone-hard heart,
To revel in the entrails of my lambs.
But that still use of grief makes wild grief tame,
230   My tongue should to thy ears not name my boys
Till that my nails were anchored in thine eyes,
And I, in such a desp'rate bay of death,
Like a poor bark of sails and tackling reft,
Rush all to pieces on thy rocky bosom.

RICHARD
235   Madam, so thrive I in my enterprise
And dangerous success of bloody wars
As I intend more good to you and yours
Than ever you or yours were by me harmed!

QUEEN ELIZABETH
What good is covered with the face of heaven,
240   To be discovered, that can do me good?

RICHARD
The advancement of your children, gentle lady.

QUEEN ELIZABETH
Up to some scaffold, there to lose their heads.

RICHARD
Unto the dignity and height of fortune,
The high imperial type of this earth's glory.

QUEEN ELIZABETH

True, when a king who defies God is choosing that destiny. My children would have enjoyed a better death if God had blessed you with a purer life.

RICHARD

You speak as if *I* had killed my nephews.

QUEEN ELIZABETH

Nephews, indeed, cheated by their uncle of comfort, kingdom, relatives, freedom, and life. Whichever hand literally stabbed their tender hearts, you're the one who gave the order. No doubt the murderous knife was blunt till it was sharpened on your stony heart—you reveled in my lambs' bloody guts. But constant expression of wild grief will only make it tame, so I'm not going to say any more about my boys until I've gouged your eyes out with my bare hands. Like a sailboat that has lost its sails, I will throw myself on your rocky bosom—and get torn to pieces.

RICHARD

Madam, if I do as well as I think I'm going to do in these dangerous, violent wars, you and your relatives will have more good at my hands than you've ever had bad!

QUEEN ELIZABETH

What good does heaven have in store that can do me any good now?

RICHARD

The advancement of your children, noble lady.

QUEEN ELIZABETH

Advancement to some scaffold, to lose their heads.

RICHARD

No, advancement to the dignity and height of honor, to a high, imperial kind of glory.

QUEEN ELIZABETH

245   Flatter my sorrow with report of it.
   Tell me what state, what dignity, what honor,
   Canst thou demise to any child of mine?

RICHARD

   Even all I have— ay, and myself and all—
   Will I withal endow a child of thine;
250   So in the Lethe of thy angry soul
   Thou drown the sad remembrance of those wrongs
   Which thou supposest I have done to thee.

QUEEN ELIZABETH

   Be brief, lest that the process of thy kindness
   Last longer telling than thy kindness' date.

RICHARD

255   Then know that from my soul I love thy daughter.

QUEEN ELIZABETH

   My daughter's mother thinks it with her soul.

RICHARD

   What do you think?

QUEEN ELIZABETH

   That thou dost love my daughter from thy soul.
   So from thy soul's love didst thou love her brothers,
260   And from my heart's love I do thank thee for it.

RICHARD

   Be not so hasty to confound my meaning.
   I mean that with my soul I love thy daughter
   And do intend to make her Queen of England.

QUEEN ELIZABETH

   Well then, who dost thou mean shall be her king?

RICHARD

265   Even he that makes her queen. Who else should be?

QUEEN ELIZABETH

   What, thou?

RICHARD

   Even so. How think you of it?

QUEEN ELIZABETH

Flatter me in my mourning: tell me what dignity or honor you could possible bring to any child of mine?

RICHARD

The dignity of everything I own. In fact, I will give a child of yours everything plus myself, provided you forget the wrongs you imagine I have done to you.

QUEEN ELIZABETH

Well, explain—but do it fast so that your puny store of kindness isn't used up by talking about it.

RICHARD

Then know that from my soul I love your daughter.

QUEEN ELIZABETH

I believe it.

RICHARD

What do you believe?

QUEEN ELIZABETH

That you love my daughter to spite your soul. That's the way you loved my brothers. And that's the way I thank you for it.

RICHARD

Don't be so quick to twist my meaning. I mean that I love your daughter *with* all my soul. I intend to make her queen of England.

QUEEN ELIZABETH

Tell me, who will be the king?

RICHARD

The one who makes her queen, of course. Who else should it be?

QUEEN ELIZABETH

What, you?

RICHARD

Yes, exactly. Me. What do you think, madam?

QUEEN ELIZABETH
How canst thou woo her?

RICHARD
                              That would I learn of you,
As one being best acquainted with her humor.

QUEEN ELIZABETH
270   And wilt thou learn of me?

RICHARD
Madam, with all my heart.

QUEEN ELIZABETH
Send to her, by the man that slew her brothers,
A pair of bleeding hearts; thereon engrave
"Edward" and "York." Then haply she will weep.
275   Therefore present to her—as sometime Margaret
Did to thy father, steeped in Rutland's blood—
A handkerchief, which say to her did drain
The purple sap from her sweet brother's body,
And bid her wipe her weeping eyes withal.
280   If this inducement move her not to love,
Send her a letter of thy noble deeds;
Tell her thou mad'st away her uncle Clarence,
Her uncle Rivers, ay, and for her sake
Mad'st quick conveyance with her good aunt Anne.

RICHARD
285   You mock me, madam. This is not the way
To win your daughter.

QUEEN ELIZABETH
                              There is no other way,
Unless thou couldst put on some other shape
And not be Richard, that hath done all this.

RICHARD
Say that I did all this for love of her.

QUEEN ELIZABETH
290   Nay, then indeed she cannot choose but hate thee,
Having bought love with such a bloody spoil.

QUEEN ELIZABETH

How would you woo her?

RICHARD

That's what I want to find out from you, who knows her best.

QUEEN ELIZABETH

And *will* you learn from me?

RICHARD

Madam, with all my heart.

QUEEN ELIZABETH

Okay, then. Do this: send her a pair of bleeding hearts. Make clear they come from the man who killed her brothers. Write "Edward" and "York" on them. That will get her to weep. Then present her with a handkerchief, like the one Margaret gave your father, which was steeped in his son Rutland's blood. Tell her this handkerchief sopped up the blood of her sweet brother's body and urge her to dry her weeping eyes with it. If this encouragement doesn't move her to love you, send her a description of your other noble deeds. Tell her how you secretly dispensed with her uncle Clarence, her uncle Rivers, and, for her sake, her good aunt Anne.

RICHARD

Come, come, you're making fun of me. This is not the way to win your daughter.

QUEEN ELIZABETH

There isn't any other way, unless you took on another form and became someone else.

RICHARD

But suppose I did all the things you named out of love for her.

QUEEN ELIZABETH

Then she has no choice but to hate you, as you purchased her love with murder.

RICHARD
        Look what is done cannot be now amended.
        Men shall deal unadvisedly sometimes,
        Which after-hours give leisure to repent.
295   If I did take the kingdom from your sons,
        To make amends I'll give it to your daughter.
        If I have killed the issue of your womb,
        To quicken your increase I will beget
        Mine issue of your blood upon your daughter.
300   A grandam's name is little less in love
        Than is the doting title of a mother.
        They are as children but one step below,
        Even of your metal, of your very blood,
        Of all one pain, save for a night of groans
305   Endured of her for whom you bid like sorrow.
        Your children were vexation to your youth,
        But mine shall be a comfort to your age.
        The loss you have is but a son being king,
        And by that loss your daughter is made queen.
310   I cannot make you what amends I would;
        Therefore accept such kindness as I can.
        Dorset your son, that with a fearful soul
        Leads discontented steps in foreign soil,
        This fair alliance quickly shall call home
315   To high promotions and great dignity.
        The king that calls your beauteous daughter wife
        Familiarly shall call thy Dorset brother.
        Again shall you be mother to a king,
        And all the ruins of distressful times
320   Repaired with double riches of content.
        What, we have many goodly days to see!
        The liquid drops of tears that you have shed
        Shall come again, transformed to orient pearl,
        Advantaging their love with interest
325   Of ten times double gain of happiness.
        Go then, my mother; to thy daughter go.

RICHARD

Whatever has already been done can't be undone now. Men act imprudently sometimes, then realize their mistakes when they have time to think about them. If I took the kingdom from your sons, I'll give it to your daughter to make up for it. If I have killed your children, I will have children with your daughter. A grandmother is loved hardly less than a mother is. Your grandchildren will be just one step removed from your own children—they share your character, your blood, and require the same effort minus that one night of labor, like that which you suffered through for your own daughter. Your children caused you trouble in your youth, but mine will bring you comfort in your old age. The only loss you've had is that your son was not king. Because of that loss, your daughter will be queen. I can't make up for everything that I'd like to, so accept such kindness as I can offer. Your son Dorset, who fled in fear to join an army in France against me, could come home to high promotions and great dignity. The king who calls your beautiful daughter "wife" will call Dorset "brother." And you will be the mother to a king again, with all the miseries of unhappy times not just repaired, but also improved. Indeed, we have many good days to look forward to! The tears you have shed will be transformed into pearls. Your happiness will be like a loan that has grown through interest to ten times its original size. Go, then, mother, to your daughter.

Make bold her bashful years with your experience;
Prepare her ears to hear a wooer's tale;
Put in her tender heart th' aspiring flame
330   Of golden sovereignty; acquaint the Princess
With the sweet silent hours of marriage joys;
And when this arm of mine hath chastisèd
The petty rebel, dull-brained Buckingham,
Bound with triumphant garlands will I come
335   And lead thy daughter to a conqueror's bed,
To whom I will retail my conquest won,
And she shall be sole victoress, Caesar's Caesar.

QUEEN ELIZABETH
What were I best to say? Her father's brother
Would be her lord? Or shall I say her uncle?
340   Or he that slew her brothers and her uncles?
Under what title shall I woo for thee,
That God, the law, my honor and her love
Can make seem pleasing to her tender years?

RICHARD
Infer fair England's peace by this alliance.

QUEEN ELIZABETH
345   Which she shall purchase with still-lasting war.

RICHARD
Tell her the king, that may command, entreats—

QUEEN ELIZABETH
That, at her hands, which the king's King forbids.

RICHARD
Say she shall be a high and mighty queen.

QUEEN ELIZABETH
To vail the title, as her mother doth.

RICHARD
350   Say I will love her everlastingly.

Give her the benefit of your experience, and prepare her to hear me court her. Make her aspire to be queen. Tell the princess about the sweet, silent hours of joy there are in marriage. And when my army has chastised the petty rebel, that stupid Buckingham, I will return wreathed in victory crowns and lead your daughter to a conqueror's bed. She will be the only victor over my triumphs. She will be the ruler of a Caesar.

QUEEN ELIZABETH

What should I say to her? That her father's brother wants to be her husband? Or should I say it's her uncle? Or should I describe you as the one who killed her brothers and her uncles? How can I describe you that will make you appeal to the young woman and will also agree with God, the law, my honor, and her feelings?

RICHARD

Claim fair England's peace depends on this alliance.

QUEEN ELIZABETH

She will purchase that peace with an everlasting war.

RICHARD

Tell her that the king, who has the power to command people, asks her.

QUEEN ELIZABETH

He asks her to do what God forbids.

The Church forbid marriage between uncle and niece.

RICHARD

Say she will be a high and mighty queen.

QUEEN ELIZABETH

Only to watch that title become worthless, as her mother has.

RICHARD

Say I will love her everlastingly.

QUEEN ELIZABETH
But how long shall that title "ever" last?

RICHARD
Sweetly in force unto her fair life's end.

QUEEN ELIZABETH
But how long fairly shall her sweet life last?

RICHARD
As long as heaven and nature lengthens it.

QUEEN ELIZABETH
355   As long as hell and Richard likes of it.

RICHARD
Say I, her sovereign, am her subject low.

QUEEN ELIZABETH
But she, your subject, loathes such sovereignty.

RICHARD
Be eloquent in my behalf to her.

QUEEN ELIZABETH
An honest tale speeds best being plainly told.

RICHARD
360   Then plainly to her tell my loving tale.

QUEEN ELIZABETH
Plain and not honest is too harsh a style.

RICHARD
Your reasons are too shallow and too quick.

QUEEN ELIZABETH
O no, my reasons are too deep and dead—
Too deep and dead, poor infants, in their graves.

RICHARD
365   Harp not on that string, madam; that is past.

QUEEN ELIZABETH
Harp on it still shall I till heart-strings break.

RICHARD
Now by my George, my Garter, and my crown—

QUEEN ELIZABETH
Profaned, dishonored, and the third usurped.

QUEEN ELIZABETH
But how long will "ever" last?

RICHARD
Until her beautiful life's end.

QUEEN ELIZABETH
But how long will her beautiful life last?

RICHARD
As long as heaven and nature extend it.

QUEEN ELIZABETH
As long as hell and Richard want it.

RICHARD
Tell her that I, her king, am her lowly subject.

QUEEN ELIZABETH
But she, your subject, hates such a king.

RICHARD
Be eloquent on my behalf.

QUEEN ELIZABETH
An honest tale succeeds best when it is told simply.

RICHARD
Then tell her my loving story in simple terms.

QUEEN ELIZABETH
You can't tell a story simply when it's a lie.

RICHARD
Your answers are too shallow and too hasty.

QUEEN ELIZABETH
Oh no, my reasons are deep and as permanent as death.
They're buried as deep as my poor infants in their grave.

RICHARD
Don't harp on that point, madam—it's past.

QUEEN ELIZABETH
I will harp on it till my heartstrings break.

RICHARD
Now, by St. George, my knighthood, and my crown—

QUEEN ELIZABETH
The first you profaned, the second you dishonored,
and the third you stole.

RICHARD
　　I swear—

QUEEN ELIZABETH
　　　　By nothing, for this is no oath.
370　Thy George, profaned, hath lost his lordly honor;
　　Thy garter, blemished, pawned his knightly virtue;
　　Thy crown, usurped, disgraced his kingly glory.
　　If something thou wouldst swear to be believed,
　　Swear then by something that thou hast not wronged.

RICHARD
375　Then, by myself—

QUEEN ELIZABETH
　　　　　　Thyself is self-misused.

RICHARD
　　Now, by the world—

QUEEN ELIZABETH
　　　　　　'Tis full of thy foul wrongs.

RICHARD
　　My father's death—

QUEEN ELIZABETH
　　　　　　Thy life hath it dishonored.

RICHARD
　　Why then, by God.

QUEEN ELIZABETH
　　　　　　God's wrong is most of all.
　　If thou didst fear to break an oath by Him,
380　The unity the king my husband made
　　Thou hadst not broken, nor my brothers died.
　　If thou hadst feared to break an oath by Him,
　　Th' imperial metal circling now thy head
　　Had graced the tender temples of my child,
385　And both the princes had been breathing here,
　　Which now, two tender bedfellows for dust,
　　Thy broken faith hath made the prey for worms.
　　What canst thou swear by now?

RICHARD

I swear—

QUEEN ELIZABETH

By nothing, because this is no oath. St. George loses his holiness once *you* have sworn by him; you've ruined the emblem of the knighthood, and the crown lost its kingly glory once you stole it. If you want me to believe something you'll swear to, then swear by something you haven't wronged.

RICHARD

Then, by myself—

QUEEN ELIZABETH

You've misused yourself.

RICHARD

Now, by the world—

QUEEN ELIZABETH

It's full of your ugly wrongdoings.

RICHARD

By my father's death—

QUEEN ELIZABETH

Your life has dishonored his death.

RICHARD

Why then, by God—

QUEEN ELIZABETH

You wrong God most of all. If you had been afraid to break an oath with him, you wouldn't have ruined the united front the king, my husband, created before he died, and you wouldn't have killed my brothers. If you had been afraid to break an oath with him, the crown you are currently wearing would have graced the head of my child, and both princes would still be alive, not preyed on by worms. What can you swear by now?

RICHARD

                              The time to come.

QUEEN ELIZABETH

    That thou hast wrongèd in the time o'erpast;

390   For I myself have many tears to wash

    Hereafter time, for time past wronged by thee.

    The children live whose fathers thou hast slaughtered,

    Ungoverned youth, to wail it in their age;

    The parents live whose children thou hast butchered,

395   Old barren plants, to wail it with their age.

    Swear not by time to come, for that thou hast

    Misused ere used, by times ill-used o'erpast.

RICHARD

    As I intend to prosper and repent,

    So thrive I in my dangerous affairs

400   Of hostile arms! Myself myself confound,

    Heaven and fortune bar me happy hours,

    Day, yield me not thy light, nor night thy rest,

    Be opposite all planets of good luck

    To my proceedings if, with dear heart's love,

405   Immaculate devotion, holy thoughts,

    I tender not thy beauteous princely daughter.

    In her consists my happiness and thine.

    Without her follows to myself and thee,

    Herself, the land, and many a Christian soul,

410   Death, desolation, ruin and decay.

    It cannot be avoided but by this;

    It will not be avoided but by this.

    Therefore, dear mother—I must call you so—

    Be the attorney of my love to her:

415   Plead what I will be, not what I have been;

    Not my deserts, but what I will deserve.

    Urge the necessity and state of times,

    And be not peevish found in great designs.

RICHARD

By the future.

QUEEN ELIZABETH

You've already wronged that by what you did in the past. I myself have many tears to cry in the time to come, because of what you've done. There are children living whose fathers you have slaughtered. When they are grown, they will wail about a childhood in which no one watched out for them. There are parents living whose children you have butchered; they are now old withered plants who will moan over their losses as they grow old. Don't swear by the future, because you've ruined it before it has even arrived.

RICHARD

May I only do well in these dangerous battles if my intention to repent and prosper is sincere! Let me destroy myself, let heaven and destiny deprive me of happy hours, let day remain dark and night sleepless, and let me have nothing but terrible luck if I do not love with a pure heart, clean devotion, and holy thoughts your beautiful royal daughter. My happiness and yours lie in her. If I do not win her, death, desolation, and decay will descend on this land and on me, you, herself, and many a Christian soul. Ruin cannot be avoided unless I marry her. It *will not* be avoided unless I marry her. Therefore, good mother—I must call you that—advocate for me. Plead with your daughter about what I will be, not what I have been. Don't talk about my just desserts but about what I *will* deserve. Tell her how necessary this marriage is at this time, and don't be small-minded about such important plans.

QUEEN ELIZABETH
Shall I be tempted of the devil thus?

RICHARD
420   Ay, if the devil tempt you to do good.

QUEEN ELIZABETH
Shall I forget myself to be myself?

RICHARD
Ay, if your self's remembrance wrong yourself.

QUEEN ELIZABETH
Yet thou didst kill my children.

RICHARD
But in your daughter's womb I bury them,
425   Where, in that nest of spicery, they will breed
Selves of themselves, to your recomforture.

QUEEN ELIZABETH
Shall I go win my daughter to thy will?

RICHARD
And be a happy mother by the deed.

QUEEN ELIZABETH
I go. Write to me very shortly,
430   And you shall understand from me her mind.

RICHARD
Bear her my true love's kiss; and so, farewell.

Exit QUEEN ELIZABETH
Relenting fool and shallow, changing woman!

Enter RATCLIFFE, *with* CATESBY *behind*

How now, what news?

QUEEN ELIZABETH
>Shall I be tempted by the devil?

RICHARD
>Yes, if the devil tempts you to do good.

QUEEN ELIZABETH
>Shall I forget the wrongs you've done to me so that I can be the mother of a king again?

RICHARD
>Yes, if your memories do you no good.

QUEEN ELIZABETH
>Yet you killed my children.

RICHARD
>But in your daughter's womb I will bury them. In that rich nest they shall grow again, to console you.

QUEEN ELIZABETH
>Should I go convince my daughter to marry you?

RICHARD
>And be a happy mother by doing so.

QUEEN ELIZABETH
>I'm going. Write to me very soon and I'll let you know what she thinks.

RICHARD
>Give her a kiss from me, her true love. And so, goodbye.

>*QUEEN ELIZABETH exits.*
>Weak-willed fool! Shallow, fickle woman!

>*RATCLIFFE enters, with CATESBY following.*

>Hello! What's the news?

RATCLIFFE
>   Most mighty sovereign, on the western coast
> 435   Rideth a puissant navy. To our shores
>   Throng many doubtful hollow-hearted friends,
>   Unarmed and unresolved to beat them back.
>   'Tis thought that Richmond is their admiral;
>   And there they hull, expecting but the aid
> 440   Of Buckingham to welcome them ashore.

RICHARD
>   Some light-foot friend post to the duke of Norfolk—
>   Ratcliffe, thyself, or Catesby. Where is he?

CATESBY
>   Here, my good lord.

RICHARD
>   Catesby, fly to the duke.

CATESBY
> 445   I will, my lord, with all convenient haste.

RICHARD
>   Ratcliffe, come hither. Post to Salisbury.
>   When thou com'st thither
>   — *(to* CATESBY*)* Dull, unmindful villain,
>   Why stay'st thou here and go'st not to the duke?

CATESBY
> 450   First, mighty liege, tell me your Highness' pleasure,
>   What from your Grace I shall deliver to him.

RICHARD
>   O true, good Catesby. Bid him levy straight
>   The greatest strength and power that he can make
>   And meet me suddenly at Salisbury.

CATESBY
> 455   I go.

Exit

RATCLIFFE

My noble king, a powerful fleet of ships sails on the western coast. Many former friends of ours have gathered to meet the fleet and aren't willing to beat it back. Word is that Richmond is the navy's admiral. The ships are drifting off the coast, sails unfurled, only waiting for Buckingham to help them come ashore.

RICHARD

Norfolk was a York loyalist—he stood behind Edward IV and Richard III, and he died fighting for Richard.

Someone who can ride fast, go to the duke of Norfolk. You go, Ratcliffe, or Catesby. Where is Catesby?

CATESBY

Here, my good lord.

RICHARD

Catesby, fly to the duke.

CATESBY

I will my lord, as fast as I can.

RICHARD

Ratcliffe, come here. Ride to Salisbury. When you get there—*(to* CATESBY*)* Stupid, distracted rascal, why are you still standing there? Why haven't you left for the duke's?

CATESBY

First, mighty king, tell me what you want me to tell him.

RICHARD

Oh, right, good Catesby. Tell him to gather together the greatest army he can muster in a hurry and meet me right away at Salisbury.

CATESBY

I'm off.

He exits.

RATCLIFFE
What, may it please you, shall I do at Salisbury?

RICHARD
Why, what wouldst thou do there before I go?

RATCLIFFE
Your Highness told me I should post before.

RICHARD
My mind is changed.

Enter STANLEY

Stanley, what news with you?

STANLEY
460   None good, my liege, to please you with the hearing,
Nor none so bad but well may be reported.

RICHARD
Hoyday, a riddle! Neither good nor bad.
What need'st thou run so many mile about
When thou mayst tell thy tale the nearest way?
465   Once more, what news?

STANLEY
Richmond is on the seas.

RICHARD
There let him sink, and be the seas on him!
White-livered runagate, what doth he there?

STANLEY
I know not, mighty sovereign, but by guess.

RICHARD
Well, as you guess?

STANLEY
470   Stirred up by Dorset, Buckingham, and Morton,
He makes for England, here to claim the crown.

RATCLIFFE

What would you like me to do at Salisbury?

RICHARD

Why, what is there to do before I get there?

RATCLIFFE

Your Highness just told me that I should ride there before you.

RICHARD

I changed my mind.

STANLEY *enters.*

Stanley, what news do you have?

STANLEY

Nothing that you want to hear, my lord, but nothing so bad that I can't mention it.

RICHARD

Well, how nice, a riddle! Neither good nor bad. Why do you go around in circles when you could get to the point? Once again, what's the news?

STANLEY

Richmond is sailing on the sea.

RICHARD

Let him sink there so the sea will cover him! Lily-livered coward, what's he doing there?

STANLEY

I don't know, mighty king. I can only guess.

RICHARD

Well, what do you guess?

STANLEY

That, stirred up by Dorset, Buckingham, and Morton, he's coming to England to claim the crown.

RICHARD
Is the chair empty? Is the sword unswayed?
Is the king dead, the empire unpossessed?
What heir of York is there alive but we?
475 And who is England's king but great York's heir?
Then tell me, what makes he upon the seas?

STANLEY
Unless for that, my liege, I cannot guess.

RICHARD
Unless for that he comes to be your liege,
You cannot guess wherefore the Welshman comes.
480 Thou wilt revolt and fly to him, I fear.

STANLEY
No, my good lord. Therefore mistrust me not.

RICHARD
Where is thy power, then, to beat him back?
Where be thy tenants and thy followers?
Are they not now upon the western shore,
485 Safe-conducting the rebels from their ships?

STANLEY
No, my good lord. My friends are in the north.

RICHARD
Cold friends to me. What do they in the north
When they should serve their sovereign in the west?

STANLEY
They have not been commanded, mighty king.
490 Pleaseth your Majesty to give me leave,
I'll muster up my friends and meet your Grace
Where and what time your Majesty shall please.

RICHARD
Ay, thou wouldst be gone to join with Richmond,
But I'll not trust thee.

suspision

RICHARD

Is the throne empty? Is the army without a leader? Is the king dead, the empire dispossessed? What heir of the York family is there alive other than myself? And who is England's king but an heir of the great York? Therefore, tell me, what is he doing at sea?

STANLEY

Unless it's what I said, your Majesty, I have no idea.

RICHARD

Unless he's coming to be your leader you can't guess why the Welshman's coming? You plan to revolt and join him, I'm afraid.

Richmond was a descendent of the Welshman Owen Tudor.

STANLEY

No, mighty king, do not distrust me.

RICHARD

Where is your army, then, to beat him back? Where are your tenants and your followers? Aren't they at this very moment on the western shore helping the rebels land safely from their ships?

STANLEY

No, my good lord, my friends are in the north.

RICHARD

Then they're cold friends to me. What are they doing in the north when they should be in the west serving their king?

STANLEY

They haven't been commanded to go to the west, mighty king. If your Majesty would like, I'll muster up my friends and meet you wherever and whenever you like.

RICHARD

Yes, you want to go join Richmond. But I'm not going to trust you.

STANLEY

                              Most mighty sovereign,
495   You have no cause to hold my friendship doubtful.
         I never was nor never will be false.

RICHARD

         Go then and muster men, but leave behind
         Your son George Stanley. Look your heart be firm.
         Or else his head's assurance is but frail.

STANLEY

500   So deal with him as I prove true to you.

                                              Exit

Enter a MESSENGER

MESSENGER

         My gracious sovereign, now in Devonshire,
         As I by friends am well advisèd,
         Sir Edward Courtney and the haughty prelate,
         Bishop of Exeter, his elder brother,
505   With many more confederates are in arms.

Enter SECOND MESSENGER

SECOND MESSENGER

         In Kent, my liege, the Guilfords are in arms,
         And every hour more competitors
         Flock to the rebels, and their power grows strong.

Enter THIRD MESSENGER

THIRD MESSENGER

         My lord, the army of great Buckingham—

RICHARD

510   Out on you, owls! Nothing but songs of death.
         He striketh him
         There, take thou that till thou bring better news.

STANLEY

Most mighty sovereign, you have no reason to doubt my friendship. I was never disloyal, and I never will be.

RICHARD

Then go gather your men, but leave behind your son, George Stanley. Make sure your faith is firm, or he has little chance of keeping his head.

STANLEY

Treat him as my loyalty toward you calls for.

He exits.

A MESSENGER *enters.*

MESSENGER

My noble king, my friends have informed me that Sir Edward Courtney and his brother, the haughty Bishop of Exeter, are now in Devonshire, where they have assembled an army.

Devonshire: a county in south-west England

A SECOND MESSENGER *enters.*

SECOND MESSENGER

My king, the Guildfords in Kent have armed themselves, and every hour new associates flock to their aid, and their army increases.

Kent: a county southeast of London

A THIRD MESSENGER *enters.*

THIRD MESSENGER

My lord, the duke of Buckingham's army—

RICHARD

Enough, you owls! Do you have nothing but songs of death? *(he strikes the* THIRD MESSENGER*)* Take that until you bring me better news.

The cry of the owl was thought to be a death omen.

THIRD MESSENGER
> The news I have to tell your Majesty
> Is that by sudden floods and fall of waters
> Buckingham's army is dispersed and scattered,
515 > And he himself wandered away alone,
> No man knows whither.

RICHARD
>   I cry thee mercy.
> There is my purse to cure that blow of thine.
> *He gives money*
> Hath any well-advisèd friend proclaimed
> Reward to him that brings the traitor in?

THIRD MESSENGER
520 > Such proclamation hath been made, my lord.

Enter FOURTH MESSENGER

FOURTH MESSENGER
> Sir Thomas Lovell and Lord Marquess Dorset,
> 'Tis said, my liege, in Yorkshire are in arms.
> But this good comfort bring I to your Highness:
> The Breton navy is dispersed by tempest.
525 > Richmond, in Dorsetshire, sent out a boat
> Unto the shore to ask those on the banks
> If they were his assistants, yea or no—
> Who answered him they came from Buckingham
> Upon his party. He, mistrusting them,
530 > Hoisted sail and made his course for Brittany.

RICHARD
> March on, march on, since we are up in arms,
> If not to fight with foreign enemies,
> Yet to beat down these rebels here at home.

Enter CATESBY

THIRD MESSENGER

The news I have to tell your majesty is that Buckingham's army has dispersed from sudden floods and heavy rainfall. Buckingham himself has wandered away alone to who knows where.

RICHARD

I beg your pardon. Here's some money to make up for that blow I gave you. *(he gives money)* Has any intelligent friend of ours offered a reward to whoever catches the traitor?

THIRD MESSENGER

Yes, your Highness.

A **FOURTH MESSENGER** *enters.*

FOURTH MESSENGER

It's been reported that Sir Thomas Lovell and Lord Marquess Dorset have assembled an army in Yorkshire, my lord. But I bring your Grace this comfort: a storm has dispersed the navy from Brittany. And Richmond, who is in Dorsetshire, sent a boat to shore to ask the men on the banks if they were on his side, yes or no. They said they were with Buckingham. Richmond didn't trust them. He hoisted sail again and sailed back to Brittany.

Yorkshire: a town in northern England

Dorsetshire: a county on England's south coast

RICHARD

Let's keep marching since we're prepared to fight. Even if we don't fight foreign enemies, we'll beat down these rebels at home.

CATESBY *returns.*

CATESBY

My liege, the duke of Buckingham is taken.
535   That is the best news. That the earl of Richmond
Is with a mighty power landed at Milford,
Is colder tidings, yet they must be told.

RICHARD

Away towards Salisbury! While we reason here,
A royal battle might be won and lost.
540   Someone take order Buckingham be brought
To Salisbury. The rest march on with me.

Flourish. Exeunt

CATESBY

Your Majesty, the duke of Buckingham has been captured—that's the best news. The fact that the earl of Richmond has landed in Milford with a mighty army is less good news, but it must be told.

Milford Haven is on the coast of Wales.

RICHARD

Away toward Salisbury! While we're talking here, a royal battle could be won and lost. Someone deliver the order that Buckingham be brought to Salisbury. Everyone else, march on with me.

A trumpet plays.

They all exit.

ACT 4, SCENE 5

Enter STANLEY *and Sir* CHRISTOPHER.

STANLEY
Sir Christopher, tell Richmond this from me:
That in the sty of the most deadly boar
My son George Stanley is franked up in hold;
If I revolt, off goes young George's head;
5   The fear of that holds off my present aid.
So get three gone. Commend me to thy lord.
Withal, say that the queen hath heartily consented
He should espouse Elizabeth her daughter.
But, tell me, where is princely Richmond now?

CHRISTOPHER
10   At Pembroke, or at Ha'rfordwest in Wales.

STANLEY
What men of name resort to him?

CHRISTOPHER
Sir Walter Herbert, a renownèd soldier;
Sir Gilbert Talbot, Sir William Stanley,
Oxford, redoubted Pembroke, Sir James Blunt,
15   And Rice ap Thomas, with a valiant crew,
And many other of great name and worth;
And towards London they do bend their power,
If by the way they be not fought withal.

STANLEY
(gives him a paper) Well, hie thee to thy lord. I kiss
20   his hand. My letter will resolve him of my mind.
Farewell.

Exeunt

ACT 4, SCENE 5

STANLEY *and Sir* CHRISTOPHER *enter.*

STANLEY

Sir Christopher, relay this message to Richmond: My son George Stanley is penned up in the bloody boar's sty. If I revolt, off goes young George's head. My fear of that prevents me from helping Richmond at this time. But, tell me, where is the noble Richmond now?

CHRISTOPHER

At Pembroke, or at Harfordwest in Wales.

STANLEY

Which noblemen have joined him?

CHRISTOPHER

Sir Walter Herbert, a renowned soldier; Sir Gilbert Talbot; Sir William Stanley; Oxford; the highly feared Pembroke; Sir James Blunt; Rice ap Thomas, with a valiant crew; and many other famous and powerful noblemen. They plan to head straight to London, assuming they don't encounter any resistance on the way.

STANLEY

(giving him a paper) Return to your lord. Give him my best regards. Tell him the queen has given her heart-felt consent to his marriage to her daughter, Elizabeth. And these letters will let him know what my thinking is. Goodbye, and take care.

They exit.

ACT FIVE

SCENE 1

Enter BUCKINGHAM *with* SHERIFF *and halberds, led to execution*

BUCKINGHAM
Will not King Richard let me speak with him?

SHERIFF
No, my good lord. Therefore be patient.

BUCKINGHAM
Hastings and Edward's children, Grey and Rivers,
Holy King Henry and thy fair son Edward,
5   Vaughan, and all that have miscarrièd
By underhand, corrupted, foul injustice,
If that your moody, discontented souls
Do through the clouds behold this present hour,
Even for revenge mock my destruction.—
10   This is All Souls' Day, fellow, is it not?

SHERIFF
It is.

BUCKINGHAM
Why, then All Souls' Day is my body's doomsday.
This is the day which, in King Edward's time,
I wished might fall on me when I was found
15   False to his children and his wife's allies.
This is the day wherein I wished to fall
By the false faith of him who most I trusted.
This, this All Souls' Day to my fearful soul
Is the determined respite of my wrongs.
20   That high All-seer which I dallied with
Hath turned my feignèd prayer on my head
And given in earnest what I begged in jest.

ACT FIVE

SCENE 1

BUCKINGHAM *enters with* SHERIFF *and guards leading him to his execution.*

BUCKINGHAM

Won't King Richard let me speak with him?

SHERIFF

No, my good lord. So be calm.

BUCKINGHAM

Hastings and Edward's children, Rivers and Grey, holy King Henry and your fine son Edward, Vaughan, and all who have died from underhanded, corrupt, fiendish injustice, if your angry souls are witnessing this moment through the clouds, enjoy the revenge— laugh at my ruin! This is All-Souls' day, fellows, isn't it?

A Catholic day of prayer for souls stuck in between Heaven and Hell

SHERIFF

It is, my lord.

BUCKINGHAM

Why, then, it's my body's doomsday. Today I'm going to get what I said I wished would happen to me if I was ever false to King Edward's children or his wife's allies. This is the day I'm going to get what I wished for when I wished that the person I most trusted would betray me. This, this All-Souls' day, is my just desserts. I tried to play games with God, and he turned my fake prayer on my head, giving me for real what I'd asked for as a joke.

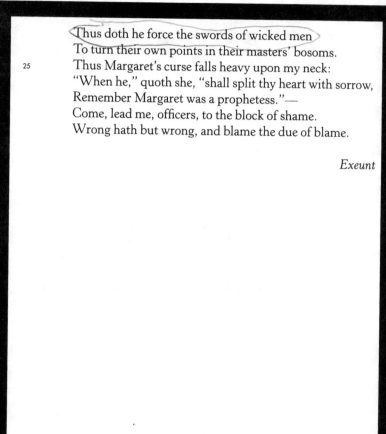

Thus doth he force the swords of wicked men
To turn their own points in their masters' bosoms.
25 Thus Margaret's curse falls heavy upon my neck:
"When he," quoth she, "shall split thy heart with sorrow,
Remember Margaret was a prophetess."—
Come, lead me, officers, to the block of shame.
Wrong hath but wrong, and blame the due of blame.

Exeunt

This is how God forces wicked men to turn their swords against themselves. Margaret's curse has come true. "When Richard has split your heart in two with grief," she said, "you'll know that Margaret was a prophetess." Come, sirs, bring me to this block of shame. I have done wrong, so I will suffer wrong. I have been blamed because I deserved to be.

They all exit.

ACT 5, SCENE 2

Enter RICHMOND, OXFORD, BLUNT, HERBERT, *and others,*
with drum and colors

RICHMOND

Fellows in arms, and my most loving friends,
Bruised underneath the yoke of tyranny,
Have we marched on without impediment,
Thus far into the bowels of the land
5   And here receive we from our father Stanley
Lines of fair comfort and encouragement.
The wretched, bloody, and usurping boar,
That spoiled your summer fields and fruitful vines,
Swills your warm blood like wash, and makes his trough
10   In your embowelled bosoms—this foul swine
Is now even in the center of this isle,
Near to the town of Leicester, as we learn.
From Tamworth thither is but one day's march.
In God's name, cheerly on, courageous friends,
15   To reap the harvest of perpetual peace
By this one bloody trial of sharp war.

OXFORD

Every man's conscience is a thousand men,
To fight against this guilty homicide.

HERBERT

I doubt not but his friends will turn to us.

BLUNT

20   He hath no friends but who are friends for fear.
Which in his dearest need will fly from him.

RICHMOND

All for our vantage. Then, in God's name, march.
True hope is swift, and flies with swallow's wings.
Kings it makes gods, and meaner creatures kings.

Exeunt

ACT 5, SCENE 2

RICHMOND, OXFORD, BLUNT, HERBERT, *and others enter with drummers and flag bearers.*

RICHMOND

Fellow soldiers and my loyal friends suffering under that tyrant Richard, we have marched all the way to the center of England without encountering any opposition. And now we receive encouraging news from my stepfather Stanley: Richard—that violent, greedy boar who roots through your summer fields and ripening vines, guzzles your warm blood, and makes his trough in your disemboweled bellies—is now near the town of Leicester, only one day's march from us here in Tamworth. In God's name, let's continue on in high spirits, my courageous friends. Our aim is to achieve everlasting peace from this one violent war.

Tamworth is in central England.

OXFORD

Every man's conscience is a thousand swords against this murderer.

HERBERT

I suspect his friends will join us.

BLUNT

He has no friends except those who are too afraid to defy him. In his greatest need, even they will desert him.

RICHMOND

All to our advantage. So, in God's name, let's march. Hope with good cause is swift; it flies as fast as a swallow. It turns kings into gods and men of lower rank into kings.

They all exit.

ACT 5, SCENE 3

Enter RICHARD, *in arms, with* NORFOLK, RATCLIFFE,
SURREY, *and soldiers*

RICHARD
Here pitch our tent, even here in Bosworth field.—
My Lord of Surrey, why look you so sad?

SURREY
My heart is ten times lighter than my looks.

RICHARD
My Lord of Norfolk—

NORFOLK
5   Here, most gracious liege.

RICHARD
Norfolk, we must have knocks, ha, must we not?

NORFOLK
We must both give and take, my loving lord.

RICHARD
Up with my tent!—Here will I lie tonight.
But where tomorrow? Well, all's one for that.
10   Who hath descried the number of the traitors?

NORFOLK
Six or seven thousand is their utmost power.

RICHARD
Why, our battalia trebles that account.
Besides, the king's name is a tower of strength
Which they upon the adverse party want.
15   Up with the tent!—Come, noble gentlemen,
Let us survey the vantage of the ground.
Call for some men of sound direction.
Let's lack no discipline, make no delay,
For, lords, tomorrow is a busy day.

Exeunt

ACT 5, SCENE 3

RICHARD, *dressed in his armor, enters with* NORFOLK, SURREY, *and others.*

RICHARD

Let's pitch our tents right here in Bosworth Field. My Lord of Surrey, why do you look so sad?

SURREY

My heart is ten times lighter than my looks.

RICHARD

My Lord of Norfolk—

NORFOLK

Here, most gracious king.

RICHARD

Norfolk, we're going to have a few blows, right?

NORFOLK

We've got to give them and take them, my lord.

RICHARD

Put my tent up! I'll lie here tonight. But where will I lie tomorrow? Well, it doesn't matter. Does anyone know the number of the enemy's troops?

NORFOLK

Six or seven thousand, at most.

RICHARD

Why, our troops amount to three times that. Besides, the king's name is a tower of strength; the opposition doesn't have that advantage. Put up my tent! Come, noble gentlemen, let us look at our battle plan and get some experienced officers to help us figure out the best strategy. Let's be disciplined and not delay, because tomorrow is a busy day.

They all exit.

Enter RICHMOND, *Sir William Brandon,* OXFORD, DORSET,
HERBERT, BLUNT, *and others. Some of the soldiers pitch*
RICHMOND'*s tent*

RICHMOND

20   The weary sun hath made a golden set,
        And by the bright track of his fiery car,
        Gives token of a goodly day tomorrow.—
        Sir William Brandon, you shall bear my standard.—
        Give me some ink and paper in my tent;
25   I'll draw the form and model of our battle,
        Limit each leader to his several charge,
        And part in just proportion our small power.
        My Lord of Oxford, you, Sir William Brandon,
        And you, Sir Walter Herbert, stay with me.
30   The earl of Pembroke keeps his regiment—
        Good Captain Blunt, bear my goodnight to him,
        And by the second hour in the morning
        Desire the earl to see me in my tent.
        Yet one thing more, good captain, do for me.
35   Where is Lord Stanley quartered, do you know?

BLUNT

        Unless I have mista'en his colors much,
        Which well I am assured I have not done,
        His regiment lies half a mile, at least,
        South from the mighty power of the king.

RICHMOND

40   If without peril it be possible,
        Sweet Blunt, make some good means to speak with him,
        And give him from me this most needful note.
        He hands him a paper

BLUNT

        Upon my life, my lord, I'll undertake it.
        And so God give you quiet rest tonight!

RICHMOND, *Sir William Brandon*, OXFORD, DORSET,
HERBERT, BLUNT, *and others enter on the other side of
the stage. Some soldiers pitch* RICHMOND*'s tent.*

RICHMOND

The sunset was golden and left a bright track in the
sky, which indicates that tomorrow will be a good day.
Sir William Brandon, you will carry my flag. Bring
some ink and paper to my tent, and I'll draw a model
of our battle, appoint each leader to his particular
command, and carefully divide up our small army.
My Lord of Oxford, you, Sir William Brandon, and
you, Sir Walter Herbert, are going to stay with me.
The earl of Pembroke will stick with his regiment.
Good Captain Blunt, tell the earl goodnight from me,
and tell him that by two in the morning I would like
him to visit my tent. One more thing before you go,
Blunt—where is Lord Stanley lodging, do you know?

BLUNT

Unless I've mistaken his battle flags, which I'm sure I
haven't, his regiment lies at least half a mile south of
the king's mighty army.

RICHMOND

If it's possible to do this without putting yourself in
danger, dear Captain Blunt, say goodnight to him
from me and give him this important note.
He hands him a paper.

BLUNT

Upon my life, my lord, I'll do it. Have a restful night!

RICHMOND
45   Good night, good Captain Blunt.

BLUNT *exits*

Come, gentlemen,
Let us consult upon tomorrow's business
Into my tent. The dew is raw and cold.

Enter, to his tent, RICHARD, NORFOLK, RATCLIFFE, CATESBY,
and others

RICHARD
What is 't o'clock?

CATESBY
50   It's suppertime, my lord. It's nine o'clock.

RICHARD
I will not sup tonight. Give me some ink and paper.
What, is my beaver easier than it was?
And all my armor laid into my tent?

CATESBY
It is, my liege, and all things are in readiness.

RICHARD
55   Good Norfolk, hie thee to thy charge.
Use careful watch. Choose trusty sentinels.

NORFOLK
I go, my lord.

RICHARD
Stir with the lark tomorrow, gentle Norfolk.

NORFOLK
I warrant you, my lord.

Exit

RICHARD
60   Catesby.

RICHMOND

Good night, dear Captain Blunt.

Blunt exits.

Come, gentlemen, let's discuss tomorrow's action in my tent. The night air is too raw and cold for us to stay outdoors.

RICHARD, NORFOLK, RATCLIFFE, CATESBY, *and others enter in* RICHARD's *tent.*

RICHARD

What time is it?

CATESBY

It's dinnertime, my lord. It's nine o'clock.

RICHARD

I'm not going to eat dinner tonight. Give me some ink and paper. Is the visor of my helmet working better now? And has my armor been put in my tent?

CATESBY

Yes, my lord. Everything's ready.

RICHARD

My good man Norfolk, hurry to your post. Be careful whom you choose as guards—make sure they're trustworthy.

NORFOLK

I'm off, my lord.

RICHARD

Get up early tomorrow—at the sound of the lark—noble Norfolk.

NORFOLK

I will, my lord.

He exits.

RICHARD

Catesby.

CATESBY
My lord.

RICHARD
Send out a pursuivant-at-arms
To Stanley's regiment. Bid him bring his power
Before sunrising, lest his son George fall
65   Into the blind cave of eternal night.

Exit CATESBY

(to soldiers) Fill me a bowl of wine. Give me a watch.
Saddle white Surrey for the field to-morrow.
Look that my staves be sound, and not too heavy.—
Ratcliffe.

RATCLIFFE
70   My lord.

RICHARD
Sawst thou the melancholy Lord Northumberland?

RATCLIFFE
Thomas the earl of Surrey and himself,
Much about cockshut time, from troop to troop
Went through the army cheering up the soldiers.

RICHARD
75   So, I am satisfied. Give me a bowl of wine.
I have not that alacrity of spirit
Nor cheer of mind that I was wont to have.
Set it down. Is ink and paper ready?

RATCLIFFE
It is, my lord.

RICHARD
80   Bid my guard watch. Leave me.
Ratcliffe, about the mid of night come to my tent
And help to arm me. Leave me, I say.

Exeunt Ratcliffe and the other attendants. RICHARD *sleeps.*

CATESBY

Yes, my lord?

RICHARD

Send a junior officer to Stanley's regiment to tell Stanley to bring his men here before sunrise—if he wants to see his son George alive.

CATESBY *exits.*

(to soldiers) Get me some wine. Get a soldier to stand watch outside my tent. Saddle my white horse Surrey for battle tomorrow. Make sure the shafts of my lances are solid, but not too heavy. Ratcliffe!

RATCLIFFE

Yes, my lord?

RICHARD

Did you see the gloomy Lord Northumberland?

RATCLIFFE

Thomas, the earl of Surrey, and he were moving from troop to troop around twilight cheering up the soldiers.

RICHARD

Good, I'm satisfied. Give me some wine—I don't feel as energetic as I used to. Set it down. Is my ink and paper ready?

RATCLIFFE

It is, my lord.

RICHARD

Make sure my guard is on duty and leave me alone. Ratcliffe, around midnight come to my tent and help me put on my armor. Now leave me alone, as I said.

RATCLIFFE *and the other attendants exit.* **RICHARD** *sleeps.*

Enter STANLEY *to* RICHMOND *in his tent, lords and others attending*

STANLEY
Fortune and victory sit on thy helm!

RICHMOND
All comfort that the dark night can afford
85   Be to thy person, noble father-in-law.
Tell me, how fares our loving mother?

STANLEY
I, by attorney, bless thee from thy mother,
Who prays continually for Richmond's good.
So much for that. The silent hours steal on,
90   And flaky darkness breaks within the east.
In brief, for so the season bids us be,
Prepare thy battle early in the morning,
And put thy fortune to the arbitrament
Of bloody strokes and mortal-staring war.
95   I, as I may—that which I would I cannot,—
With best advantage will deceive the time,
And aid thee in this doubtful shock of arms.
But on thy side I may not be too forward,
Lest, being seen, thy brother, tender George,
100   Be executed in his father's sight.
Farewell. The leisure and the fearful time
Cuts off the ceremonious vows of love
And ample interchange of sweet discourse,
Which so-long-sundered friends should dwell upon.
105   God give us leisure for these rites of love!
Once more, adieu. Be valiant, and speed well.

RICHMOND
Good lords, conduct him to his regiment:
I'll strive with troubled thoughts to take a nap,
Lest leaden slumber peise me down tomorrow,
110   When I should mount with wings of victory.

STANLEY *enters and goes to* RICHMOND*'s tent, where lords and others are waiting on him.*

STANLEY

Let fortune and victory be yours!

RICHMOND

I wish you all the comfort that such a dark night as this can offer, noble father-in-law. Tell me, how is my mother?

STANLEY

Your mother sends her blessings. She prays continually on your behalf. Enough about that—morning will be here soon. To be brief—as the occasion requires—prepare to fight early in the morning, when your future will be decided. I can't do everything I want to, but I'll help you as well as I can. But I can't be too obvious about being on your side without risking the life of your stepbrother, young George. If I'm seen helping you, George will be killed right in front of my eyes. Farewell. The lack of time and the risk I'm under will have to keep us from bonding and catching up on each other's news the way we usually would after not seeing each other for so long. I hope we have the time some day! Again, goodbye. Be brave and do well!

RICHMOND

Good lords, escort him to his regiment. I'm going to try to take a nap despite my racing thoughts so that exhaustion won't get the better of me tomorrow, when I'll need to ride as if my horse had wings.

Once more, good night, kind lords and gentlemen.

Exeunt all but RICHMOND

O Thou, whose captain I account myself,
Look on my forces with a gracious eye.
Put in their hands thy bruising irons of wrath,
115   That they may crush down with a heavy fall
The usurping helmets of our adversaries!
Make us thy ministers of chastisement,
That we may praise thee in the victory!
To thee I do commend my watchful soul,
120   Ere I let fall the windows of mine eyes.
Sleeping and waking, O, defend me still!
Sleeps

Enter the GHOST OF PRINCE EDWARD, *son to* KING HENRY VI

GHOST OF PRINCE EDWARD
(to RICHARD*)* Let me sit heavy on thy soul tomorrow!
Think how thou stabbed'st me in my prime of youth
At Tewkesbury. Despair therefore, and die!
(to RICHMOND*)*
125   Be cheerful, Richmond, for the wrongèd souls
Of butchered princes fight in thy behalf.
King Henry's issue, Richmond, comforts thee.

Exit

Enter the GHOST OF KING HENRY VI

GHOST OF KING HENRY VI
(to RICHARD*)* When I was mortal, my anointed body
By thee was punchèd full of deadly holes.
130   Think on the Tower and me. Despair, and die!
Harry the Sixth bids thee despair and die.
(to RICHMOND*)*
Virtuous and holy, be thou conqueror.
Harry, that prophesied thou shouldst be king,
Doth comfort thee in thy sleep. Live and flourish.

Again, good night, kind lords and gentlemen.

Everyone exits except RICHMOND.

Oh God, whose side I think I'm fighting on, look kindly on my forces. Fuel them with dangerous fury, so they can crush the enemy. Make us your agents of revenge, so we can praise you when we're victorious! Before I fall asleep, I entrust my soul to you. Defend me, God, both when I'm asleep and when I'm awake. *He sleeps.*

The GHOST OF PRINCE EDWARD, *King Henry VI's son, enters.*

GHOST OF PRINCE EDWARD

(to RICHARD*)* I will weigh heavily on your soul tomorrow. Remember how you stabbed me at Tewksbury, when I was just a young man. Despair, and die! *(to* RICHMOND*)* Be cheerful, Richmond—butchered princes fight for you. I, King Henry's son, will provide you with comfort.

The GHOST OF KING HENRY VI *enters.*

GHOST OF KING HENRY VI

(to RICHARD*)* When I was still alive, you punctured my body, the body of God's blessed king, full of holes. Remember the Tower and me there. Despair, and die! Harry the Sixth commands you to despair and die! *(to* RICHMOND*)* Because you are virtuous and holy, you must be the conqueror! Harry, who prophesied that you would be king, comforts you in your sleep: live and prosper!

Exit

Enter the GHOST OF CLARENCE

GHOST OF CLARENCE

135   *(to* RICHARD*)* Let me sit heavy in thy soul tomorrow,
         I, that was washed to death with fulsome wine,
         Poor Clarence, by thy guile betrayed to death.
         Tomorrow in the battle think on me,
         And fall thy edgeless sword. Despair, and die!
140   *(to* RICHMOND*)* Thou offspring of the house of Lancaster,
         The wrongèd heirs of York do pray for thee
         Good angels guard thy battle. Live and flourish.

Exit

Enter the GHOSTS OF RIVERS, GRAY, *and* VAUGHAN

GHOST OF RIVERS
         (to RICHARD*)* Let me sit heavy in thy soul tomorrow,
         Rivers, that died at Pomfret. Despair, and die!

GHOST OF GREY
145   *(to* RICHARD*)* Think upon Grey, and let thy soul despair!

GHOST OF VAUGHAN
         (to RICHARD*)*
         Think upon Vaughan, and with guilty fear
         Let fall thy lance. Despair, and die!

ALL
         (to RICHMOND*)*
         Awake, and think our wrongs in Richard's bosom
         Will conquer him! Awake, and win the day.

Exeunt

Enter the GHOSTS OF *the two young* PRINCES

He exits.

The GHOST OF CLARENCE *enters.*

GHOST OF CLARENCE

(to RICHARD*)* I hope I weigh heavily on your soul tomorrow! It's me, drowned to death in a nauseating barrel of wine. It's me, poor Clarence, whom you betrayed to death! Tomorrow in battle, think of me and drop your useless sword. Despair, and die! *(to* RICHMOND*)* Offspring of the House of Lancaster, the wronged heirs of York pray for you. Good angels protect your fight! Live and prosper!

He exits.

The GHOSTS *of* RIVERS, GRAY, *and* VAUGHAN *enter.*

GHOST OF RIVERS

(to RICHARD*)* I will weigh heavily on your soul tomorrow—I, Rivers, who died at Pomfret. Despair, and die!

GHOST OF GREY

(to RICHARD*)* Think about Grey, and despair!

GHOST OF VAUGHAN

(to RICHARD*)* Think about Vaughan, and drop your lance from fear and guilt. Despair, and die!

ALL

(to RICHMOND*)* Awaken, and have faith that the wrongs Richard carries in his heart will defeat him! Awaken, and win the day!

They exit.

The GHOSTS OF *the two young* PRINCES *enter.*

GHOSTS OF PRINCES
(to RICHARD*)*
150   Dream on thy cousins smothered in the Tower.
         Let us be lead within thy bosom, Richard,
         And weigh thee down to ruin, shame, and death.
         Thy nephews' souls bid thee despair and die.
         (to RICHMOND*)*
         Sleep, Richmond, sleep in peace and wake in joy.
155   Good angels guard thee from the boar's annoy.
         Live, and beget a happy race of kings.
         Edward's unhappy sons do bid thee flourish.

                                                    Exeunt

Enter the GHOST OF HASTINGS

GHOST OF HASTINGS
         (to RICHARD*)* Bloody and guilty, guiltily awake,
         And in a bloody battle end thy days.
160   Think on Lord Hastings. Despair and die!
         (to RICHMOND*)* Quiet, untroubled soul, awake, awake.
         Arm, fight, and conquer for fair England's sake.

Enter the GHOST OF ANNE

GHOST OF ANNE
         (to RICHARD*)*
         Richard, thy wife, that wretched Anne thy wife,
         That never slept a quiet hour with thee,
165   Now fills thy sleep with perturbations.
         Tomorrow, in the battle, think on me,
         And fall thy edgeless sword: Despair and die!
         (to RICHMOND*)* Thou quiet soul, sleep thou a quiet sleep.
         Dream of success and happy victory.
170   Thy adversary's wife doth pray for thee.

                                                      Exit

GHOSTS OF PRINCES

(to RICHARD*)* Dream about your nephews, smothered in the Tower. Let us rest in your heart as heavily as lead, Richard, and drag you down to ruin, shame, and death! Your nephews' souls command that you despair and die! *(to* RICHMOND*)* Sleep, Richmond, sleep in peace and wake in joy. Good angels will protect you from the boar's attacks! Live, and give birth to a whole, happy race of kings! Edward's unlucky sons want you to flourish.

They exit.

The GHOST OF HASTINGS *enters.*

GHOST OF HASTINGS

(to RICHARD*)* You violent, guilty man, wake up full of guilt and end your days in a bloody battle! Think about Lord Hastings. Despair, and die! *(to* RICHMOND*)* Quiet untroubled soul, wake up! Arm yourself, fight, and win for beautiful England's sake!

He exits.

The GHOST OF ANNE *enters.*

GHOST OF ANNE

(to RICHARD*)* Richard, your wife, your wretched wife, Anne, who never enjoyed a quiet hour of sleep with you, now fills your sleep with disturbing thoughts. Tomorrow in battle think of me and fall on your sword: despair, and die! *(to* RICHMOND*)* You quiet soul, sleep a quiet sleep. Dream of success and happy victory. Your enemy's wife is praying for you.

She exits.

Enter the GHOST OF BUCKINGHAM

GHOST OF BUCKINGHAM
>   *(to* RICHARD*)* The last was I that helped thee to the crown;
>   The last was I that felt thy tyranny.
>   O, in the battle think on Buckingham,
>   And die in terror of thy guiltiness.
175   Dream on, dream on, of bloody deeds and death.
>   Fainting, despair; despairing, yield thy breath.
>   *(to* RICHMOND*)* I died for hope ere I could lend thee aid,
>   But cheer thy heart, and be thou not dismayed.
>   God and good angels fight on Richmond's side,
180   And Richard fall in height of all his pride.

Exit

RICHARD *starts out of his dream*

RICHARD
>   Give me another horse! Bind up my wounds!
>   Have mercy, Jesu!—Soft, I did but dream.
>   O coward conscience, how dost thou afflict me!
>   The lights burn blue. It is now dead midnight.
185   Cold fearful drops stand on my trembling flesh.
>   What do I fear? Myself? There's none else by.
>   Richard loves Richard; that is, I and I.
>   Is there a murderer here? No. Yes, I am.
>   Then fly! What, from myself? Great reason why:
190   Lest I revenge. What, myself upon myself?
>   Alack, I love myself. Wherefore? For any good
>   That I myself have done unto myself?
>   O, no! Alas, I rather hate myself
>   For hateful deeds committed by myself.
195   I am a villain. Yet I lie. I am not.
>   Fool, of thyself speak well. Fool, do not flatter.

The GHOST OF BUCKINGHAM *enters.*

GHOST OF BUCKINGHAM

(to RICHARD*)* I was the first to help you to the crown and the last to feel the effects of your tyranny. Think of Buckingham when you're fighting tomorrow, and die terrified of the sins you've committed! Tonight, dream of bloody deeds and death. Tomorrow, when you lose heart, fall into despair and then death. *(to* RICHMOND*)* I died before I could help you as I was hoping to. But be cheerful and don't worry. God and good angels fight on your side, and Richard will fall at the height of his false pride.

He exits.

RICHARD *starts up out of his dream.*

RICHARD

Give me another horse! Bandage my wounds! Have mercy, Jesus!—Wait, I was only dreaming. Oh cowardly conscience, how you're torturing me! The candles burn blue—that means it's the dead of night. I'm sweating and trembling with fear. But what am I afraid of? Myself? There's no one else here. Richard loves Richard, that is, there's just me and myself here. Is there a murderer here? No. Yes, I am. Then run away. What, from myself? Yes, to avoid taking revenge on myself. Unfortunately, I love myself. Why? Did I do anything good to myself? Oh, no. Alas, I hate myself instead, because of the hateful deeds I've committed. I am a villain. But I'm lying; I'm not a villain. Fool, speak well of yourself. Fool, do not flatter yourself.

My conscience hath a thousand several tongues,
And every tongue brings in a several tale,
And every tale condemns me for a villain.
200 Perjury, perjury, in the highest degree;
Murder, stern murder, in the direst degree;
All several sins, all used in each degree,
Throng to the bar, crying all, "Guilty! guilty!"
I shall despair. There is no creature loves me,
205 And if I die no soul will pity me.
And wherefore should they, since that I myself
Find in myself no pity to myself?
Methought the souls of all that I had murdered
Came to my tent, and every one did threat
210 Tomorrow's vengeance on the head of Richard.

Enter RATCLIFFE

RATCLIFFE
My lord.

RICHARD
Zounds, who is there?

RATCLIFFE
Ratcliffe, my lord, 'tis I. The early village cock
Hath twice done salutation to the morn.
215 Your friends are up and buckle on their armor.

RICHARD
O Ratcliffe, I have dreamed a fearful dream!
What think'st thou, will our friends prove all true?

RATCLIFFE
No doubt, my lord.

RICHARD
O Ratcliffe, I fear, I fear.

RATCLIFFE
220 Nay, good my lord, be not afraid of shadows.

My conscience has a thousand different tongues, and every tongue has a different tale to tell, but every one of them condemns me. They find me guilty of perjury in the highest degree and murder in the highest degree, and several others sins, all committed in every possible degree. The sins throng the court. They all say, "Guilty! Guilty!" It's time to despair. No one loves me, and if I die, no one will pity me. And why should they, since even I myself can't muster any pity for myself? I dreamed that the souls of everyone I'd murdered flocked to my tent, and every one of them threatened to take revenge on me tomorrow.

RATCLIFFE *enters.*

RATCLIFFE

My lord.

RICHARD

Damn it, who's there?

RATCLIFFE

Ratcliffe, my lord, it's me. The rooster has already crowed twice. Your friends are up and buckling on their armor.

RICHARD

Oh Ratcliffe, I had a terrifying dream! What do you think, will my friends prove loyal?

RATCLIFFE

No doubt, my lord.

RICHARD

Oh Ratcliffe, I'm afraid, I'm afraid—

RATCLIFFE

No, my good lord, don't be afraid of dreams.

RICHARD
By the apostle Paul, shadows tonight
Have struck more terror to the soul of Richard
Than can the substance of ten thousand soldiers
Armed in proof and led by shallow Richmond.
225   'Tis not yet near day. Come, go with me;
Under our tents I'll play the eavesdropper
To see if any mean to shrink from me.

Exeunt

Enter the lords to RICHMOND, *sitting in his tent*

LORDS
Good morrow, Richmond.

RICHMOND
Cry mercy, lords and watchful gentlemen,
230   That you have ta'en a tardy sluggard here.

A LORD
How have you slept, my lord?

RICHMOND
The sweetest sleep and fairest-boding dreams
That ever entered in a drowsy head
Have I since your departure had, my lords.
235   Methought their souls whose bodies Richard murdered
Came to my tent and cried on victory.
I promise you, my soul is very jocund
In the remembrance of so fair a dream.
How far into the morning is it, lords?

LORDS
240   Upon the stroke of four.

RICHMOND
Why, then 'tis time to arm and give direction.
His oration to his soldiers
More than I have said, loving countrymen,
The leisure and enforcement of the time
245   Forbids to dwell upon. Yet remember this:

RICHARD

> By St. Paul, ghosts have struck more terror in my soul tonight than ten thousand of worthless Richmond's soldiers could, dressed up in their most sword-proof armor. It's not yet daylight. Come with me; I'll spy under the tents to see if any of my own people plan to desert me.

They exit

RICHMOND'S LORDS *enter his tent and go to where he is sitting.*

LORDS

> Good morning, Richmond.

RICHMOND

> Pardon me, lords and gentlemen who stayed awake. You've caught me oversleeping.

A LORD

> How did you sleep, my lord?

RICHMOND

> Since you left, I've been enjoying the sweetest sleep and most promising dreams I've ever had, my lords. I dreamed the souls of the people Richard murdered came to my tent and promised me victory. I tell you, I feel very jolly remembering such a beautiful dream. How late is it, lords?

A LORD

> It's almost four.

RICHMOND

> Why, then, it's time to put on my armor and instruct the troops. (*to his soldiers*) I can't tell you much right now, loyal countrymen, because we don't have time. But know this:

God and our good cause fight upon our side.
The prayers of holy saints and wrongèd souls,
Like high-reared bulwarks, stand before our faces.
Richard except, those whom we fight against
250 Had rather have us win than him they follow.
For what is he they follow? Truly, gentlemen,
A bloody tyrant and a homicide;
One raised in blood, and one in blood established;
One that made means to come by what he hath,
255 And slaughtered those that were the means to help him;
A base foul stone, made precious by the foil
Of England's chair, where he is falsely set;
One that hath ever been God's enemy.
Then if you fight against God's enemy,
260 God will, in justice, ward you as his soldiers.
If you do sweat to put a tyrant down,
You sleep in peace, the tyrant being slain.
If you do fight against your country's foes,
Your country's fat shall pay your pains the hire.
265 If you do fight in safeguard of your wives,
Your wives shall welcome home the conquerors.
If you do free your children from the sword,
Your children's children quits it in your age.
Then, in the name of God and all these rights,
270 Advance your standards. Draw your willing swords.
For me, the ransom of my bold attempt
Shall be this cold corpse on the earth's cold face;
But if I thrive, the gain of my attempt
The least of you shall share his part thereof.
275 Sound drums and trumpets boldly and cheerfully;
God and Saint George! Richmond and victory!

Exeunt

We have God and a good cause on our side. The prayers of saints and those that Richard wronged support us like high-walled fortresses. Other than Richard, even those whom we fight against would rather we won. Because who is this man they follow? Truly, gentlemen, a violent tyrant and a murderer, who rose to his high position by shedding blood and kept the position the same way. He rose to the top by means of others and then slaughtered them. He's like a worthless stone, who only seems like a valuable gem because he's on the throne, where he doesn't belong. He has always been God's enemy. And when you fight God's enemy, God will protect you. If you struggle to bring down a tyrant, you will sleep peacefully when the tyrant is killed. When you fight against your country's enemies, you will be paid for your efforts with your country's wealth. If you fight to protect your wives, your wives will welcome you home as conquerors. When you free your children from the sword, your grandchildren will repay you in your old age. So, in the name of God and all the good that will come of this battle, march with your flags high and draw your swords. As for me, if I fail, the only ransom I will offer the enemy is my corpse. But if I succeed, every one of you will share in the profit. Play boldly and cheerfully, drummers and trumpeters. Here's to God and Saint George! To Richmond and victory!

In the Middle Ages, noblemen taken in battle often could go free afterward if they paid the enemy. Richmond says if Richard captures him, he will die rather than pay for his freedom.

They all exit.

Enter King RICHARD, RATCLIFFE, *attendants and forces*

RICHARD
What said Northumberland as touching Richmond?

RATCLIFFE
That he was never trainèd up in arms.

RICHARD
He said the truth. And what said Surrey then?

RATCLIFFE
280   He smiled and said "The better for our purpose."

RICHARD
He was in the right, and so indeed it is.

The clock striketh

Tell the clock there. Give me a calendar.

He looks in an almanac

Who saw the sun today?

RATCLIFFE
Not I, my lord.

RICHARD
285   Then he disdains to shine, for by the book
He should have braved the east an hour ago
A black day will it be to somebody. Ratcliffe!

RATCLIFFE
My lord.

RICHARD
The sun will not be seen today.
290   The sky doth frown and lour upon our army.
I would these dewy tears were from the ground.
Not shine today? Why, what is that to me
More than to Richmond, for the selfsame heaven
That frowns on me looks sadly upon him.

RICHARD, RATCLIFFE, *attendants, and soldiers enter.*

RICHARD

What did Northumberland say about Richmond?

RATCLIFFE

That he was never trained as a soldier.

RICHARD

That's true. And what did Surrey say to that?

RATCLIFFE

He smiled and said, "The better for us."

RICHARD

He's right, and that's how it is.

The clock strikes.

Read the time there. Give me an almanac. *(looking in an almanac)* Did anyone see the sun today?

RATCLIFFE

I didn't, my lord.

RICHARD

Then it refuses to shine. According to this almanac, it should have risen an hour ago. It'll be a black day for somebody today. Ratcliffe!

RATCLIFFE

My lord?

RICHARD

The sun will not appear today. The sky frowns and scowls on our army. I wish there wasn't so much dew on the ground. So, the sun won't shine today! Well, why should that be worse for me than it is for Richmond? The same heaven that's frowning on me looks gloomily on him.

Enter NORFOLK

NORFOLK
295   Arm, arm, my lord. The foe vaunts in the field.

RICHARD
Come, bustle, bustle. Caparison my horse.—
Call up Lord Stanley; bid him bring his power.—
I will lead forth my soldiers to the plain,
And thus my battle shall be orderèd:
300   My foreward shall be drawn out all in length,
Consisting equally of horse and foot;
Our archers shall be placèd in the midst.
John Duke of Norfolk, Thomas Earl of Surrey,
Shall have the leading of this foot and horse.
305   They thus directed, we will follow
In the main battle, whose puissance on either side
Shall be well wingèd with our chiefest horse.
This, and Saint George to boot—What think'st thou,
Norfolk?

NORFOLK
310   A good direction, warlike sovereign.

He sheweth him a paper

This found I on my tent this morning.

RICHARD
(reads)
Jockey of Norfolk, be not so bold.
For Dickon thy master is bought and sold.
A thing devisèd by the enemy.—
315   Go, gentlemen, every man unto his charge.
Let not our babbling dreams affright our souls.
Conscience is but a word that cowards use,
Devised at first to keep the strong in awe.
Our strong arms be our conscience, swords our law.

NORFOLK *enters.*

NORFOLK

Get ready, my lord. The enemy is making its appearance on the battlefield.

RICHARD

Hurry, hurry—prepare my horse. Tell Lord Stanley to bring his army. I will lead my soldiers to the field and the battle formation will be like this: the vanguard will extend in a line that is equal parts horsemen and foot soldiers. The archers will stay in the middle. John Duke of Norfolk and Thomas Earl of Surrey will lead the horsemen and foot soldiers. I'll follow in the center of the troop formation, which I'll defend with my best horse, and with Saint George on my side, as well! What do you think, Norfolk?

NORFOLK

A good plan, warrior king. I found this pinned to my tent this morning.

He shows RICHARD *a piece of paper.*

RICHARD

(reads) "Jackie of Norfolk, don't be too bold, for Dick your master has been betrayed." Something the enemy devised. Go, gentleman, every man to his command. Don't let babbling dreams frighten us—conscience is just a word that cowards use to intimidate the strong. The strong fight we put on will be our conscience, our swords will be our law.

320 March on. Join bravely. Let us to it pell mell
If not to heaven, then hand in hand to hell.
His oration to his army
What shall I say more than I have inferred?
Remember whom you are to cope withal,
325 A sort of vagabonds, rascals, and runaways,
A scum of Bretons and base lackey peasants,
Whom their o'er-cloyèd country vomits forth
To desperate ventures and assured destruction.
You sleeping safe, they bring to you unrest;
330 You having lands and blessed with beauteous wives,
They would restrain the one, distain the other.
And who doth lead them but a paltry fellow,
Long kept in Brittany at our mother's cost,
A milksop, one that never in his life
335 Felt so much cold as overshoes in snow?
Let's whip these stragglers o'er the seas again,
Lash hence these overweening rags of France,
These famished beggars weary of their lives,
Who, but for dreaming on this fond exploit,
340 For want of means, poor rats, had hanged themselves.
If we be conquered, let men conquer us,
And not these bastard Bretons, whom our fathers
Have in their own land beaten, bobbed, and thumped,
And in record, left them the heirs of shame.
345 Shall these enjoy our lands, lie with our wives,
Ravish our daughters?

Drum afar off

Hark! I hear their drum.
Fight, gentlemen of England.—Fight, bold yeomen.—
Draw, archers, draw your arrows to the head.—
350 Spur your proud horses hard, and ride in blood.
Amaze the welkin with your broken staves—

March on, be brave in battle, and let's go pell-mell to heaven, if not hand in hand to hell. (*to his army*) What more can I say? Remember who you're dealing with— a random bunch of bums, rascals, runaways, Breton scum, and peasant hangers-on whom an overcrowded nation vomits out to populate every desperate, sure-to-fail enterprise. You have been sleeping soundly, and they bring unrest. You own land they want to steal. Those of you who are blessed with beautiful wives, they want to defile them. And who's leading them but an inconsequential fellow who for the longest time lived in Brittany at his mother's expense? A girly man, a man who never in his life felt more cold than seeps into one's boots in the snow? Let's send these stragglers back over the sea. Let's whip these arrogant relics of France—these starving beggars, tired of their lives, who would have hanged themselves, poor rats, if it weren't for this foolish enterprise they've been dreaming about—back to France. If we're going to be conquered, let men conquer us, and not these French bastards whom our forefathers already beat, thrashed, and pummeled on their own turf, and shamed them forever in the history books. Should these people enjoy our lands? Sleep with our wives? Rape our daughters?

Drum heard far off.

Listen! I hear their drums. Fight, gentlemen of England! Fight, brave landlords! Draw your bows all the way back, archers! Spur your proud horses hard, horsemen, and ride in blood. Startle even the sky with the sound of your lances cracking.

Enter a MESSENGER

What says Lord Stanley? Will he bring his power?

MESSENGER
My lord, he doth deny to come.

RICHARD
Off with his son George's head!

NORFOLK
355   My lord, the enemy is past the marsh.
After the battle let George Stanley die.

RICHARD
A thousand hearts are great within my bosom.
Advance our standards. Set upon our foes.
Our ancient word of courage, fair Saint George,
360   Inspire us with the spleen of fiery dragons.
Upon them! Victory sits on our helms.

Exeunt

A MESSENGER *enters.*

What does Lord Stanley say? Will he bring his army?

MESSENGER

My lord, he refuses to come.

RICHARD

Off with his son George's head!

NORFOLK

My lord, the enemy has already passed the marsh. Let George Stanley die after the battle.

RICHARD

A thousand hearts beat in my chest. Let's advance our flags, set upon our enemies, and have our ancient saint of courage, good Saint George, inspire us with the fury of fiery dragons! Let's go! Victory is with us.

They all exit.

ACT 5, SCENE 4

Alarum. Excursions. Enter NORFOLK *and forces fighting; to him* CATESBY

CATESBY
Rescue, my lord of Norfolk, rescue, rescue!
The king enacts more wonders than a man,
Daring an opposite to every danger.
His horse is slain, and all on foot he fights,
5   Seeking for Richmond in the throat of death.
Rescue, fair lord, or else the day is lost!

Alarums. Enter RICHARD

RICHARD
A horse, a horse, my kingdom for a horse!
CATESBY
Withdraw, my lord. I'll help you to a horse.
RICHARD
Slave, I have set my life upon a cast,
10   And I will stand the hazard of the die.
I think there be six Richmonds in the field;
Five have I slain today instead of him.
A horse, a horse, my kingdom for a horse!

Exeunt

ACT 5, SCENE 4

Blasts of military music (trumpets and drums) and flurries of soldiers fighting. NORFOLK *and* CATESBY *enter with soldiers fighting.*

CATESBY

Help, my lord of Norfolk, help, help! The king performs more wonders than seem humanly possible, challenging every enemy he sees. His horse is killed, so he's fighting on foot, risking his life to search out Richmond. Help, dear lord, or the battle will be lost!

Blasts of military music (trumpets and drums).

RICHARD *enters.*

RICHARD

A horse, a horse, I'd give my kingdom for a horse!

CATESBY

Get off the field, my lord. I'll find you another horse.

RICHARD

Peasant, I have gambled my life on this one throw of the dice, and I'm willing to take what comes. I think there are six Richmonds on the field. I've killed five that looked like him, anyway. A horse, a horse! I'd give my kingdom for a horse!

They all exit.

ACT 5, SCENE 5

Alarum. Enter RICHARD *and* RICHMOND. *They fight.* RICHARD
is slain. Retreat and flourish. Enter RICHMOND, STANLEY
bearing the crown, with divers other lords and soldiers

RICHMOND

God and your arms be praised, victorious friends!
The day is ours; the bloody dog is dead.

STANLEY

(offering him the crown)
Courageous Richmond, well hast thou acquit thee.
Lo, here this long-usurpèd royalty
5   From the dead temples of this bloody wretch
Have I plucked off, to grace thy brows withal.
Wear it, enjoy it, and make much of it.

RICHMOND

Great God of heaven, say amen to all!
But tell me, is young George Stanley living?

STANLEY

10   He is, my lord, and safe in Leicester town,
Whither, if it please you, we may now withdraw us.

RICHMOND

What men of name are slain on either side?

STANLEY

John Duke of Norfolk, Walter, Lord Ferrers,
Sir Robert Brakenbury, and Sir William Brandon.

RICHMOND

15   Inter their bodies as becomes their births.
Proclaim a pardon to the soldiers fled
That in submission will return to us.
And then, as we have ta'en the sacrament,
We will unite the white rose and the red.

ACT 5, SCENE 5

Blasts of military music (trumpets and drums). RICHARD *and* RICHMOND *enter; they fight.* RICHARD *is killed. The trumpet sounds to signal a retreat.* RICHMOND *retreats.* RICHMOND *and* STANLEY, *bearing the crown, return with several lords.*

RICHMOND

God and your work be praised, victorious friends. The day is ours. The bloody dog is dead.

STANLEY

(offering him the crown) Courageous Richmond, you fought well. Here, I've taken back the stolen crown from that violent lowlife so it can grace your brows. Wear it, enjoy it, and make much of it.

RICHMOND

Great God of heaven, say amen to all this! But, tell me, is young George Stanley alive?

STANLEY

He is, my lord, and safe in Leicester, where, if you'd like, we can retreat to.

RICHMOND

Which gentlemen on each side have been killed?

STANLEY

John Duke of Norfolk, Walter Lord Ferrers, Sir Robert Brakenbury, and Sir William Brandon.

RICHMOND

Bury them in a manner appropriate to their noble births. Proclaim that I'll pardon the soldiers who fled if they will return and submit to my rule. As I vowed, I will unite the York and Lancaster families.

20   Smile heaven upon this fair conjunction,
      That long have frowned upon their enmity.
      What traitor hears me and says not "Amen?"
      England hath long been mad and scarred herself.
      The brother blindly shed the brother's blood.
25   The father rashly slaughtered his own son.
      The son, compelled, been butcher to the sire.
      All this divided York and Lancaster,
      Divided, in their dire division.
      O, now let Richmond and Elizabeth,
30   The true succeeders of each royal house,
      By God's fair ordinance conjoin together,
      And let their heirs, God, if thy will be so.
      Enrich the time to come with smooth-faced peace,
      With smiling plenty and fair prosperous days!
35   Abate the edge of traitors, gracious Lord,
      That would reduce these bloody days again,
      And make poor England weep in streams of blood!
      Let them not live to taste this land's increase,
      That would with treason wound this fair land's peace.
40   Now civil wounds are stopped, peace lives again.
      That she may long live here, God say amen.

                                              Exeunt

Heaven, for a long time you have frowned upon the hatred between them. Smile, then, on this beautiful union. What traitor hears me and doesn't say amen? England has long been so crazy that she was willing to hurt herself, brothers blindly shed their brothers' blood, fathers rashly slaughtered their own sons, sons were forced to butcher their fathers. All this further divided the two families, which were already so badly divided. Now let Richmond and Elizabeth, the true heirs of each royal house, be joined together! And let their heirs, if you are willing, God, enrich the future with peace and plenty! Gracious Lord, blunt the swords of those traitors who mean to tear poor England apart again! Let those who would mar this fair land's peace with treason die before they can enjoy its wealth. Civil wounds now can heal, and peace can live again. So that England may live a long life like this, let God say amen!

They all exit.

SPARKNOTES LITERATURE GUIDES

1984

The Adventures of
 Huckleberry Finn

The Adventures of Tom
 Sawyer

The Aeneid

All Quiet on the Western
 Front

And Then There Were
 None

Angela's Ashes

Animal Farm

Anna Karenina

Anne of Green Gables

Anthem

Antony and Cleopatra

Aristotle's Ethics

As I Lay Dying

As You Like It

Atlas Shrugged

The Autobiography of
 Malcolm X

The Awakening

The Bean Trees

The Bell Jar

Beloved

Beowulf

Billy Budd

Black Boy

Bless Me, Ultima

The Bluest Eye

Brave New World

The Brothers Karamazov

The Call of the Wild

Candide

The Canterbury Tales

Catch-22

The Catcher in the Rye

The Chocolate War

The Chosen

Cold Mountain

Cold Sassy Tree

The Color Purple

The Count of Monte
 Cristo

Crime and Punishment

The Crucible

Cry, the Beloved Country

Cyrano de Bergerac

David Copperfield

Death of a Salesman

The Death of Socrates

The Diary of a Young Girl

A Doll's House

Don Quixote

Dr. Faustus

Dr. Jekyll and Mr. Hyde

Dracula

Dune

Edith Hamilton's
 Mythology

Emma

Ethan Frome

Fahrenheit 451

Fallen Angels

A Farewell to Arms

Farewell to Manzanar

Flowers for Algernon

For Whom the Bell Tolls

The Fountainhead

Frankenstein

The Giver

The Glass Menagerie

Gone With the Wind

The Good Earth

The Grapes of Wrath

Great Expectations

The Great Gatsby

Grendel

Gulliver's Travels

Hamlet

The Handmaid's Tale

Hard Times

Harry Potter and the
 Sorcerer's Stone

Heart of Darkness

Henry IV, Part I

Henry V

Hiroshima

The Hobbit

The House of Seven
 Gables

I Know Why the Caged
 Bird Sings

The Iliad

Inferno

Inherit the Wind

Invisible Man

Jane Eyre

Johnny Tremain

The Joy Luck Club

Julius Caesar

The Jungle

The Killer Angels

King Lear

The Last of the Mohicans

Les Miserables

A Lesson Before Dying

The Little Prince

Little Women

Lord of the Flies

The Lord of the Rings

Macbeth

Madame Bovary

A Man for All Seasons

The Mayor of
 Casterbridge

The Merchant of Venice

A Midsummer Night's
 Dream

Moby Dick

Much Ado About Nothing

My Antonia

Narrative of the Life of
 Frederick Douglass

Native Son

The New Testament

Night

Notes from Underground

The Odyssey

The Oedipus Plays

Of Mice and Men

The Old Man and the Sea

The Old Testament

Oliver Twist

The Once and Future
 King

One Day in the Life of
 Ivan Denisovich

One Flew Over the
 Cuckoo's Nest

One Hundred Years of
 Solitude

Othello

Our Town

The Outsiders

Paradise Lost

A Passage to India

The Pearl

The Picture of Dorian
 Gray

Poe's Short Stories

A Portrait of the Artist as
 a Young Man

Pride and Prejudice

The Prince

A Raisin in the Sun

The Red Badge of
 Courage

The Republic

Richard III

Robinson Crusoe

Romeo and Juliet

The Scarlet Letter

A Separate Peace

Silas Marner

Sir Gawain and the Green
 Knight

Slaughterhouse-Five

Snow Falling on Cedars

Song of Solomon

The Sound and the Fury

Steppenwolf

The Stranger

Streetcar Named Desire

The Sun Also Rises

A Tale of Two Cities

The Taming of the Shrew

The Tempest

Tess of the d'Ubervilles

The Things They Carried

Their Eyes Were
 Watching God

Things Fall Apart

To Kill a Mockingbird

To the Lighthouse

Treasure Island

Twelfth Night

Ulysses

Uncle Tom's Cabin

Walden

War and Peace

Wuthering Heights

A Yellow Raft in Blue
 Water

Notes

Notes

Notes

Notes